ROYAL BOROUGH OF GREEN

Follow us on twitter @greenwichlibs

Please return by the last date shown

Nov 2017 Lovelock -- DEC 2017		
EL 6/22 10 JAN 2023 - 8 JUN 2023 18 JUN ~~for~~ ? renewed 13 Jul. Jun 15 Sep		

and needs to be read in Westminster as much as Leeds, ~~~
or Sheffield'   Glenn Moore, *World Soccer* connist

'This is a wonderful book, at its heart about why we love ousport
with such a pa~~~'   ~~~ Caplan, *forty20*

Anṫght history before becoming a journalist, autḣt. His previous books are *Promised Land: A Nort* which was named both Football Book of the Yeaṙk of the Year by the National Sporting Club, and ̇i Know You're Here?*, which was shortlisted for Footḣe Year. He was an arts writer for the *Independent* and ẇort and culture for, amongst others, the *Guardian*, *Timė.atesman*.

By the same author

Promised Land: A Northern Love Story

Does Your Rabbi Know You're Here?:
̇he Story of English Football's Forgotten Tribe

MOVING THE GOALPOSTS

A Yorkshire Tragedy

Anthony Clavane

riverrun

First published in Great Br
This paperback edition pul

r

riverrun

an imprint of
Quercus Publishing Ltd
Carmelite House
50 Victoria Embankment
London EC4Y 0DZ

An Hachette UK company

A CIP catalogue record for this book is available
from the British Library

ISBN 978 1 84866 514 9
EBOOK ISBN 978 1 78429 104 4

Every effort has been made to contact copyright holders.
However, the publishers will be glad to rectify in future
editions any inadvertent omissions brought to their attention.

Quercus Publishing Ltd hereby exclude all liability to the extent permitted
by law for any errors of omissions in this book and for any loss,
damage or expense (whether direct or indirect) suffered by a
third party relying on any information contained in this book.

10 9 8 7 6 5 4 3 2 1

Typeset by CC Book Production

Printed and bound in Great Britain by Clays Ltd, St Ives plc

To Elaine Clavane and Hazel Mostyn,
my two favourite Yorkshirewomen.

And on the pedestal these words appear:
'My name is Ozymandias, king of kings:
Look on my works, ye Mighty, and despair!'
Nothing beside remains. Round the decay
Of that colossal wreck, boundless and bare
The lone and level sands stretch far away.

'Ozymandias', Percy Bysshe Shelley, 1818

'Economics are the method. The object is to change the soul.'

Margaret Thatcher, 1981

'Casper, get off those bloody goalposts.'

Mr Sugden, in Kes, 1970

Contents

Introduction: Billy Casper's Goalposts

'In an age of change, the urban, industrial North became a symbol of what was being lost: an imaginary world of honesty, authenticity and working-class community, a world where people spoke plainly and stood by their word.'

Dominic Sandbrook,
The Great British Dream Factory, 2015

Billy Casper wakes up in the bed he shares with his older brother, Jud. Jud has to get up early to go down the pit. After doing his paper round Billy goes to school where he is interviewed by the Youth Employment Officer. The officer suggests he considers 'the good opportunities in mining'. During a football match in his games lesson, he is put in goal by Mr Sugden, the bullying sports master. Whilst swinging from the goalposts he lets in a goal and is punished by Sugden. In an English lesson Mr Farthing, a more sympathetic teacher, encourages Billy to tell the class about his pet kestrel. At breaktime he gets into a fight with a boy on a coke heap. After school, on top of a deserted hill overlooking a South Yorkshire council estate, Farthing visits Billy's shed. The bird, Billy tells him, is not a pet. It is more than just his sport. It is a symbol of hope.

To understand where it all went wrong we need to go back to the 1980s, the decade when a county synonymous with deeply rooted notions of collectivism, solidarity and sporting achievement became associated with division, defeat and disaster. A large number of Yorkshire villages, towns and cities were left permanently scarred by the social, economic and cultural changes of that turbulent, reckless, revolutionary era. In the ensuing years there have been some notable sporting feats, the occasional White Rose triumph even. But the underlying story has been anomie.

We must, of course, define our terms. It is my view that, since the eighties, sport has 'gone wrong' in the sense that it has become increasingly infected by greed, rampant individualism and amorality. Huge sections of society have been disenfranchised by a new sporting order in which money, rather than collective endeavour, determines success. To some of its supporters a kind of deregulated paradise, this new order has surrendered to an array of deadly sins: financial doping, match-fixing, cover-ups, corruption, etc. Just like its great industries, many of Yorkshire's great football teams have never fully recovered from the harrowing of their region. Although enjoying fleeting success during the boom years of the 1990s, they have lurched from well-publicised financial disaster to despair. As a very small group of mega-brands came to dominate the richest league in the world, some went into meltdown, ignominiously hurtling down the divisions. Attendances at rugby league matches have fallen; despite its Sky-sponsored Super League makeover, the region's 'national sport' remains an overlooked, mostly invisible, game, lacking the financial power of its southern-based, Establishment rival. The county cricket team have, admittedly, enjoyed a recent revival, winning back-to-back championships. But, like the 'living-the-dream' football clubs, they have paid a price for monetising these dreams; not only have they run up a hefty debt but they remain haunted by the ghosts of a civil war that, for three decades, cast them into the wilderness.

Throughout this book I will be referring to 'Old Yorkshire' as an idea rather than a place. Each chapter tells the story of a particular town or city that exemplifies this idea: a raw, rugged, nonconformist, fiercely local, collectivist sensibility forged during the industrial revolution. As in Richard Hoggart's pioneering 1957 cultural study *The Uses of Literacy*, which provided the book's inspiration, my aim is to present the universal – the rise and fall of a powerful, solidaristic, working-class culture – through the particular. Although written sixty years ago, Hoggart's compelling evocation of working-class Hunslet remains an influential study of a world, as one contemporary reviewer put it, 'brimming over with extended family life, warmth and neighbourliness'. Although, as Hoggart acknowledged, that world was already beginning to fray at the edges by the time his book was published, its communitarian ethos survived until the eighties.

It would be wrong to entirely blame the collapse of that ethos on the sea change that took place during the 'Thatcher decade'. The post-war, social-democratic consensus – a mixed economy, full employment, strong welfare state – had already taken a big hit in the seventies, when economic crises struck on both sides of the Atlantic. Neoliberalism, a term which was coined as long ago as 1938, actually entered the British mainstream after the IMF bailed out the mid-seventies, Callaghan–Healey Labour government – and, in keeping the Iron Lady's deregulatory, supply-side reforms in place, the Blair–Brown New Labour governments noticeably upheld her legacy. And yet the Thatcher decade was undoubtedly a watershed moment, widening the gap between rich and poor, north and south and haves and have-nots, marking the end of the 'Old Britain' and the first steps towards a new one.

It was during this decade that Old Yorkshire became a kind of shorthand for the Old Britain that lay beyond, and got left behind by, London and the home counties. To some it stood for a pre-eighties, prelapsarian idyll, to others an anachronistic, almost vaudevillian, version of the class struggle. The truth is, as always, somewhere in between. But as the county's economic lifeblood drained away, and its heartland sank into a psychological depression, even former Thatcherites came to regret its passing. 'The new broom swept, and it swept pretty clean,' lamented *Mail on Sunday* political commentator Peter Hitchens. 'In towns I know well, car assembly lines, railway workshops, glassworks engineering plants, chocolate factories vanished or shrank to nothing. A journey across the heart of England, once an exhilarating vista of muscular manufacturing, especially glorious by night, turned into archaeology. Now, if it looked like a factory, it was really a ruin.'

The emasculation of a militant trade union – Arthur Scargill's National Union of Mineworkers – was one thing; the destruction of traditional, mutually self-sustaining, local communities quite another. For more than a century, it had been the exertions of these communities that had both spurred Britain's industrial development and transformed the broad acres into a sporting powerhouse, a counter-magnet to the swaggering, self-important capital. Their myriad institutions, based on the trinity of work, leisure and family, had provided working-class families with a context of social solidarity and cooperation. From the Industrial Revolution onwards, the communitarian ethos had been expressed through country fairs, mechanics' institutes, welfare halls, Methodist churches, friendly societies, mutual insurers, retail, saving and agricultural co-operatives and trade unions. In the following century it was embodied by credit unions, community halls, labour clubs, workers' educational association classes, brass bands, libraries, leisure centres, seaside holidays and pop groups. The county's pubs, too, had been breeding grounds for communal games like quoits (throwing rings over pegs), dog racing, pigeon flying, pitch and toss – and of course football, rugby league and cricket. Football in particular, as the sports historian Matthew Taylor has written, had been 'built upon the peculiarly tight-knit community identities characteristic of British working-class life. Local teams could provide a focus for community consciousness, linking together disparate groups of individuals in a common cause every week.' Many round- and oval-ball clubs originated from working-class community associations and local institutions such as schools, churches and workplaces.

There is a tendency to romanticise what could often be stiflingly claustrophobic neighbourhoods, pockmarked by overcrowding, poverty and bigotry. Life was frequently grim and the work that supported them backbreaking and dangerous. They also changed considerably over the course of the twentieth century: slum clearance, for example, triggered a relocation from back-to-back, inner-city areas to new, remote, suburban estates. But there remained a fundamental sense that, guided by a spirit of mutual aid and collective co-operation, working-class communities could determine their own history. As the educationalist Brian Jackson argued, the fact that 'industrial workers over ten generations made so much out of such squalor and indignity [was] one of the little miracles of British social history'.

In *The Making of the English Working Class*, the historian E. P. Thompson saluted the new proletariat's 'collective self-consciousness' as 'the great spiritual gain of the industrial revolution'. This narrative rescued Old Yorkshire from the condescension of that legion of middle-class Victorian writers who, during their intrepid journeys up north, had recoiled at the 'satanic' excesses of a smog-infested, strike-ridden region. The county, it has to be said, played up to its muck-and-nettles image, reinforced by John Ruskin's description of Sheffield as 'the dirty picture in the golden frame'. In *Books Do Furnish a Room*, Anthony Powell wrote: 'It is not what happens to people that is significant, but what they think happens to them.' Everyone, Powell elaborated, has a personal myth. He was writing about fictional characters but the axiom can be equally applied to regional character. Yorkshire liked, still likes, to see itself as a melting pot of society's undervalued, perennially tasked with the responsibility of keeping British sport honest. It has particularly revelled in its role as the backbone of English cricket; hence the timeworn, if largely inaccurate, maxim: 'A strong Yorkshire means a strong England.' It has proudly expressed its identity through its football, cricket and rugby league teams. Sport has always been and remains, despite the tragedy of the past three decades, its cultural adrenalin.

Local, collective pride is hardly unique to Yorkshire. The northeast, the north-west, Devon, the Welsh Valleys and the Scottish Highlands, to name but five sport-obsessed regions, all have their own, similar, personal myths. Indeed, up until the nineteenth century, as Roy Hattersley noted, 'there were no immutable economic laws which united Barnsley, Bridlington and Boroughbridge and yet somehow distinguished them from what lay east of the Pennines and south of the Humber . . . no common cultural heritage or spiritual yearning that embraced Hull, Haworth and Halifax.' But, from the formation of Sheffield FC, the world's first modern football club, in 1857, to the Hillsborough tragedy 132 years later, 'God's own county' made a particular point of presenting itself as the alternative to a snobbish, hypocritical, southern-based Establishment. Its amateur and professional teams have tended to represent society's have-nots, conveying a solidarity society rooted in the synchronised labour of the factory, mill, mine and shipyard.

Its traditional sporting culture was the product of a social bargain struck between employers and workforce – the latter enduring appalling working conditions and, in return, expecting the former to subsidise their churches, welfare halls and sporting organisations. Yorkshire, gradually, became to London what Sparta had been to Athens: a harsher, tougher society. As Hattersley observed, the county stood for something 'when all that was hard, heavy and arduous . . . began to flourish in the country – coal cut from deep seams, blooms and billets of hot steel manhandled under massive steam hammers, wool spun and woven not at home but during long days spent in the company's cold sheds. To survive any or all of that, the families that lived in the lath and plaster back-to-back houses had to espouse the oppressive virtues and the stern values.' The idea of a shared, muscular culture came into its own between 1945 and the mid-1970s. For all its neuroses, amongst them a penchant for self-flagellating, declinist doom-mongering, Britain was, back then, a relatively stable, unified country. The post-war Labour government's redistribution of wealth changed the terms of trade between the haves and have-nots. This is often referred to as sport's golden age. In football, rugby league and cricket there was a hunger for community and belonging. In most parts of the country, these sports offered stability, normality and familiarity. There was an extra intensity and hardness about the teams' style of play as fans flocked to the dilapidated grounds in huge numbers. The immediate decade after the conflict was a period of peak attendance at football matches; supporters born between 1950 and 1970, who became young adult fans in the mid-eighties, were part of a universal culture imbibed with a sense of collective responsibility for the health of the game. There was a spirit of egalitarianism abroad: seven different clubs won the Football League championship in the first seven years after the war. 'The ground was the working man's theatre,' wrote Andrew Ward and John Williams, 'and the pitch his stage.'

The idea for this book came when I read out this quote from *Football Nation: Sixty Years of the Beautiful Game* to a group of children who attended the school where *Kes*, the classic 1970 Ken Loach movie, had been filmed. The week-long, residential writing course involved a trip to their local football club. At the beginning of the week most of the kids declared their allegiances to elite clubs like Manchester United, Arsenal, Liverpool and even Chelsea. But when we visited Barnsley FC's Oakwell stadium, to be greeted by a large sign sporting the legend 'My Town, My Team, My Blood', their latent Casper-ness suddenly came to the surface. It was clear that the film, an unsentimental, and unsurpassed, depiction of a South Yorkshire mining community, had been burned into their consciousness, reinforcing their sense of their beleaguered town, indeed the whole of Yorkshire, as a place apart, misunderstood and wronged.

One session was taught by Ian McMillan, the Bard of Barnsley, who used to be the club's poet-in-residence. *A Kestrel for a Knave,* the Barry Hines book the classic film was based on, was, he explained, 'our defining myth. It's our *Moby-Dick*, our *Great Expectations*, our *Things Fall Apart*, our *Great Gatsby*, our *Grapes of Wrath*. It's our creation myth. Billy Casper's story reminds us that we are worth writing about. Here is our little town presented as a place where epic things can happen.' Set at the end of the sixties, Hines' novel tells the story of a half-boy, half-pigeon who is bullied both at home and at school and seeks solace in the rolling fields and rich woods beyond the pithead. Hines, the son of a miner, grew up near Barnsley and was the last of that great generation of post-war working-class writers to barge through the privileged ranks of the metropolitan elite. Along with Hoggart's seminal tome, and other masterly accounts of traditional working-class life by sociologists such as Michael Young and Norman Dennis, who co-wrote a groundbreaking study of Featherstone, these social realist writers breathed new life into cultural stereotypes about the 'lower orders'.

Kes is often misread as a gritty, depressing, grim-up-north film. Its depiction of Old Yorkshire is certainly brutal and unsparing. But it is, chiefly, a movie about the possibility of redemption, entirely in tune with the social upheavals of an era belligerently challenging the residual inequalities of post-war Britain. 'I thought I would like to show that these kids can do something which is in fact very skilful,' said Hines. 'They can do all kinds of things if only they're given opportunities.' Both the book and film offered a glimpse of what it was like to rise, soar even, above a hopeless situation. You did not have to accept your fate, know your place or be battered into submission, especially on a football pitch by a Manchester United-supporting bully. In the film's most famous scene, Brian Glover's callous PE teacher, Mr Sugden – 'I'm scheming this morning, all over the field, just like Charlton used to do. Anyway, Denis Law's in the wash this week' – insists on being both referee and team captain, taking every free kick and blowing his whistle whenever he's tackled.

After a comically inept performance in goal, Billy is pushed into the shower and Sugden turns the thermostat to cold. The youngster's two-fingered riposte waymarked the industrial militancy of the coming decade. In 1972 a human blockade, organised by the Yorkshire NUM, closed down Saltley coke depot, forcing Ted Heath's Conservative government to award striking miners a 21 per cent pay rise. Two years later, 'King Coal', as the media had taken to calling Scargill's troops, played a large part in bringing down that government. This was a decade of affordable housing, low unemployment, free health care, free higher education, low levels of crime and greater equality. In 2004, the New Economics Foundation concluded that Britain had been a happier country in 1976 than it has been in the twenty-eight years since. 'Inflation was high but so were pay settlements,' said Andy Beckett, a chronicler of the era. 'People had the money, particularly in the second half of the 70s when the economy was better, to become interested in buying their own home, having a bigger car . . . living standards for most Britons in the 1970s were probably growing more than they had done in the previous 60 or 70 years.'

Since the eighties, however, the forward march of labour has not only been halted but gone into reverse. Social mobility has fallen by the wayside. A northern working-class hero is no longer something to be. 'You see a lot of people who look like whippets around here,' said McMillan. 'They look thin and haunted. You see Billy Casper everywhere.' A few months after the writing course I actually saw the 'real' Casper walking around in Barnsley. David Bradley, who had been chosen from hundreds of local 'whippets' to play the lead role in *Kes*, returned to his old school to see the students perform their work. Forty years after his beguiling portrayal, his instantly recognisable, unforgettably pinched, shrewd, hungry face still reminded me of Arthur Hopcraft's description of Stanley Matthews in *The Football Man*: 'A worker's face like a miner's, never really young, tight against a brutal world even in repose.'

Kes' famous football scene was filmed on the school's muddy playing fields. Bradley pointed out the goalposts he had swung from as a reluctant goalkeeper. 'Look,' he laughed, 'you can still see the dink in the crossbar.' He talked with great enthusiasm about his lifelong support for Barnsley FC. At the beginning of the shoot he had carried on with his part-time job selling programmes at Oakwell, but the film crew eventually paid him off. *Kes* was his big break. A few years ago he returned to Barnsley. 'I've not been to Oakwell over the last season and a half,' he admitted. 'I can't afford it.' That 'confession' speaks to the tragedy at the heart of this book. In a country radically transfigured, over three decades, by the most dramatic shift of resources since Henry VIII closed the monasteries, a great swathe of British society has ended up priced out of, and alienated from, the new sporting order.

At the beginning of my research for the book, I learned that Casper's school had been demolished. There was a half-hearted attempt to preserve the goalposts but they, too, were eventually knocked down, leaving a sizeable hole in Old Yorkshire's – and the nation's – psychological landscape.

Wivenhoe and Leeds, April 2016

Act One:

Division

'All fixed, fast-frozen relations, with their train of ancient and venerable prejudices and opinions, are swept away, all new-formed ones become antiquated before they can ossify. All that is solid melts into air . . .'

Karl Marx and Friedrich Engels,
The Communist Manifesto, 1848

4 May 1979. On her arrival at 10 Downing Street, Margaret Thatcher sonorously quotes from Saint Francis of Assisi: 'Where there is discord, may we bring harmony.' The high-priestess of neoliberalism turns out to be the most divisive prime minister in post-war British. history. Dominated by industrial strife, social conflict, race riots and an economic policy that lays waste to large swathes of the north, her decade in power culminates in a divisive tax which, ultimately, prompts her downfall. A famous 1978 Tory poster had shown a snaking queue of jobless head-lined 'Labour isn't working'. But the introduction of monetarist economic policies precipitates an escalation in unemployment, from 1.3 million in 1979 to over 3 million in 1983. The Chancellor of Exchequer, Geoffrey Howe, cuts the top rate of income tax from 83p to 60p in the pound. VAT is increased from 8 to 15 per cent. The government removes all controls over the exchange of foreign currency. Individualism is all the rage, symbolised by the advent of the Sony Walkman. By the end of 1982, Britain has more video recorders per head than any other country in the world. Midway through the first term, in the middle of a long and deep recession, 364 university economists write a letter to the government warning that the monetarist experiment will 'deepen the depression, erode the industrial base of our economy and threaten its social and political stability'. Riots break out in Brixton, Southall, Leeds, Toxteth and Moss Side. As an old world lays dying, and a new one begins to be born, New Britain becomes polarised, fractured, fragmented. And as its heavy industry, the lifeblood of so much of the region, begins to feel its pulse faltering, Old Yorkshire falls prey to turbulence.

1

Old Faithful

'Old faithful, we roam the range together.
Old faithful, in any kind of weather.
When the round-up days are over,
And the Boulevard's white with clover,
For you, old faithful pal of mine.'

'Old Faithful', Hull FC anthem

HULL'S BIG DAY OUT

3 May 1980. Wembley. The Challenge Cup final. Hull FC vs Hull Kingston Rovers. Airlie Birds vs The Robins. Black-and-whites vs red-and-whites. The Battle of Hull. 'Will the last person to leave,' a banner draped over a bridge on the A63 asks the myriad marauders crashing south, 'please turn out the lights?' Steve Hubbard bursts through for Rovers for the first try of the match. He then knocks a penalty over to give the Robins a 5-0 lead. Another Hubbard penalty and, after less than a quarter of the game, Rovers are 7-0 up. The match swings when Tim Wilby goes over for Hull FC, but Sammy Lloyd can't convert. As half-time approaches, Roger Millward slots over an important drop-goal to make it 8-3. Lloyd adds a penalty to bring Hull closer at 8-5. With five minutes to go, the Airlie Birds are penalised and Hubbard, once again, converts to increase the lead to 10-5. A few minutes before the end, Hubbard collapses in a heap and is stretchered off.

Keith Tindall was on the losing side in the Battle of Hull and 'that lot over the river' have never let him forget it. 'A red-and-whiter said I was on Facebook but I'm too old for all that stuff,' the Hull FC legend tells an amused group of black-and-whiters being shown around the giant, shopping plaza-like KC Stadium.* 'What he meant

---

* There are three clubs in Hull: Hull FC and Hull Kingston Rovers (both rugby league) and Hull City A.F.C. (football). Hull FC used to play at the Boulevard, and now play at the KC Stadium; Rovers were formerly based at Old Craven Park and have since moved to a new ground called Craven Park; and City once called Boothferry Park home, and now share the KC with Hull FC.

was he'd seen this picture of me on Facebook, coming out of the "10-5" pub. The "10-5" – cheeky buggers. I hadn't realised it was called that. Someone had invited me in for a drink. A mean trick.' Tindall tells me how much 'Hull's big day out', as he calls it, still means to both sides of the city, some three-and-a-half decades on. He is frequently asked about it, even though he played in several other, far more memorable, finals. During his hour-long tour, someone had mentioned Hull City, the club's co-tenants at the stadium. 'I'm okay with City but I don't like to mention Mr Allam,"* he snapped. 'Unfortunately, he doesn't do us any favours.' All becomes clear when we visit the Whiteley Suite. The walls are decorated with framed photographs of John Whiteley or, as Tindall prefers to call him, 'the chosen one'. A year or so ago, he took a tour group into the suite and was shocked to find that the pictures of Hull's greatest-ever rugby league player had been removed and replaced by football photos. 'I think Mr Allam wanted to charge Hull FC something like £350 a photograph,' he explains. 'They were taken down, but after we protested they put 'em back up.' I tell him my next port of call is the Royal Hotel to meet Steve Hubbard, the Rovers player who touched down the winner in 1980. 'Tell him to give that Oscar back,' Tindall winks. 'Ask him why he pretended to get injured at the end.' I walk for a mile up the battered Anlaby Road, which in the eighties was Kingston upon Hull's major western artery. Hubbard is waiting for me in the foyer. A grand Italianate building, opened by Queen Victoria in 1851 and commemorated in Phillip Larkin's poem 'Friday Night in the Royal Station Hotel', the hotel no longer exudes the provincial self-confidence described by the Hull University librarian.

---

* Assem Allam, the Hull City A.F.C. owner since 2010.

It remains, however, an oasis of calm, its silence, as one of the twentieth century's great poets noted, 'laid like carpet'. On the way into the hotel I had passed a statue of Larkin, mid-dash, notebook clutched under an arm, overcoat flapping open and a hat swinging from his left hand. 'What Larkin found,' wrote his biographer Andrew Motion, 'was a city at the end of one kind of life, waiting for another to begin.'

LONDON 0 HULL 4

In 1980, for the first time in history, Hull's two rugby league clubs met in the Challenge Cup final. The media, inevitably, homed in on the Tale of Two Cities angle, highlighting the intense, longstanding rivalry between the teams. Their different geographical locations were discussed at great length: Hull FC, on the west side of the river, were wedded to the Hessle Road trawlermen – Rovers, their bitter adversaries on the east side, were the coastal fishermen's team. The city's economic decline, however, had decimated both communities and the old Wembley Stadium – if an aerial photograph had been taken from the top of its white, concrete towers – would have resembled a giant comfort blanket of red, black and white; the teams' colours seemed to merge into one as two warring tribes came together in a moving show of Hullensian solidarity. The whole city, it appeared, had migrated en masse to London, briefly taking possession of a self-regarding capital believed, by its transient occupiers, to be living off the honest toil of the downtrodden north. This was the day Hull let the world know that, despite the countless hard knocks it had received over the years – the latest being the disappearance of its fishing fleet – it was not yet ready, in the words of the A63 banner, to turn out the lights.

Both Tindall and Hubbard, although on opposite sides, used the same phrase to sum up the big day: 'It showed the city hadn't given in.' Regardless of the outcome (a famous Rovers victory) the match allowed a downtrodden, besieged city its moment, providing a national platform for its wounded civic pride in an era when a rugby cup final still meant something; since the 1980s, the showpiece, like its soccer equivalent, has hugely declined in importance. 'On that day, every year, London was full of fans,' explained Tindall. 'Not just from Hull but from all over the country.' The number of neutral supporters attending the event has, like his team's support base, drastically shrunk. Before the new era of Sky and the Super League, it was one of the most important days in the sporting calendar.

Although it prompted a revival in both clubs' fortunes, the final had the feel of a last hurrah. This most northern of sports was, like Hull itself, reaching the end of one kind of life, and would soon have to adapt to the demands of a new, globalised, sporting order. Only one year away from his own swansong, after five colourful decades commentating on a game he'd played a key role in popularising, Eddie Waring – better known than any football, let alone rugby league, presenter is today – provided a suitably wistful commentary. Lamenting the passing of a once-great maritime port, he invoked the 'sailing ships of days gone by' and compared the teams walking out of the Wembley tunnel to 'two ships coming into the port of Hull'. The idea of tribal warfare in a remote, east Yorkshire port had an obvious appeal to the media. And yet, as the final suggested, the city was keen to present a united front in front of the watching millions. To many Hullensians, the real divide was not between Hull and

Rovers, or the east and west sides of the river, but between 'them' – the London-based elite – and 'us'. The Housemartins might not have had this occasion in mind when, six years later, they released their first album, *London o Hull 4*, but its title perfectly encapsulated the moment the plucky, underdog, oval-ball city invaded the Big Smoke.

Waring's lament betrayed a hazy yearning for a lost post-war world of full employment, social mobility and rapidly rising living standards. The BBC's rugby league commentator for five decades, his jocular persona, relentlessly satirised by TV comedians, tended to wind up over-earnest northern fundamentalists. But, as his biographer, Tony Hannan, pointed out, he saw rugby league as 'more than just a simple social pleasure. The particularly working-class phenomenon . . . was both a symbolic expression of personal identity and a crucial component in an entire way of life . . . rugby league told of who you were and from where you came.' Waring had campaigned all his life to get the north's 'national sport' taken more seriously. At the beginning of his broadcasting career, in the last year of the war, he made a famous emotional address to the overseas troops listening to his Yorkshire Cup final commentary on the BBC World Service. 'For those lads from Hunslet who are serving abroad,' he declared, 'I want to tell them that I am sitting in the old pavilion. There's 9,000 people here and I am going to open the window so you can hear the Parkside roar.' In Waring's version of Old Yorkshire, sport was not only a diversion from industry's dirty, dangerous, back-breaking jobs, but a symbol of the county's resolute fighting spirit.

At the end of the rail network, and the beginning of the long crossing to northern Europe, Hull has, historically, enjoyed flicking two fingers up at London. The English Civil War began in 1642 when its merchants slammed shut the gates in the face of King Charles' tax collectors. In the early nineteenth century, local MP William Wilberforce led the campaign against the slave trade. In 1895, Hull FC took part in a rebellion which led to the formation of a new rugby league, a guerrilla organisation called the Northern Union; fifty years later, rising from the wreckage left by the Luftwaffe, the city's revival was inspired by Whiteley's black-and-whites. Up until a decade ago, before its football team's intoxicating adventures, it was the parochial oval-ball game that shaped the city's identity. Like the parliamentarians who opposed the king and the abolitionists, Hull FC were at the forefront of a late-nineteenth-century resistance – both to the southern gentleman-amateurs who objected to rugby players being compensated for missing their Saturday morning shifts and the round-ball interlopers determined to breach their stronghold. Before the mid-seventies cod war Hull had tended to turn its back on the capital, preferring to look out to the North Sea for its prosperity – either through whaling, fishing or merchant ships that traded with neighbours in the Low Countries. As Waring's colleague Tony Gubba explained, in an eve-of-final documentary, the 'fleets of 150 trawlers which made Hull fish docks famous ten years ago have now dwindled to less than two dozen. And catches are actually brought in by road to be gutted and cleaned by men with unshakable loyalties.'

The conflict with Iceland had destroyed its trawler fleets, an augury of the chill winds of globalisation about to blow through Britain's industrial heartlands – and Westminster had stood by. The Labour government, under pressure from the Americans, who needed Iceland as a bulwark against the Soviet Union, allowed the Nordic country to impose a 200-mile fishing limit, causing swathes of Hull's staple industry to rot and 15,000 jobs to disappear. The city had once been a major centre of shipping. In the sixties and seventies, there had been a steady southward migration, a depopulation in which thousands of young, ambitious, working-class men and women had disembarked to the London, exacerbating north–south tensions. Goal-kicker Sammy Lloyd remembered the frisson in the Hull camp when a posse of Buckingham Palace officials breezed into the changing room just before the final. 'One of them said he wanted a word with us,' said Lloyd. '"Now, chaps," he said, "you are going to be presented to Her Majesty the Queen Mother. Now, she will offer her hand. It is not for you chaps to shake her hand manfully." It was as if we were all northern heathens and we were going to be bouncing her up and down. And then, with a look in his eye, he turned across to look at Paul Woods, who was one of our best assassins. It was as if he were warning Paul to be on his best behaviour.'

On the inner sleeve of *London o Hull 4*, Heaton had printed the legend 'Take Jesus, Take Marx, Take Hope'. 'We're interested in the inspirational side,' he explained. 'The power, the collective power . . . the footballing side of it.' A city which had endured heavy bombing during the war (93 per cent of its homes were blitzed), post-war civic vandalism and the ravages of de-industrialisation was not going to take its latest subordination to London lying down. In this sense, although renowned for its out-on-a-limb, maverick tendencies – epitomised by its creamy-white phone boxes – Hull was, and remains, northern defiance writ large.

In the early eighties such unilateralist truculence had become the trademark of the city's musical, as well as sporting, nonconformists. Like The Housemartins, Everything But The Girl were a critically acclaimed Hull-based band who revelled in the city's sense of apartness. Their singer Tracey Thorn observed that its:

lack of any rock glamour to speak of meant that we were forever left off the tour circuit. In all the time I was there I can remember going to see Haircut 100, The Polecats and, er, that's it. One result of this situation was that Ben [Watt] and I began to evolve in a musical isolation that was both good and bad for us. And like some bizarre Darwinian experiment we gradually became more and more like ourselves and less and less like anyone else, anywhere else. The seeds of our separation from the main developments in pop music through the 1980s can perhaps be traced in part back to this separation, our sense of being set apart; that 'you and me against the world' attitude.

These two unfashionably belligerent indie bands, like several of their Sheffield counterparts, operated in a parallel universe to the New Romantic, Thatcher-inspired mainstream. As bright, shiny, shoulder-padded London groups like Spandau Ballet, Culture Club and Wham! became the toast of the pop world, Old Yorkshire romantics like Thorn, Heaton and Pulp's Jarvis Cocker continued to stick two fingers up at the very idea of international stardom.

THE FISH DOCK TEAM

In the mid-eighties, after being rebuked by the Independent Broadcasting Authority for a lewd on-air remark about the south's prime minister, Heaton retorted: 'They should come and see some of the housing estates in Hull. That's what I call obscene.' Twenty-five years later, these estates, which had been built during the urban renewal programme of the sixties and seventies and suffered years of decline and depopulation, were singled out by *The Idler* magazine as a particular lowlight of Britain's 'crappest town'. Property guru Kirstie Allsopp, the presenter of popular TV show *Location, Location, Location*, then declared Hull to be the worst place to live in the country. As a rejoinder, and to promote its UK City of Culture campaign, the local council produced a promotional video narrated by the actor Tom Courtenay. 'People are slow to leave it,' intoned Courtenay, quoting a line from a Larkin essay, 'but quick to return.'

There was a certain irony to this homage, but it was heartfelt. Courtenay had made his name in the sixties social realist film *Billy Liar*, a huge influence on *Kes*, in which a young, working-class dreamer attempts to escape his Old Yorkshire backwater and seek his fame and fortune down south. In the movie, Billy bottles out of catching the train to the capital, but in real life Courtenay became a huge success in Swinging London and then Hollywood. In a beautifully written memoir, he paid tribute to the Airlie Birds for keeping him grounded during this heady ascent. 'Dad and I always had our love of sport in common,' he wrote. 'It was the one thing that connected us powerfully.' He might have left Hull, but it had never left him.

In *Dear Tom*, he recalled how, in his Hessle Road neighbourhood, all the families worked, played, learned and shopped together. Within inhaling distance of the reeking River Humber, the community had created a rugby team in its own image – Hull FC –which was known to locals as 'the fish dock team'. Hull's growth during the Industrial Revolution had been driven, like other northern towns and cities, by the local trinity of home, work and leisure, a dense fabric bound together by Hessle Road, St Andrew's Dock and the Boulevard, a 10,000-capacity stadium built shortly after Hull FC joined the rebel Northern Union. Powered by its fertile catchment area, the fish dock team quickly became one of the new league's pre-eminent forces, reaching three consecutive cup finals between 1908 and 1910. In 1913 they signed the game's biggest star, Billy Batten, who repaid the club a year later by leading them to a first-ever Challenge Cup win. In 1921, they won the championship. They then lost back-to-back finals but lifted the Yorkshire Cup and again topped the league table. After winning the Yorkshire League in 1926–7, they endured a lean spell but won their third Championship title in 1935–6. Before the Second World War broke out, they were runners-up in the Yorkshire Cup and League. After the war they continued to win trophies and reach finals until the seventies when, mirroring the port's decline, they stagnated. A nadir was reached in 1974 when only 721 people turned up at the Boulevard to watch an encounter with bottom-of-the-league club Huyton.

'I saw Hessle Road's demise at first hand,' said Hubbard, whose winning try triggered the most successful period in Hull Kingston Rovers' history. The red-and-whites, like their black-and-white rivals, also suffered during the seventies. Late developers in the game, having to wait until 1964 before making their first visit to Wembley, their traditional heartland was on the dry side of the river, where shore gangs worked to catch the tide. Hubbard, who was born on the west side, began his working life as a wages clerk at St Andrews dock, a quarter of a mile from Hessle Road, where he witnessed what he called the 'double whammy' of housing relocation and economic decline, which 'tore the whole of the neighbourhood apart'. From the window of his office, where he kept an eye on the diminished fleet of trawlers entering the basin, he witnessed 'the death of the fishing industry. It happened, really, the year I worked there, around 1974–5. They had different shops on the dock. I took the wages each week to the shops and saw the queues get smaller as the fishing industry began to fold. The amount of work dropped drastically. It went from being a vibrant, incredibly busy dock to disappearing in front of our eyes.'

Hubbard doesn't think it strange that Humberside, as the area was then known, briefly emerged as a rugby league superpower after the 1980 final. 'It was our way of fighting back, of regrouping,' he explained. 'The city was having a terrible time.' Hull's most notorious serial killer, Bruce Lee, had been convicted of twenty-six charges of manslaughter following a spree of arson attacks. Rioting youths battled police. 'The city centre on a Saturday evening was not for the weak,' wrote City fan Shaun Todroff. 'The area was ruled by gangs intent on causing as much damage to each other as they could. Fighting was a way of life . . . [this] generation of Hessle Road youth didn't flock to the sea with the same enthusiasm or in the same numbers as their forebears. Instead they looked for shore-based jobs, shaved their heads and laced up their boots. These skinheads would virtually wipe out the fishermen culture along with the after-effects of the cod war, which decimated the industry in Hull.'

And yet this was a time when the fish dock team became one of the most powerful rugby league sides in the country, commanding gates of almost 13,000. They were champions in 1983 and runners-up either side of that year. They won the Challenge Cup in 1982 and were finalists in 1983 and 1985. Rovers, who averaged around 8,000 a game, won back-to-back titles in 1984 and 1985 and lost at Wembley in 1981 and 1986. Hubbard thinks the all-Hull final sparked a 'reawakening, which put the city back on the national map'. Towards the end of the decade, however, both teams, like the city itself, spiralled into decline. Since the formation of the Super

League, in 1996, he feels that 'something has gone from the game. The commitment from Hull and Rovers players when the two teams play each other now is nowhere near what it used to be. I feel that kind of spirit is history. The game today is really hyped up. It's Super League, but I can't get my head round it at all. It doesn't have a sense of community any more.'

In *Dear Tom*, Courtenay paid tribute to the academic Richard Hoggart who, while teaching at Hull University in the late fifties, had written *The Uses of Literacy*. Hoggart had predicted the rise of an individualised, privatised world based on consumerism, status-seeking and acquisitiveness. He feared it would destroy the collective ties that held working-class society together. Metropolitan advertisers and the national media were already, he argued, robbing local communities of their identity and people within them of inherited values. As a result, the individuals of the future would believe 'nothing and [be] able to honour almost no one; in such circumstances we stand on nothing and so can stand for nothing.' Hoggart's boyhood rugby league team, Hunslet, which he portrayed as the embodiment of working-class collectivity at play, were the apotheosis of this 'common culture'.

The street corners of Courtenay's childhood were, like Hoggart's Hunslet, dotted with idyllic corner shops: butchers, general stores, hairdressers and bakers, all providing a social meeting point for a community that lived in each other's pockets. This was a world where people spoke plainly and stood by their word. At Crimliss' fish and chip shop, fish dock workers would bring home a 'fry' to share with their neighbours. Everyone claimed to know Amy Johnson, the Hessle Road tomboy who grew up to become one of the world's great aviators and whose plane mysteriously plunged into the Thames during the Second World War.

In the sixties, thousands of families were uprooted from working-class districts, including Hessle Road, and relocated to soulless suburban estates. These sprawling housing areas had been built on requisitioned farmland miles away from the town centre to redress the destruction of the war. 'There was a migration from Hessle Road,' recalled Dave Windass, a local playwright.

All the kids used to play outside and they had families connected to the fishing industry. Families were forced to move to estates on the edge of Hull. It was a systematic clearance of densely-populated streets, two-up, two-down terraces, really packed places with big families, which went on for about two or three years. Going to a football game or rugby game was and is part of the working-class ritual. You knew where you were with life back then. Life was a lot simpler and it evolved around the working week. If you start dismantling that then the fabric of everyday working life starts slipping away. That's not specific to Hull, but to the industrial north.

The demolished neighbourhood's conviviality has undoubtedly been exaggerated over time. Many families would have been relieved to leave their squalid, unsanitary housing and move into homes with a bath, inside toilet and running hot water. But its disappearance broke the bond linking home to work. By the time the rugby league historian Tony Collins had left Hull in 1980, he was aware that 'a lot of the traditional housing areas were ending as big communities.' Only the third part of the local trinity, the Boulevard, had remained intact. 'The stadium gave those broken-up communities some type of meaning,' said Collins, 'something to cling on to.'

For a while, being moved across the river to the remote and inhospitable east Hull towers actually intensified the former Hessle Road residents' fervour for the fish dock team. 'They still stayed black-and-white,' said Tindall. 'These double-decker buses came out of the new Bransholme estate and when there was a Hull FC game you could see everyone pressed against the window. They were full to the gunnels with supporters. The community spirit died a bit later than that, just after the end of my playing days in the mid-eighties. But, at first, you had all these people who came to the Boulevard from the east. After a game, they didn't want to go home. They went on to Hessle Road for a drink before the game and after it they went back to Hessle Road again, back to where their old neighbourhood used to be. All those pubs were absolutely crammed. How they ever got home, across the other side of the city, God only knows. Today, though, it's not the same. This new lot of fans, I'm afraid, have no memory of those Hessle Road days.'

A LOST WORLD

Outside a west Hull pub in the early fifties, during the middle of Hull FC's post-war renaissance, a large crowd gathered around a hole in the ground. As a tall man in an apron emerged up a ladder, holding an empty beer keg on his shoulder, he was greeted by a crescendo of applause. It was The Chosen One, 'Gentleman John' Whiteley. The Hull loose forward, who scored 156 tries in 417 games, retains a special place in the city's folk memory. He started out as a filleter on the docks and didn't even get a signing-on fee when Hull snapped him up in 1950. The club, however, agreed to pay him £100 when he first played for Great Britain's under-21s. On receiving the payment, he gave all the money to his mother. 'She immediately bought a four-ringed gas cooker,' he said. 'We lived down Gordon Street near the Boulevard. Our kitchen was full of women for the next seven days all wanting to look at it. I also got her a radiogram and a week's holiday at Butlin's at Farley, which is also gone. It was just after the war and there was this fervour for looking for a local sportsman to play in the black-and-white shirt, to play at international level. I couldn't go anywhere. All the fans adopted me. I was still filleting on the fish dock but being an international rugby player wasn't conducive to standing around all day long in the freezing cold, filleting fish, so they got me a job in the brewery, humping barrels of beer. I loved it.'

Whiteley is not an Old Romantic. He refuses to pine for the crumbling terraces, rickety stands and primitive toilets of the Boulevard. But he does miss its atmosphere and sense of community. 'It was a hard, tough culture but also very warm,' he remembered. In 2002, he spoke in favour of the proposed move to the KC Stadium, pointing out that the club's heritage would never be forgotten; the smell of the fish docks might no longer blow off the Humber, he said, but their 67-year-old anthem, 'Old Faithful', would always be sung at matches. The song has played a crucial role in sustaining the bond between the club and its supporters. It speaks to the latter's pride and loyalty, to continuity and tradition, to the camaraderie of a time when trawlermen were kings and sporting heroes were both local and loyal. After working flat out to clear away all the bought fish, filleters would take their minds off their cold, wet work by breaking out into the chart-topping, cowboy melody. 'Old Faithful' is a valedictory cry. 'It was made famous by Gene Autry, the film star,' said Lloyd, who now tours the east Yorkshire clubs as a folk singer. 'He sings the song to his horse because he's a cowboy. "Old Faithful, pal of mine." He's about to put it to sleep, because it's at the end.' It's a symbol of a lost world, a lament to a dying breed, a community that might have been sold out by 'that London', but still lives on in the hearts of its dwindling fan base. It evokes an era of extended family life, belonging and neighbourliness, before the great upheaval of slum clearance, the traumatic decline of the docks and New Britain's assault on the inherited values of a common culture. The song also struck a chord because of the west Hull community's identification with cowboy life. 'The rough rawhide cowhand had to brand the cattle and struggle against the elements,' explained local historian Alec Gill. 'Equally, the tough trawler deckhand had to gut the fish and battle against the elements. A number of other parallels can be drawn: the wide-open spaces, (hated) owners, uncertainty of life, boozy behaviour, saloon fights, and strained relationships with women. In addition, there was perhaps an affinity between the cowboy and his horse; and the trawlerman and his ship – riding the range or riding the waves.'

It was sung by Hull trawlermen as they battled freezing winds and roaring seas. When Whiteley was a player, 120 ships would set off to ply their trade in the treacherous waters of the North Sea and the Arctic. With their distinctive suits – made to measure by local tailoring shops – heavy drinking and cowboy nicknames, these 'three-day millionaires', as they were known, worked hard and played hard. They enjoyed a reputation as the last of the hunters, embarking on wild spending sprees during their three-day breaks, jumping into cabs and letting the meters run as they worked their way through the profits of a bountiful trip – before hitting the Boulevard. The dock was their rite of passage, a gateway to a world of adventure – but also to a potential watery death. The hardships they endured during their trips made deep-sea fishing the most dangerous profession in Britain. Nine hundred trawlers sunk between 1830 and 1980, leaving thousands of men dead. There was a lower life expectancy than average and a very high incidence of stomach cancer, lung cancer and heart disease. 'They were away for three weeks,' recalled Whiteley. 'So every day ten or fifteen trawlers landed, and they all lived in the vicinity of the Boulevard. It was like a Mecca. It was their life. They would come down the North Sea, flat out, to catch the tide for the match, singing "Old Faithful". They'd be stoking the fire up like an old American train. Just to get home for the match. They'd go straight off the dock. They'd been away for three weeks – but they'd go straight to the match.'

According to legend, 'Old Faithful' had first been sung to one loyal local hero in particular, the dependable goal kicker Joe Oliver, during a narrow victory over Wigan in 1936. Overjoyed with the win, Hull fans spontaneously began to serenade their points machine.

Lloyd, a former miner who moved to Hull from Castleford, was taught 'Old Faithful', now a staple of his repertoire, on his first day at the Boulevard. 'I'd played there so many times with Cas,' he said.

And you'd hear the Hull crowd singing it for their boys. And we'd come off and we'd be having a few beers with the Hull lads and we always used to say 'Fucking hell, I wish we had a song for Cas that's like that.' When my mate Knocker Norton, who played for Hull, persuaded me to go over he said 'Sammy, they'll love you to bits. And when you hear "Old Faithful", well . . .' You automatically get this affinity with this strange song. It's about a guy getting a horse to kneel down. The story goes that one horribly wet day, Hull are playing Bramley. As the wind was lashing into their faces some of the folks on the old Threepenny Stand were wondering just what they were doing there. Then Oliver, their ever reliable full-back, caught another ball and drove it out – and one of the wags started singing 'Old Faithful, he roams the range . . .' It was just the affection they had for him. He was stable, he was rock steady. 'Old Faithful, we roam the range together.' It's what Hull fans do. They might not have as big a following but they still follow the team all over the rugby league circuit together.

HULL CITY RIP

The Big Day Out was Rovers against Hull, east against west, coastal fishermen against deep-sea trawlermen. Since the 1980 final, however, the city has been defined by another battle: Old Yorkshire against New Britain. Hull used to be an oval-ball town. J. B. Priestley described a rugby league crowd in the 1920s as 'stocky men with short upper lips and jutting long chins who roll a little in their walk and carry their heads stiffly, twelve stone of combative instinct.' During the Great Depression of the 1930s, the Bradford-born writer embarked on a lengthy, rambling journey around England. 'These people are pleasant but queer,' he wrote of Hullensians. 'They are queer because they are not quite Yorkshire but not quite anything else.' It is true that the old fishing port's geographical isolation has always set it apart from the rest of the region; stuck out at the end of a fifty-mile cul-de-sac, its focus is as much on the sea beyond as the hinterland that surrounds it. But its rugby league queerness – or, put another way, its refusal to sacrifice a longstanding, fierce and hard-won independence to the incoming forces of globalisation – is a quintessential Old Yorkshire trait.

Football was still seen as the interloper long after Hull City A.F.C had been formed in 1904. 'We believe we can become one of the top clubs in the country,' City's first president, Alfred E. Spring, had declared. They were, however, to spend almost a century outside the top flight – although in 1910 they came agonisingly close to breaking into the elite, failing to win promotion by 0.29 of a goal. They have never won a title outside the third tier of English football. City's Division Three championship in 1965–6 and Third Division (North) wins in 1932–3 and 1948–9, when the league still included New Brighton and Gateshead, remained, until the last decade, their greatest achievements.

Despite the club's recent Premier League exploits, many fans look back fondly to the mid-sixties as a golden age. This was the era when they stormed the Third Division championship, breaking all records, including the divisional one for attendance: 49,655 turned up to watch a Christmas Day clash with Rotherham. Cliff Britton's team, with its two legendary strikers, Chris Chilton and Ken Wagstaff, produced one of the most exciting periods in the Tigers' history, coinciding with a boom in English football as it geared itself up for the 1966 World Cup. Hull were even, for a short time, considered to be fashionable. According to the Chelsea match programme for an FA Cup quarter-final tie against City, the Swinging Londoners' opponents were 'the Third Division club with the Second Division outlook and the First Division ground'.

The man who had transformed their fortunes was Harold Needler, a wealthy local businessman and lifelong fan. From the moment he joined his brother Henry on the board in 1945, to his death thirty years later, 'Big Aitch' was openly ambitious for the club. He bought the great Raich Carter for £6,000 in 1948. He invested thousands of pounds in the team during the sixties as they tried, in vain, to get into the First Division. A successful builder, he oversaw the creation of Boothferry Park, which quickly gained a reputation as one of the best surfaces in the country. The new stadium benefited from an era when the docks still overflowed with fish. 'The drainage improved when they dug it up and laid a layer of rotten fish on top of cinders,' wrote local journalist and City fan Mike Ulyatt. 'It became a very good pitch. You'd think it might smell a bit but there was plenty of soil on top. Mind you, there was always a whiff of fish in those days if the wind was in the right direction.'

And yet the club spent virtually the whole of the twentieth century in the shadow of both rugby league teams, failing to make any real inroads into the city's sporting psyche. Hull became a byword for soccer underachievement, notorious for being the biggest city in Europe never to have hosted top-flight football. As the city emptied for the 1980 final, a few thousand black-and-amber diehards defied the mass exodus, filing into Boothferry Park for a bottom-of-the-table third division clash. City spent most of the seventies and eighties in the lower leagues, fighting off bankruptcies. In 1982, the year Hull FC beat Widnes to finally, after a sixty-eight-year wait, lift the Challenge Cup, the then Fourth Division team became the first Football League club to call in the receivers (Yorkshire neighbours Halifax Town and Bradford City would soon follow). It was in this year that the deepest recession for half a century took a heavy toll. Unemployment figures reached 3 million for the first time since the

1930s, leaving one in eight out of work, and social unrest simmered on the nation's streets. During the 1981–2 season City's crowds consistently fell below the 4,000 mark. The imposing North Stand was condemned to make way for an ugly-looking supermarket and protesters marched to the ground carrying a coffin draped in a banner that read 'Hull City RIP'. There was a revival under manager Brian Horton, who guided the team to sixth in the old Division Two in 1986, but a squad littered with promise was disbanded at the end of the decade as City were relegated to the third tier. In 1992, they became the first English club to go into administration. After that it was a long slide towards the bottom of the Football League.

THE DRINKING FOUNTAIN

The opening of the KC Stadium, in 2002, confirmed a remarkable shift in the balance of sporting power. The spanking, state-of-the-art amphitheatre was hailed by council leader Pat Doyle as 'a beacon of hope, a vindication of those who believe in the future of our great city'. In this future, a new enterprise culture would usher in 'an exciting new era'. To fill the vacuum created by its post-industrial decline, Hull would embrace a new identity, using football to regenerate itself in the twenty-first century. Its archetypal low-wage, high-welfare economy, broken seemingly beyond repair, would be revived, restructured and rebranded.

In Old Yorkshire, the potency of Hull's rugby league giants had been taken for granted. The emergence of a more assertive, commercially driven, outward-looking, sporting vision, however, had gradually sidelined those fading Victorian institutions. 'Their success had provided a way of keeping the community together,' said Collins. 'You may not still be living down Hessle Road or Greatfield Estate, where a lot of Rovers fans once lived, but you were keeping hold of what you had and you were keeping traditions going.' After the black-and-whites decided to join City in the new, £44 million stadium, the final link in the home-work-leisure trinity was broken. A few years later the Boulevard's beloved 'cathedral' was demolished and its diminished band of worshippers relocated to what *Guardian* journalist David Conn called 'a multi-million pound island of glitz, fenced off from its rundown surroundings'. The Boulevard's demise, wrote Dave Hadfield in *Up and Over*, one of the most entertaining books written about rugby league, meant there was now, 'nothing to hold the immediate area together. I suppose that, if you live in Fulham or Chelsea, a football or rugby ground might seem to lower the tone; in parts of Rugby League Land, it is the only thing that keeps it up.'

All that is left of Hull's spiritual home, in fact, is a drinking fountain. It was erected in the 1870s, when local philanthropists connected to the temperance movement tried to provide an alternative to alehouses. As mains water became more readily available, some developers decided to furnish streets such as Boulevard with grand decorative fountains. The fashion for using them as commemorative items or as memorials continued into the next century. It stands, today, as a lone symbol of west Hull's decline. 'As you come to the Boulevard off Hessle Road,' Hull FC's head of media James Clark said,

> you see the terrace houses, looking dated now, but back then they were the place to live. And slap-bang in the middle is a wonderful fountain, which is fenced off. The Boulevard is now a lower-end street with boarded-up houses, but there's this won-

derful piece of architecture in the middle. There's an angel, with water coming out, and it makes you wonder what it was like when it was thriving. It makes me think of Johnny Whiteley walking down the street all those years ago, of the guys on the docks walking home after training in the morning. They all lived in that area. They walked up to the Boulevard, trained and played there two or three times a week. Work hard, play hard. That mentality was carried across in their performances on the field. There was a togetherness, a pride, a playing for the badge. You could see what it meant playing for Hull at that ground, how special that ground was, what it meant to the people of that area. Imagine if the fountain wasn't there. You wouldn't have the foggiest about rugby league and what that street meant to people. It was the heart of the community, its defining spirit.

Twelve years later, after the KC's grand opening, Doyle's prophecy appeared to have been realised. Hull had been named the City of Culture 2017 and its reborn football team had spent a handful of seasons in the Premier League, reaching their first-ever FA Cup final. At the new Wembley they were pitched against Arsenal and, according to their coach Steve Bruce, it was to be 'the greatest day in our history ... mighty Arsenal against tiny Hull.' The similarities with 1980 were unavoidable. There was another mass exodus to London – although this time it was the rugby diehards who were left behind, travelling across the Pennines to Manchester for the Hull–Rovers derby. Here, again, was a plucky underdog's two-fingered salute to a preening city-state (which, thirty-four years later, had become even more self-regarding).

In the build-up to Big Day Out: The Sequel, defender Liam

Rosenior felt obliged to remind the assembled media that, despite his team's exhilarating ascent, the local area remained rundown. 'There is not much money,' he said. 'There has been no investment in the area for a long time. Most footballers are working-class lads. We see the poverty in this area, a lot of people on the breadline, and we hope we're helping to re-invigorate some pride.' At the club's plush new training ground, hidden away in the quiet, pleasant, leafy suburb of Cottingham, Bruce talked about a 'bigger picture' and posed an intriguing question: 'Where have all the young footballers gone?' In the past decade he could recall only two from Hull: Nicky Barmby and Dean Windass, the local brickie who scored the goal that propelled them into the Premier League in 2008. In the following seven years, revealed Bruce, not one homegrown player had emerged from the club's youth ranks.

Bruce's concern about the breeding of young talent was, indeed, part of a much bigger picture. The city still topped every nefarious list going: 'crap' towns, teenage pregnancies, obesity, bad schools and low wages. In a recent cover article, written after visiting its deserted high street, disintegrating warehouses and rotting docks, an *Economist* correspondent had dismissed it as an 'urban ghost town' suitable only for abandonment. It had the highest proportion of people on Jobseeker's Allowance – 6.6 per cent – in the country. Twenty-two per cent of 16–64-year-olds were economically inactive. A report by the End Child Poverty coalition revealed that it contained some of the poorest people in the land.

Hessle Road had produced countless Casper-esque heroes over the years: Oliver, Whiteley, Johnson and Lillian Bilocca, the 'headscarf revolutionary' who had taken on the might of the fishing industry in the sixties after three trawlers had been lost at sea. But its close-knit fishing community was long gone and a new generation of Billy Caspers were now trapped in their soulless estates. 'There are loads of lovely areas around Hull, especially around our training ground,' Bruce pointed out,

but go to the outskirts and you can see how it's suffered from years of economic neglect. It's really tough for people around here to go to a football match because of money. We mustn't forget these people. We must recognise that football is their relief from the mundanities of everyday life, like it's always been. All football clubs were created, back in the day, for the average working man in the street. This area's been hit hard for years. I'm from a local council estate up in Newcastle. A tough working-class area. Everybody worked in the shipyard. Since the shipyards have gone, engineering has gone, the pits have gone, the area where I lived and grew up in is now a ghetto. It's unrecognisable. I went back there a few years ago and it's scary. Junkies and drugs. Hull reminds me so much of the north-east in the way it's been badly hit.

Still, the plucky underdog was once again ready to strut its stuff at Wembley, to advertise its enormous, wasted potential, to take possession of the capital. After going two goals up inside the first nine minutes, tiny Hull collapsed and mighty Arsenal ran out 3-2 winners. The following season, they dropped out of the Premier League. Their relegation to the Championship left Yorkshire, a county of nearly six million people – and ten professional football clubs – without any representation in the glamorous, moneyed, all-singing, all-dancing top flight.

LONDON 4 HULL 0

In 2015, Adam Pearson left his post as executive director at Leeds United to focus on his role as Hull FC's chairman. The local business community, he warned, were deserting the black-and-whites. In the past ten years, as their round-ball counterparts had yo-yoed in and out of the elite, the Airlie Birds had failed to win any trophies. The City of Culture was only two years away and sponsorship was proving hard to attract. 'We have to fight for financial support,' he said. Pearson admitted that rugby league still had a limited national appeal and was now struggling locally to compete with its globally revered rival. 'You can tinker with the format and the rules,' he said, 'but, at the end of the day, do eight, nine, ten, eleven, twelve-year-old kids in Hull want to go to Premier League football or rugby league?' The club's season ticket numbers were falling 'but we'll keep battling until we achieve success. The problem is that rugby league is less important than it used to be because of the lack of government, and governing body, funding for school programmes in the game. That's a legacy of under-investment in that area. School rugby has diminished as Premier League football has become all-encompassing.'

As the City of Culture bid illustrated, the fish dock team had struggled to come to terms with the old port's reconfigured fault lines. In the transition towards a global sporting economy, two versions of Hull – one as an insular, provincial, repository of local, communal values, the other as a dynamic, monetised brand facing out across the Humber – had hardened. The local council had prepared for the twelve-month extravaganza by demolishing the Rank Hovis flour mill, a majestic local landmark, and replacing it with the Radisson Blu hotel, which was owned by an international chain. Chancellor

George Osborne had prepared by announcing £150 million for London museums, £141 million for arts and cultural developments at the Olympic Park in east London, £100 million for a new Royal College of Arts campus in Battersea – and a measly £1 million for Hull's year as City of Culture. In the same month, the city's bid to bring Amy Johnson's plane *Jason* to her city of birth, marking seventy-five years since her death, was rejected by London's Science Museum. London 4 Hull 0.

Pearson was desperate for Hull FC to come out of the shadows of Hull City, now successfully established as the city's dominant sporting team. Assem Allam, the Tigers' multi-millionaire owner, is a product of the eighties enterprise culture. The very model of a self-made entrepreneur, he had fled to Hull from Gamal Abdel Nasser's regime in Egypt and, in 1981, bought a generator manufacturer that blossomed into the internationally successful Allam Marine Company. It supplied generators to the royal palace in Dubai and won a Queen's Award for Enterprise. In a series of newspaper interviews, he proudly pointed out a picture of himself standing above a match-day crowd. Underneath it was a quote by the French novelist Victor Hugo: 'There is nothing more powerful than an idea whose time has come.' Ever since the eighties it has been this idea, rather than a river or an ancestral sporting allegiance, which has divided Hull.

To City's old faithful that idea (in essence transforming an unfashionable, provincial, community-based team into a global brand that sells shirts and sponsorships around the world) is the antithesis of the public-spirited paternalism of the Needler era. Since Needler's son Christopher sold up in 1997, a series of ambitious, brazenly opportunistic and often divisive risk-takers – all, in their different ways, standard-bearers of the New Britain – have been chipping away at the club's identity. Writing in the magazine *When Saturday Comes*, City fan Brian Simpson wrote that the Needlers and their ilk were 'driven by civic pride, a sense of *noblesse oblige*' and concluded that 'long-term support for a club [would soon] be a thing of the past'.

Martin Fish was the first of the new breed to make his mark at City. Shortly after becoming chairman, in Christopher Needler's final years, he upset fans by allowing Bradford City's away section to take over the South Stand, traditional Tigers territory. Eventually, Fish's financial mismanagement put the club's existence at risk – until tennis-player-turned-health-club magnate David Lloyd came to the rescue. Lloyd then proceeded to fall out with the council after they blocked his plan to sell Boothferry Park and build what he called an 'American leisure city'. Fans protested by throwing tennis balls on to the pitch at home games. 'I remember one game we came back out after half-time and there were drawing pins all over the place,' recalled David Brown, whose winner against Torquay, in the final home game of the 1998–9 season, stopped the club going out of the Football League. 'There was a lot of unrest. At one stage there was a deadline for the club to be sold and everything to be agreed behind the scenes over the debts. We were playing Cardiff and that was going to be the club's last day. I think the bailiffs were there to lock up Boothferry Park and that was going to be it.' After declaring the city to be 'living in the Dark Ages', Lloyd sold up to Stephen Hinchliffe, whose company Facia was being investigated for fraud. Hinchliffe took the club into administration in 2001 and was later jailed for conspiracy to defraud and bribery.

Allam has spent more than £70 million of his own money on the club. And yet he has turned out to be the most divisive owner of them all. Three months after reaching the FA Cup final, with the

fans still basking in the afterglow of Big Day Out 2, he announced
that Hull City would be renamed Hull Tigers. In order to compete
in a Premier League now dominated by mega-wealth, and not get
left behind by an increasingly internationalised, and monetised, elite,
the Tigers had no choice but to 'go global'. In the gilded top flight,
where there were significant differences in wage bills, transfer kitties
and revenue collection, a plucky underdog no longer had a chance.
'"Hull City" is irrelevant,' he told a local paper. 'It is common. I
want the club to be special . . . "City" is a lousy identity.' Replacing
'City' with 'Tigers', he argued, would transform tiny Hull into mighty
Hull. It would boost their international marketing appeal and reach
out to an international TV audience. 'In the Premier League you
are a global club,' he explained, 'and you should act big. Global. If
you want to act as local then remain local, but I didn't buy the club
to remain local.'

A campaign group, City Till We Die, was immediately formed to
fight the proposal and a new battle of Hull commenced. 'History,
tradition and community play a vital part in why supporters are
loyal to football clubs,' one protester explained. 'They are not brands.'
The protesters were depicted as unreconstructed Luddites who lived
in a time warp. They were standing in the way of the club's long-
overdue migration into media-and-entertainment land. They were
traditionalist dinosaurs who would rather visit spit-and-sawdust
grounds in the league's nether regions than glamorous stadiums like
Old Trafford, Anfield and the Emirates. Some of this was true. Some
campaigners liked playing up to the stereotype, reminiscing about
the bits of rust that used to shower down on them from the Boothferry Park roof. 'To be honest, I'd rather see Hull City in the fourth
division playing Macclesfield and Stockport than playing Manchester

United as Hull Tigers,' admitted David Goodman, author of several books on the club. 'My dad invested so much time and so much money on City,' said Windass. 'He went for decades. These clubs are the product of the city. The owners are custodians of the club's history and heritage. My old man died before going to KC stadium, before the Wembley Cup Final. Whenever I go to the football I feel that my old man's with me. It's sentimental, I know, but the name "City" was important to him. It's a lot deeper than a name change. It crystallises what we're about as a city. And what Yorkshire is, or at least should be, about as a county.'

2

A Tale of Two Heroes

'Sadly, my lasting memory will be of the greatest of all counties reduced to a squabbling rabble; of squalid, petty arguments; of supporters, once the most loyal and sane of all memberships, torn apart by a cult that regarded one man as greater than the club and even the game itself; and of a committee which made a terrible mistake and didn't try to put things right until it was too late.'

John Hampshire, after leaving
Yorkshire County Cricket Club in 1981

THE MIRACLE OF HEADINGLEY

20 July 1981. Headingley. The Battle for the Ashes. At the start of the third Test England are dismissed for 174, 227 runs behind the tourists, and required to bat again. For 100 years, no team has ever won a Test match after following-on. On Saturday evening the electronic scoreboard flashes up odds of 500-1 for a home win. England face almost certain defeat. At 105 for 5, Ian Botham, who has already taken six Australian wickets and scored a half century in the first innings, strides in. 'Let's give it some humpty,' he tells batting partner Graham Dilley. During two hours of magical cricket Botham smashes an unbeaten 149 not out. Driven by Bob Willis, who, thundering down the slope at the Kirkstall Lane End, claims 8 for 43, England skittle Australia out for 111 to win by 11 runs.

Botham's legendary innings produced one of the most improbable sporting triumphs of all time. England rose from the ashes and Headingley – and English sport – had a new king. 'Beefy was the Roy of the Rovers type,' explains Chris Old. 'I was in when he got his century. He stood up and bashed it around. You could feel the Australians falling apart.' When we meet, three decades after his retirement, Old is living in self-imposed exile on the Cornish coast and the two great cricketing heroes who dominated his career – Botham and Geoffrey Boycott – are about to resume their media duties in the 2015 World Cup. Old, though, isn't planning to watch the tournament. 'If I could afford Sky I would watch it,' he says. 'But I can't. One of the sad things is that the normal cricketing public don't get the opportunity to see the World Cup.' 'Besides,' his wife Letitia chips in, 'why should we pay to listen to all these people he used to work with?' Quite a few of the household names from his era, and future eras, have either coached or gone on to lucrative broadcasting careers. Old has done neither and, after running a fish and chip restaurant in Cornwall with Letitia, now works part-time at his local Sainsbury's stacking shelves. After showing me a striking photograph of the bails spinning through the air as he celebrates taking one of his 143 Test wickets, Old reveals that there was no knees-up after the famous Headingley win. Far from it: he had to get up at seven the following morning to drive to Sheffield, in the teeming rain, to play in a county match. It is curious that a man who won a Wisden Cricketer of the Year award, scored the then third-fastest century of all time – the last fifty of which was knocked out in nine minutes – and was the only Englishman to feature in both Centenary Tests against Australia, should have vanished so completely from the game. 'Cricket is in my blood,' he says. 'I'd have loved to have got back into it but it does seem to be more about the money now. The game was changing just as I was ending my playing career. There wasn't the camaraderie there had been. I think money has eroded the soul of the game.' 'Chilly' – he used to appear as 'C.Old' on the scoreboard – came in as a late-order batsman in the 1981 Test with England on 252 for 8. 'Mike Brearley was on the balcony making signals,' he recalled. 'At Yorkshire, we had a wonderful signal going around at the time which basically meant "the wheels are coming off." David Bairstow, John Hampshire and me, we'd all look at each other and do this sign, which involved touching your head in a certain way. At that Test I couldn't really do it as I had my batting gloves and helmet on. But the feeling I got was that, for the Aussies, the wheels were coming off.' They were also, at the time, coming off at Headingley itself. 'I got caught in the middle of the Boycott Wars,' he says. 'It was a horrible period. At the end of my first year as captain there was a big row because we'd left Boycott out at Scarborough. On one tour we went on, Geoffrey would walk out the other door when I came in. Or, if I was in a room, he wouldn't come in until I'd gone.' Old also fell out with Botham. He thinks their rift dates back to the year before the Headingley Test, when he privately criticised Beefy's captaincy during England's unsuccessful tour of the West Indies. Botham later labelled the injury-prone bowler 'Chilly the hypochondriac', unkindly wondering whether 'those seemingly endless sick notes [were] related to some deep-rooted fear of failure.'

A MODERN ENGLISH HERO

For the first seven decades of the twentieth century, Yorkshire were the gold standard of English cricket, winning twenty-six out of sixty championships and sharing one of the others. In the 1880s, the county's supremacy had caused something of a panic at the Marylebone Cricket Club, which at that time was the world game's governing body. The MCC, an exclusive private club of landowners packed with dukes, earls and honourables, felt threatened not only by Yorkshire's dominance but their impugning of the time-honoured Gentlemen–Players divide; the former tended to be aristocrats who didn't need to work for money and the latter came mostly from skilled working-class or lower middle-class backgrounds. In 1902, Yorkshire abolished the practice of amateurs and professionals entering the field of play through separate gates. A half-century later, batsman Len Hutton became the first Player to captain the national side.

There has always been a certain chippiness towards the south – or at least the idea of the south as a condescending neighbour that sucked in the north's skill, goods and talent. In the novelist Laurence Meynell's 1951 book on England's famous cricket grounds, Headingley, astonishingly, failed to make the cut. Bramall Lane, in Sheffield, the county's headquarters until its move to Headingley in 1902, was located next to a brewery: in the depression-hit 1930s, whenever a Home Counties side were at the crease, the workers would deliberately release its foul fumes. When Ray Illingworth was England captain he made a point of bollocking the upper-middle-class Cowdrey for being an hour late for net practice. Freddie Trueman frequently railed against the gentleman class, resenting, in his biographer Simon Wilde's words, the 'posh sods who had come straight from university into a county side and never done a real day's work in their lives'. He told the Duke of Norfolk that he should be addressed as Fred or Mr Trueman, not Trueman. 'There were thousands of Fred Truemans to be found on the building sites and in the factories of England in the 1950s and 1960s,' wrote Wilde. 'They gave the foreman some lip. Sometimes maybe they took a swing at them. But they did a hard day's work.'

'In an England cricket 11,' declared Len Hutton, the greatest England batsmen of the last century, 'the flesh may be of the south, but the bone is of the north, and the backbone is Yorkshire.' And yet that time-honoured maxim – 'a strong Yorkshire means a strong England' – does not really stand up to scrutiny. When Yorkshire were strongest, winning seven titles between 1931 and 1939, England won only four Ashes Tests. And it was when Surrey were strongest, winning seven championships on the spin in the 1950s, that England had their best decade of the twentieth century. Still, the myth persists, its moral force perhaps best expressed in an introduction to the 1941 bestseller *The King's England*. 'The history of this great county is part of the history of England itself,' its author explained. 'For its people have been the backbone of the nation in its rise to power and its struggle for freedom.'

On the fourth day of the third 1981 Ashes Test, however, the myth was eclipsed – on the very ground that had nurtured it for ninety years, 'For his fearless batting and bowling,' wrote Michael Henderson, 'and for a series of magnificent walks, including the celebrated one from John O'Groats to Land's End, Botham is regarded, rightly, as a modern English hero.' The charismatic all-rounder was cricket's 'big three' – Richard Hadlee, Imran Khan and Kapil Dev – all rolled into one. He brought drama, excitement and razzmatazz to an ailing game, reshaping the way it was played, watched and sold. Old Yorkshire's holy trinity of Illingworth, Trueman and Brian Close, of course, presented an entirely different image to the world.

OLD YORKSHIRE

'In the Yorkshire philosophy of sport,' the urbane, pipe-smoking, long-serving *Yorkshire Post* cricket correspondent Jim Kilburn once explained, 'it is impossible to be too keen on winning a competitive engagement.' During the late Victorian and Edwardian eras, while the MCC's Corinthians were instructing the world to play up, chaps, and play the game, the county was developing its tough, efficient brand of cricket under the tutelage of Lord Hawke. Captain from 1893 to

1910, and then president until his death in 1938, Hawke's side won the County Championship, which became an official competition in 1890, five times between 1898 and 1905. The win-at-all-costs mentality instilled by Hawke was credited with the dominance that followed: four consecutive titles between 1922 and 1925, seven in ten seasons in the 1930s and another six in the 1960s. As an Old Etonian and former Cambridge Blue, his lordship ostensibly reinforced the notion that the public school–Oxbridge elite have always held sway in English cricket. That it was, and remains, an upper- and middle-class sport shaped by top hats and canes: a game for gentlemen played by gentlemen. In Yorkshire's case, this couldn't be further from the truth. But Hawke was the exception that proved the rule, the obligatory upper-class captain of a club that had challenged, from its inception in 1863, the amateurism, dilettantism and individualism of the 'game of Empire'.

Hawke, however, must be credited with transforming a collection of wayward individuals into the disciplined, machine-like, champion county of legend. For him and his players, cricket was more than just escapist entertainment, more than just about winning. It served a far deeper purpose as a reflection of the county's collective subconscious. In sport, as in industrial capitalism, winners prospered and losers went to the wall. Individual ability was all very well, determination and dedication a matter of course, but there was no substitute for teamwork, based on a solidarity that disdained the egotistical. This communitarian ethos echoed the values shared in communities, institutions and workplaces across the broad acres. The county's most successful phases – the years before the Great War, the 1930s and the 1960s – were periods in which this Old Yorkshire spirit flourished both on and off the pitch: side before self, strict discipline, *esprit de corps*. Their greatest players – Wilfred Rhodes, George Hirst, Percy Holmes, Herbert Sutcliffe and Hutton – were all consummate team men, keen to pass on the rudiments of their craft to the next generation. Bill Bowes and Hedley Verity were once surprised to find Rhodes and Emmott Robinson waiting for them in their hotel bedroom: the veteran duo proceeded to explain tactics with a shaving stick, toothbrush and hairbrush. 'Remember you are representing Yorkshire,' Sutcliffe told his young protégés, 'not just yourself.' Cricket was not show business. 'We'll get 'em in singles, Wilfred,' Hirst instructed Rhodes, the last man in when England needed only fifteen more runs to beat Australia in a 1902 Ashes Test. 'We wear our white rose badge defiantly,' Sutcliffe wrote in his autobiography, 'and we hope that those with whom we play understand that our defiance is based not on the success that has attended the work of our team, but on our jealous love for our county.'

The natural temptation is to romanticise Old Yorkshire. And yet, until fairly recently, its cricketing avatar was an insular, conservative, backward-looking institution which disparaged virtually every modern innovation, from limited-overs cricket to bonus points for batting and bowling, stubbornly refusing to move with the times. Up until 1991, the county's governing committee refused to field players not born in the three ridings. Its much-vaunted collectivism would often be ruthlessly implemented; the county was renowned for discarding players as soon as they passed their sell-by date. Many of its working-class heroes ended up back on the shop floor. Holmes, for example, worked in a mill in old age. Before the Second World War there were no contracts – and no guarantees of regular money until a player was capped. In 1968, Illingworth challenged this long-entrenched employment policy by asking for a three-year contract. He was offered a year-long one, declined and was exiled to Leicestershire. 'And he can take any other bugger who feels the same way as him,' declared Brian Sellers, an authoritarian administrator who brooked no dissent. 'Long service at Yorkshire,' wrote Duncan Hamilton, 'especially from the you've-never-had-it-so-good 1950s to the Thatcherite 1980s – frequently ended not with a gold watch, but with a hatchet in the back.'

This was the unsavoury side of the county's sainted egalitarianism, an example of what Marxist–Leninists might recognise, with some envy, as cricket's answer to democratic centralism. It flushed out the prima donnas, cut the Flash Harries down to size and discouraged any show ponies from getting above themselves. Illingworth insisted, however, that its benefits easily outweighed its disadvantages. 'When I first went into the Yorkshire side I was paid [on being capped] the same as Len Hutton,' he noted, 'who was the greatest batsman of the world at the time. Similarly, young players came in without one-tenth of Brian [Close]'s or Fred [Trueman]'s or my experience, and they were paid the same as us . . . it was by far the best thing for team spirit to have all capped players on the same amount.' The great sixties team of Illingworth, Close, Trueman and Boycott fought like cats and dogs behind closed doors but frowned on anyone who publicly rocked the boat.

During Close's tenure as captain in the sixties, a period when Yorkshire won four championship titles, no one was more equal than anyone else; the battle-scarred veteran led by example, literally taking hits for the team by standing suicidally close to a batsman at silly mid-off or short-leg. 'When I started playing,' said Old, 'there were nine or so internationals in the Yorkshire dressing room and there were two or three that became internationals after that. That dressing room could be difficult but out on the pitch there was harmony. There were people there with vast amounts of knowledge and there was constant talk about cricket and I was just looking at and listening to people. Really, if you didn't learn something from that, you shouldn't have been there. It was full of strong characters. Once, I saw one senior player picking another one up and sticking him on a coat hook. But that sort of thing never left the dressing room.'

THE NEW BRITON

Botham's father had actually been brought up in Yorkshire and, according to one of his many biographers, was 'as Yorkshire ingrained as could be imaginable'. There was no noticeable move on that famous day at Headingley, however, to claim him as a Yorkie. For one thing, being born in Cheshire, thirty-seven years before the county finally allowed non-native players onto its books, he was technically ineligible. More importantly, the miracle man's celebrity, as the locals grudgingly acknowledged, appeared to place him above geographical loyalty, heritage and tradition – indeed above cricket itself. He was a towering, transformational figure who acquired wealth, celebrity and status far in excess of his predecessors and became one of the biggest box-office draws of his age. It was hardly unknown for nationally revered sportsmen to succumb to the lure of fame and finance. The 'father of cricket', W. G. Grace, had lined his pockets with lucrative endorsements back in the Victorian and Edwardian eras and, after the 1950 World Cup, Stanley Matthews was paid £20 a week for wearing branded boots. But Botham was a new kind of national hero. He saw sport as a vehicle for glamour, self-expression and entertainment rather than Corinthian character-building or an archaic egalitarianism. Like the New Romantic bands who provided the electrifying, escapist soundtrack to the early Thatcher years, he was English sport's very own matinee idol. 'People wanted that in Britain in the early eighties,' explained Martin Fry. 'They wanted a strong figure. They wanted individuals. They wanted heroes.' Botham's extraordinary Leeds innings was a triumph of individual persistence against seemingly impossible odds. In the first half of 1981's heady summer, his form had been shot to pieces. His captaincy of England, it was universally agreed, had been a disaster. After an Australian victory in the first Ashes Test and a draw at Lord's, where he was dismissed for a duck in both innings, he was forced to resign his commission. Relieved from the burden of captaincy by the avuncular Mike Brearley, he began, once again, to excel. At Headingley, with Australia on the verge of going 2-0 up in the series, his unforgettable innings turned the game on its head. Two more 'miraculous' performances – a century at Manchester and five match-winning wickets at Birmingham – also rescued hopeless causes to capture the Ashes and confirm his, and England's, resurrection.

New Britain, at this point, was on the march. A new national story, based on a narrative of individualistic self-realisation, had been created on that famous day at Headingley. Coaches might demand teamwork but the public were clearly desperate for their Roy-of-the-Rovers fixes, provided by dashing, fearless, lavishly talented heroes like Botham, Seb Coe and Daley Thompson. Cricket needed Beefy, just as tennis depended on its Big Three – John McEnroe, Jimmy Connors and Björn Borg – to attract TV, sponsorship and marketing deals. In the eighties, English sport began to thrive on epic duels; from the Coe–Ovett contest in the 1980 Moscow Olympics to the classic Taylor–Davies 'black ball' snooker final five years later, which was watched by more than 18 million people, toe-to-toe rivalries now grabbed the national imagination.

It was in this era that the BBC's Sports Personality of the Year show really came into its own, venerating glamorous, larger-than-life characters like Botham, Thompson, Barry McGuigan and the ice-skating duo Torvill and Dean. As tabloid newspapers grew in size, and fought a series of increasingly bitter circulation wars, they began to elevate (and end up, often ruthlessly, cutting down to size) these newly minted sporting superstars, especially those with bleached mullets and a penchant for hunting, shooting, fishing and womanising. In the era of the Me Generation, Loadsamoney and yuppies, the media's importance in constructing a celebrity-obsessed New Britain should not be underestimated. Like the film *Chariots of Fire*, which was released the same year, Botham's Ashes helped foster a new mood of flag-waving patriotism. 'A little-fancied Brit, an underdog,' was director Hugh Hudson's description of Eric Liddell, one of the athletes venerated in the Oscar-winning movie, 'and in running he found transcendence.' Substitute 'cricket' for 'running' and he could easily have been describing this self-propelled, utterly determined outsider who smashed, swung and swiped his way out of his northern working-class background, transcending his sport to become a world-famous celebrity.

Botham's rise was, like the decade he dominated, turbulent, exciting and disturbing. He embodied the revived power of British sport in an age when industry and empire continued to fade from view. At Headingley he had turned certain defeat into stunning victory. As the eighties wore on, and his powers declined, his off-the-field fame superseded his bat-and-ball exploits to embrace countless charity walks, well-publicised romps and the occasional encounter with illegal substances. Ultimately, a rather bloated ego – fuelled by flying planes, partying with Elton, Clapton and Jagger and driving fast cars round Brands Hatch – was revealed. 'Apart from Margaret Thatcher and the Queen,' he boasted, 'I am probably the most famous person in Britain.' He was still capable of sporadic brilliance at the crease but, as his weight increased, his bowling became less penetrative and, by 1990, like Thatcher, he had become a shadow of his former world-conquering self.

NEW BRITAIN

Botham's reckless marauding at the crease had cheered up a nation beset by economic meltdown and urban riots. Like Prince Charles' marriage to Lady Diana Spencer, the Leeds test provided a timely distraction from the rise in unemployment, inflation and inner-city violence. In fact, as the battle of Headingley was raging, Thatcher, stunned by the lowest prime ministerial approval ratings in British political history, dispatched Michael Heseltine to Liverpool to investigate the reasons behind the Toxteth riots. As her environment minister toured the city, England's backs-to-the-wall comeback appeared to offer a narrative of renewal. It was a cathartic affair, the first in a series of shared national experiences that offered respite to an increasingly polarised country. A year later, the small island nation, in seemingly irreversible decline since the war, went from humiliation to triumph at the Falklands, proving it was still an important player in global affairs. Britain, gloated Thatcher, 'had found herself again in the South Atlantic and will not look back'. The departure of the taskforce had been, in Andy Beckett's words, 'an epic, brilliantly manipulative piece of public theatre . . . that would run, to credulous rave reviews in most of the British media, for the rest of the Falklands conflict, and indeed (for more than a year) right up to the next general election.'

Twenty-eight million people watched the royal wedding and, in 1985, 1.9 billion across 150 countries tuned into Live Aid, the defining cultural event of the decade. Thatcher, at first, had been slow to catch on to these moments of national uplift. Her loathing for sport – she called for a British boycott of the 1980 Olympic Games following the Soviet invasion of Afghanistan – was only matched by her disdain for popular culture. It hardly failed to escape her notice, however, that Botham's Ashes had precipitated a surge in patriotism. 'The Bulldog Breed,' thundered the *Sun,* 'bared its teeth again.' At the end of the Headingley Test, 2,000 fans invaded the pitch and sang William Blake's 'Jerusalem' in front of the pavilion. Before the series, the England cricket team had been a symbol of the country's self-fulfilling declinism, losing an unprecedented twelve Tests in a row. Now, like *Chariots of Fire* – its title inspired by Blake's powerful anthem – they were hailed as standard bearers for the New Britain.

With Coe and Ovett breaking world records, Thatcher finally began to see the value of sport as an antidote to urban anger. A 1982 Sports Council document argued how, during the worst economic slump since the 1930s, it could be a force for social cohesion, revitalising rundown areas. This was hardly a novel idea, but it gained extra credence after a year when an orgy of looting, arson and vandalism convulsed the country with rage and resentment. Even before the Falklands conflict, the world appeared to be an increasingly violent place: The Pope, John Lennon and President Reagan had all been

shot, IRA terrorism was at its height – two months before the Headingley Test, hunger striker Bobby Sands died in prison – and there
was war in Afghanistan, across Central America and southern and
western Africa, Iran and Iraq. 'It was a pretty miserable time,' Botham
reflected. 'You had the riots all over the country. It was tough for
a lot of people. Then along came cricket and 1981 and everything
changed.' As the nation's first sporting celebrity of the modern era,
and a proud patriot, he was more than happy to accept his role as
New Britain's poster boy.

THE BOYCOTT WARS

As Beefy was being crowned the new King of Headingley, it might
have been fair to assume that the old potentate was a tad put out.
Four years earlier, half the country had marvelled at the sight of
Boycott scoring his hundredth first-class hundred, against Australia,
on his home turf. He was, in many ways, the anti-Botham, embody-
ing Rhodes' aphorism: 'We don't play cricket for fun, we play to
win' (although it should be pointed out that, in his seven-year reign
as Yorkshire captain, the team actually failed to win any trophies,
humiliatingly dropping into the lower reaches of the County Championship table). In 1983, not long after they had reprimanded the
opener for slow scoring during a game against Gloucestershire, a
committee largely made up of ex-White Rose players refused to
offer him a new contract. Boycott's supporters – unlike the patri-
cian committee, drawn from more humble backgrounds – revolted,
forming a pressure group to campaign for his reinstatement. The
following year, the pro-Boycott Reform Group swept to power in a

series of rancorous elections, bringing their beloved leader back – as a committee member as well as a player. This *coup d'état* roused the Old Yorkshire establishment to regroup and, two years later, citing endless rows and recriminations, Close and Illingworth called for their former teammate's removal. 'We just couldn't carry on with a cult figure grinding out his personal glory while the rest of the players simply made up the numbers,' explained Close after Boycott had been sacked. Despite an offer to play for Derbyshire, one of the game's greatest-ever batsmen decided, at the age of forty-five, to retire.

In his final innings he was run out at the Scarborough Cricket Festival, leaving him eight short, having scored 1,000 first-class runs for a twenty-fourth consecutive season. His twenty-four-year career, in which he scored 48,426 first-class runs, including 151 first-class centuries, was undoubtedly a great one. It would have been even greater had he not been so obsessed with his own singularity. The son of a coal miner, he saw himself as something of a working-class rebel. 'The committee tried to destroy me,' he said. 'Cricket was quite autocratic for a long time with the amateurs and the landed gentry running it. The only safeguard was the members ... the members decided in their thousands to get me a contract and overturn the committee.' This version of the Boycott Wars as a below-stairs revolution ignores the fatal flaw in his character: although clearly a hero to a large majority of the public, he had become a pariah in the dressing room due to his intractable manner, his tendency to hog the strike and his penchant for running out his batting partners.

Many teammates viewed him as an introverted loner, prone to slow knocks and run-outs, more concerned with his own batting averages than the side's overall performance.

In 1967, after hitting only 246 runs off 555 balls against India at Headingley, he was dropped by the England selectors. Old, who broke into the side in the late sixties, argued that Boycott changed when he became an established England player. 'He began to feel that the longer the time he spent at the crease the more runs he would score,' he said. 'And the better the team would do. That was his reasoning. I remember when I was captain in a one-day match and I wanted him to be more positive. He said, "I can't go in and hit the first ball for four." I said: "Why not get a run off the first ball?" He said: "Then I won't see the ball for the rest of the over."'

Botham's risk-taking daredevilry might have been anathema to Boycott, but both their 'reigns' were based on the cult of the personality. 'In that decade in Yorkshire,' reflected Old, 'the individual, not the side, became important.' As Botham's star rose, King Geoffrey became mired in the warmongering that would consign his county to three decades in the wilderness. The insularity of his epic battle with Illingworth, Close and Trueman knew no bounds. As English cricket got bigger, and rival counties began to stock up on world-class foreigners, Old Yorkshire withdrew into itself, consumed by malice and bitterness, unwilling either to nurture new talent from within or replenish a declining team from without. Their antiquated rule that only those born in the county could play for it meant that no outsiders – whether overseas players, who were starting to become a force in the county game, or new English ones, who were also starting to move between clubs more frequently – could be recruited.

Boycott was accused of selfishness throughout his career. 'He fell in love with himself at an early age,' quipped the Australian fast bowler Dennis Lillee, 'and has remained faithful ever since.' According to the BBC broadcaster Don Mosey, he was 'obsessed with achieving targets and records of his own [and] was not concerned with helping younger players'. Boycott, of course, viewed things differently, insisting that his self-obsession was the result of 'a burning desire to get the best out of myself and achieve as much as possible'.

Throughout the decade horribilis, Yorkshire was split down the middle, divided between a weak, unwieldy, out-of-touch committee and a well-drilled, focused, business-like new guard, which, like Thatcher's Conservatives, refused to take any prisoners in its assault on the stuffy establishment. 'It became very political,' said Old. 'There were a lot of people pulling in different directions. The guys on the field weren't really considered. They were just the pawns.' Old himself is a classic Casper-esque hero, a relic from the last generation to be hewn from the county's rugged hills, windswept moors and decaying industrial towns. Always more at home as a character actor than a bill-topper, he seemed to be forever in someone else's shadow: first that of his older brother Alan, who was a distinguished rugby union international, then Trueman's – whose giant shoes he never quite managed to fill – and finally Boycott's.

'Boycs' was the civil war's central figure: you were either for or against him. Like Old, the *Yorkshire Post* sportswriter David Hopps tried to stay neutral. Shortly after his appointment as the paper's cricket correspondent, he was leaving his hotel during an away match against Sussex, when he was startled to see Boycott suddenly draw up in a car: 'He told me to get in and drove me three miles down the Hove seafront. He said: "I've not met you before. You've got to realise you're either for me or against me." I said I'm not going to take sides. He said: "You won't survive, don't be naïve." I said I'm going to wake up in the morning, watch the day, write what I think. I'm staying independent. "You'll learn," he said, pulling the car up so I could get out. I thought, "Bloody hell. I've got three-and-a-half miles to walk back to my sodding hotel."' Along with other reporters, Hopps was courted by both sides. 'The Reform Group served tea and biscuits in a soulless hotel just off the M1,' he said. 'The establishment preferred a rather nice pub near Harrogate, where the drinks flowed. Captain Desmond Bailey, a landowner, nearly fell into an open fire at four in [the] afternoon. It was an uproarious, Dickensian, bucolic lunch. We all went home none the wiser about the point they wanted to make. Whether you regard Geoffrey as villain or victim, he was a divisive figure. It was not just about his character though. To some extent this was a class war characteristic of its time, a breakdown of the traditional way of doing things.'

Boycott's autobiography opens with a Henry Thoreau quote about living alone for two years in a log cabin: 'If a man does not keep pace with his companions, perhaps it is because he hears a different drummer. Let him step to the music which he hears, however measured or far away.' One of the most complex individuals ever to play the game, the cussedly slow and almost pathologically aloof opener was never going to fit the criteria of a new television era which required its star performers to be cavalier and charismatic and, when called upon, possibly give it some humpty. His rise and fall was a classic eighties morality tale. Brought up in a close-knit industrial community, he was determined not to follow his father and grandfather down the pit and acquired a job in a Ministry of Pensions office in Barnsley. 'His struggles to overcome the social disadvantages of his background, the limitations in his natural talent and the contradictions in his own nature are almost epic,' wrote his biographer, Leo McKinstry. 'He set himself a goal, to become one of the greatest batsmen in the world, and in the face of numerous obstacles – many of his own making – he ultimately achieved it.' There was, however, a price to pay for his ambition.

FIELD OF DREAMS

Although he despaired at some of Boycott's antics, Hopps does not absolve the triumvirate – Trueman, Close and Illingworth – of their responsibilities. These great players did sod all for the next generation,' he said.

We lost their knowledge. None of them gave back much. Yorkshire lost the connection with its public and the Boycott Wars had a lot to do with it. In the 1980s, the old generation didn't spread its knowledge. It didn't do anything to help create the next generation. Closey was the warmest, the younger players told me. All the other great players were doing it for their own self-publicity. None of these great players became great coaches, although Illy came back as a manager. Perhaps the Yorkshire greats didn't want their successors to be better than them. Who knows? Where was that leadership? If you don't evolve you get left behind. Yorkshire cricket had ruled the roost. When the side disintegrated they blamed their deterioration on one man. He might have been a catalyst for arguments, a tragic figure, but at the same time as the Boycott argument was going on Yorkshire weren't evolving and the Boycott argument became an excuse for not modernising. Modernising doesn't have to be about closing down the mines with no other work available. It can be a good word, not a dirty word.

At the beginning of the twenty-first century, in a belated attempt to address this longstanding failure, Yorkshire finally began to embrace the m-word – and the outside world. Not only would the side continue to feature an overseas player – the born-in-Yorkshire rule having been dropped in 1992 – they would be managed by an overseas coach. The experiment paid instant dividends. In 2001, guided by the former Australian fast bowler Wayne Clark, Yorkshire won their first county championship for thirty-three years. This impressive achievement, however, proved to be a one-off, papering over the gaping cracks. The team were relegated the following year and spent four of the next ten seasons in the second division. The cost of the wilderness years was brought home when, £8 million in debt and lacking any assets, the club suddenly found themselves on the brink of bankruptcy. Decades of myopia, mismanagement and mistaken policies had come home to roost. 'Tens of thousands of pounds that could have been spent on cricket had been frittered away in an attempt to settle old scores,' wrote Stuart Rayner, a distinguished chronicler of the period, 'but all it did was widen divisions and enrich lawyers.'

At the eleventh hour, director of cricket Geoff Cope persuaded a millionaire, Costcutter founder Colin Graves, to ride to the rescue. 'Headingley was forty-eight hours from being written off,' recalled Graves. 'It was going to go.' The demise of one of the most famous, and important, venues in British sport seemed to have been confirmed by the 2002 proposal to move to a purpose-built ground on the M1 outside Wakefield. After thinking the unthinkable, however, the committee backed down. 'I don't think we have ever recovered from the Boycott wars,' said Cope, who had broken into the great sixties side with Old. 'They were very counter-productive. They cost the club a fortune. The stadium, in particular, was in a bad way.' The seeds of the conflict were sown in a previous, more successful, era, when players sometimes came to blows in the dressing room. Trueman went through a period of refusing to bowl at Boycott in the nets. But the grizzled grandees' public, and very bitter, in-fighting reached extraordinary levels during the darkest era in the county's history, ripping it apart for decades. 'Cricketers who had spent their lives dreaming of playing for or captaining Yorkshire would end up wishing they never had,' wrote Rayner. 'Promising careers ended prematurely, huge amounts of potential went unfulfilled . . . wives and children were abused and friendships broken off; teammates became enemies and fans turned on one another.' In one infamous match, frustrated at Boycott's slow scoring, the in-form batsman John Hampshire repeatedly patted the ball back to the bowlers as a protest. Not long after he became manager, Illingworth dropped Boycott on a point of principle. Smear campaigns and personal feuds were played out in both the local and national media: Boycott denounced his sacking as captain, a decision made by the committee four days after the death of his mother, on Michael Parkinson's high-profile BBC chat show. 'The committee,' he later argued, 'tried to destroy me.'

The tarnishing of Headingley's reputation had begun in the late seventies when protesters campaigning for the release of prisoner George Davis poured oil onto the pitch during a match against Australia. Over the next few years, a succession of Tests were ruined by rain. After the famous 1981 victory, Keith Boyce, its legendary groundsman, warned the committee that the pitch's central strip would deteriorate unless he was allowed to dig the square up and re-lay it. They refused to listen. 'It was all the in-fighting,' explained former umpire Dickie Bird, a friend of Boyce who had played for Yorkshire in the fifties. 'It made Keith's life very difficult. They stuck their heads in the sand. They said that it had been good enough for the Botham Test, that it had helped England beat the Aussies. They were so short-sighted. Keith finally got his way, but it was a few years later. The damage had been done. This had been a wonderful stadium – the home of legends. But, during the Boycott wars, it went into decline.'

Boycott's self-centred pursuit of greatness had undoubtedly been detrimental to the greater good but his with-me-or-against-me stance was more a symptom, than the root cause, of this disarray. His quest for personal liberation took place in an era in which cricket was beginning to be turned upside down by sponsorship, overseas players and the introduction of one-day competitions. Preoccupied with the county's existential crisis, the committee took their eye off the ball. The result was that Headingley was left behind, eventually losing its status as the only permanent Test stadium outside London. After the ECB decided to award Test matches on the basis of money rather than tradition, the debt-ridden ground ruled itself out of the bidding for both the 2013 and 2015 Ashes. 'Headingley simply can't sell tickets at Oval or Lord's prices,' said Rayner. 'Trent Bridge, Lord's and the Oval now get the big Tests because they charge more for the seats. It's because of the economics of the Yorkshire region. The Yorkshire public has been squeezed out because it's more impoverished. Headingley doesn't have as good a ground and is playing catch-up. It is shabby compared to Trent Bridge – in terms of its facilities, stands and capacity.'

The last time Leeds hosted an Ashes Test was in 2009, when England crashed to a humiliating defeat. 'After an Ashes series finished you used to look forward to four years on and think, when are we back here, when are the Aussies coming?' said Cope. 'Right, you'd think, I'll save up for that. Not for a day, for three or four days. Headingley was full for the Ashes Tests most days. Even when the Australians weren't good, you'd come and watch them.' The Australians are not due to return to Headingley until 2019, a ten-year absence which tells its own story about the ground's slide into irrelevance.

In 2001, the year a rejuvenated Yorkshire won their thirtieth title, even a celebratory introduction to a lavishly produced, beautifully illustrated commemorative book felt obliged to portray Headingley in the bleakest of terms. 'It is dour, prone to bouts of mournfulness and generally a bit odd,' declared Robert Mills. The old pavilion, he continued, had

> all the character of an airport lounge; the Main Stand . . . has for a long time looked careworn and dilapidated; the new pavilion [has been] derided as an architectural eyesore . . . and the Western Terrace went through a period when it was a no-go area for decent human beings unless they were willing to dress up as a carrot . . . in terms of creature comforts, the ground has been bottom of most people's list of test and even of county venues for years, both for members and for the general public . . . there was a time when you half expected to see Headingley's pork pies on *The Antiques Road Show*.

Nine years after the publication of Mills' tome, Duncan Hamilton, another White Rose enthusiast, informed Wisden readers that his beloved field of dreams had become 'a dowdy, mongrel of a place'.

In failing to move with the times, and in particular being out-flanked by the modernising zeal and aggressive marketing of Durham's Riverside, Cardiff's Sophia Gardens and Hampshire's Rose Bowl, Headingley had become, for many years, a metaphor for the Old Yorkshire insularity that held the county back. During the thirty or so years it took to recover from the civil war that plunged the club to the bottom of English cricket, the famous old ground became a debt-burdened also-ran. 'The Rugby Stand looks like a ramshackle oil tanker run aground,' noted Hamilton. 'It so obviously belongs to the glum, austere era of post-war England that I half-expect Fred Trueman to emerge from the dressing room.'

THE INVISIBLE HERO

And yet, back in 1981, Headingley had been a site of self-reinvention, giving birth to the decade's emergent myth: that a dynamic, for-ward-looking, miracle worker could restore the nation's self-belief, perhaps even its greatness. This myth camouflaged the fact that the wheels had started to come off the England cricket team. Botham's Ashes was swiftly followed by a series of collapses – against Australia in 1982–3, New Zealand in 1983–4, Pakistan in 1983–4, India in 1986 and the West Indies in 1988. After England made a paltry 93 in the Caribbean, the *Daily Express* back page screamed: 'How much longer can we put up with this?' 'That summer [of 1981] probably did us more harm than good,' wrote Pat Gibson, the paper's cricket correspondent. 'The selectors believed Botham could do anything, and he could at that time. But they spent ten years looking for his replacement . . . we were still looking for miracles a decade later.'

According to Australian bowler Geoff Lawson, Botham's frenzied, daredevil, high-octane heroics had only 'wallpapered over the widening cracks of the system – individual performances often do that in team sports.' And yet they had been exhilarating water-cooler moments, national cultural events which had planted the seeds for cricket's dramatic transformation. Since the eighties, the traditional English summer game, previously limited to this country and the Commonwealth, has gone global, flowering into a pay-TV money tree. Following in the wake of Kerry Packer's late-seventies game-changing World Series Cricket, Botham's Ashes helped pave the way for the fast-moving, priapic Twenty20, the Sky Sports shake-up and the billion-pound Indian Premier League – developments that would create new marketing opportunities and prompt a revolution in the way cricket and other sports were consumed.

The instinctively aggressive Beefy became cricket's first corporate marketing tool, sprinkling some much-needed stardust onto a dull, rundown sport, elevating it to the point where sponsors and TV stations felt able to piggyback onto his appeal. A new, more exciting TV experience – every angle covered, cameras at both ends of a ground – triggered a brighter, more positive approach to the game. The tedious, Boycottite batting of old had been replaced by reverse sweeps, scoops, paddle shots and switch hits. The problem is that this magical experience is not open to all cricket fans. Every England international since 2005 has been shown exclusively on Sky; the broadcaster's 2015 deal enriched the ECB by £280m while locking both the England team and the county game behind a paywall. Terrestrial coverage had come to an end ten years earlier after Andrew 'Freddie' Flintoff provided the belief that England could, after almost two decades of defeats, finally beat the seemingly impregnable

Australians. An audience of 7.4 million watched the climax to the final Ashes Test of that 2005 series, five times more than the number who watched the 2009 denouement. The final day of England's victory in the first Ashes Test of the 2015 series had viewing figures of just 467,000.

This removal of a crucial source of cricketing inspiration for youngsters, many of whose parents can't afford pay TV, has led to a reduction in the number of people playing the game. 'Flintoff was very exciting in the 2005 series,' said Old. 'We had our café, a business, so we obviously couldn't watch it. People were coming in saying we wouldn't be seeing them for three days because they were going to be sitting in front of the telly watching the Test. The entertainment was brilliant. It was like 1981 all over again. Now you've got to pay to watch it on Sky. People go on about participation in sport declining. Well, surely interest in the game has dwindled because they can't see it.'

When Old made his debut, as a seventeen-year-old in 1966, thirteen of the seventeen-strong Yorkshire side were registered as working-class professionals. A half-century later, three of the five Yorkshiremen selected for the Ashes series – Jonny Bairstow, Gary Ballance and Joe Root – were privately educated. 'The game of cricket now is played in public schools,' commented Old. 'There's very little played in state schools, which is a problem we've got. The cricket board got a lot of money after signing with Sky. Top players are getting huge amounts of money, but the grass roots game doesn't seem to have benefited in any way. It trickled down for a while but suddenly they've cut it out. We need to get the money back into the grass roots. That's where the future Bothams will come from. Mind you, at least we've got Joe Root. He could be the next Botham.'

It has needed another Australian outsider, Jason Gillespie, appointed ten years after Clark's title win, to re-establish Yorkshire's dominance and Root, a Sheffield-born batsman, was the key early figure in his Hawkesian transformation of the county. 'In my country,' said Gillespie, 'when you get asked about English county cricket, the first thought that always comes into your head is Yorkshire County Cricket Club. It's a big county with a rich tradition. It should be winning things.' Root is New Britain's latest hero, elevated by his extraordinary native talent to the England team. His is a rousing story of how a cheeky South Yorkshire lad was plucked from his state school, via a sporting scholarship to Worksop College, to become one of the world's leading batsmen. According to legend, Boycott passed down a chest pad to the former Yorkshire and England captain Michael Vaughan, who then bequeathed it to Root. Unlike his two predecessors, however, Root is an invisible hero. For two years Yorkshire fans were unable to watch him turn out for the county in a four-day game – because he was a fixture in international cricket. He has also become invisible to terrestrial TV audiences, which is why the world's number one batsman failed to make the 2015 BBC Sports Personality of the Year shortlist (despite winning the Ashes Man of the Series award); two-thirds of households have no access to Sky Sports, the home of international cricket.

Although he became a global celebrity, Botham was the star of an England team that represented English society. Today's side, by contrast, is widely viewed as a boys' club run by an Old Boys' club, a perception confirmed by a former ECB chairman's description of Alastair Cook and his family as 'very much the sort of people we want the England captain and his family to be'. Nine of the twelve players used in the 2005 Ashes went to state schools. Ten years on, the ratio had been reversed, with the national team over-dependent on the 7 per cent of the population who attend private schools. 'If a nation is shaped by its institutions,' wrote the *Daily Telegraph* columnist Simon Briggs before the 2015 Ashes, 'then today's Britain is increasingly dominated by the products, and recruits, of our elite public schools . . . it is in sport that the imbalance is most obvious. Seven per cent of British children are privately educated, and yet the figure in [the] England Test team stood at 73 per cent . . . today, a more accurate axiom might be "When public school cricket is strong, England is strong."'

The seeds of this new class divide were sown in the eighties when the sport was shunned in state schools; according to a survey, three decades later, less than 10 per cent of them were playing 'meaningful cricket'. During the Conservative governments of 1979 to 1997, extra-curricular activities, the traditional seedbed for sporting development, were continually cut; more than 10,000 school playing fields were sold off by cash-strapped councils and a further 200 were discharged in the New Labour years. Cricket, always an expensive game, has become the preserve of those private schools that can afford to pay for playing facilities, equipment and specialist coaches. Between 1968, when they completed a hat-trick of titles, and the 2001 championship, Yorkshire drifted away from their vast hinterland of amateur cricket. 'Yorkshire cricket used to be more embedded in the community,' said Hopps. 'I remember playing local cricket in the 1970s and we'd come in off the field and there was always someone who'd turn on the radio to see how Yorkshire were getting on. Today there is a disconnect between the grass roots and the county cricket club.' 'Root is the new hero of English cricket,' said Rayner. 'But he's almost not a Yorkshire player nowadays. In twenty years' time you won't get a Joe Root. In ten years' time even. If you haven't seen these top Yorkshire cricketers playing in your backyard, and you haven't got Sky, it will be difficult to get the whole cricket bug. So where are all the next generation of Roots going to come from?'

3

The Showman Cometh

'Although it certainly can be a beautiful game, people do not follow teams like Rotherham United for aesthetic reasons.'

Julian Baggini, *Welcome to Everytown*, 2008

20 March 1982. Stamford Bridge. Chelsea vs Rotherham United. A crowd of 11,900 are at the Bridge to watch the Division Two clash between west London's fallen giants and the league's surprise pacesetters. After twenty-three minutes, the Blues take the lead with a goal from Peter Rhoades-Brown. Five minutes later Billy McEwan equalises for Rotherham. Then, in a decisive ten-minute spell, the visitors' Ronnie Moore, the £100,000 striker, scores twice to put United all but out of reach – and Tony Towner knocks one in with only a minute to make it 4-1 and complete Chelsea's misery. The thrashing propels Emlyn Hughes' promotion-hunting side to fourth in the table and pushes Chelsea down to thirteenth. The Blues' under-pressure manager John Neal says he is not worried about sliding into the relegation zone, but admits: 'It was men against boys.'

John Breckin doesn't remember a great deal about Rotherham United's most famous win. In fact, the only memory of that momentous day to have fully lodged in his consciousness was the sight of Stamford Bridge's iconic East Stand, a symbol of the stylish, early-seventies, Chelsea side he loved watching. Ten years on, the Blues were no longer the glamour boys of Swinging London, their King's Road panache and Hollywood connections – Raquel Welch, Dickie Attenborough and Michael Caine had all visited the Bridge – a fading memory. 'We pulled up at the ground and there was this new stand there, or new to us,' recalls Breckin. 'It had lifts going up and down. We were used to Millmoor. I remember my teammate Gerry Forrest looking at me and saying "Look, Breck, look at those lifts". I looked up at the lifts and I thought, "Bloody hell." Lifts in a magnificent stand. Stamford Bridge. I was looking at this shrine of a place and thinking of that seventies Chelsea team. You think: "Did we really hammer them? Pinch me."' We are talking in the press room at Rotherham's New York Stadium, built a few years ago around the shell of the club's eerie, haunting, disused Millmoor ground. To get there I drove past the gigantic Magna Science Adventure Centre, once the site of the great Steel, Peech and Tozer steelworks and, like United's state-of-the-art venue, a symbol of reinvention. The stadium's name conjures up an unlikely Sinatra-esque world of glitz, glamour and cool – 'New York, New York' greets the team every time they enter the arena – but it actually refers to the nineteenth-century designation for the local area. On the wall I spot a large, framed, black-and-white photograph of a game at Millmoor sometime in the late 1970s. 'Ah yes,' says Breckin, 'me mum and dad should be in that enclosure.' He tries to pick out Jim and Vera behind the dugout. 'I had mates at certain parts of the ground. You'd go to pick a ball up for a throw-in and they'd shout "Awright, Breck, you out tonight?" You were that close to them. They were the ones who used to get on at you. My brother would be there watching me. I knew that if I'd done 'owt wrong during the match I daren't look across.' Breckin joined the club as a fourteen-year-old member of the groundstaff, working his way up to become a first-team player, then coach, head of the youth team, assistant manager and caretaker manager. He suddenly remembers 1979 and the lead-up to Rotherham's two great matches against Chelsea:

Ian Porterfield had signed Ronnie [Moore] for a lot of money, and a few others, and I remember saying to someone: 'Hey, we've got a bit of a chance here.' Anton Johnson, the owner, took the shackles off and let Porters spend the money. Big money in them days. We got on this wave and got going. Porters left and we attracted Emlyn Hughes, who was a very big name in football. It lifted everybody in the town. And then [in 1981] we slaughtered Chelsea, 6-0 at home and 4-1 away [in 1982]. A 10-1 thrashing overall. But there's a massive gap now, isn't there? It's unbelievable to think it happened, really. Unbelievable.

LONDON 4 OLD YORKSHIRE 0

While the 6-0 away defeat in October 1981 is the standout scoreline for pre-Abramovich Chelsea diehards obsessed with 'Where were you when we were crap?' one-upmanship contests, the 4-1 rout at the Bridge has a far greater resonance for Rotherham fans. For it proved that the initial hammering had not been a David-versus-Goliath, FA Cup-type, giant-killing, one-off fluke. Almost twenty years since the sides had last met at the Bridge, it formed part of a four-match unbeaten sequence against the west Londoners, confirming the club's meteoric ascent under Johnson. Founded in 1925 as a merger between Rotherham Town and Rotherham County, who had been playing at Millmoor since 1907, Rotherham United's evolution was fuelled by the town's mining, iron and steel industries. Town were initially known as Lunar Rovers – because the team were mostly shopkeepers who worked on Saturday afternoons and played their matches in the evenings by moonlight. The Millers have never been in the top flight. They ended their brilliant 1981–2 campaign, however, only four points away, in seventh place. In the following three and a half decades they have not come anywhere close to emulating this achievement. The season after the Chelsea double, they dropped back into the Third Division and the two sides' paths have not crossed since.

In 1982, as Johnson was funding Rotherham's unlikely rise from Third Division nobodies to swaggering Chelsea-slayers, the Blues, on a downward trajectory since their early-seventies heyday, only narrowly avoided relegation. In 2015, three decades after the East Stand had almost finished them off – its construction left them £3.5 million in the red – and owned by a Russian oligarch worth $9 billion, they captured another league championship to confirm their place in the global elite. As Chelsea celebrated a fourth Premier League title win, and the Bridge continued to revel in its status as a slick, internationally famous, Champions League brand, home to football's super-rich, a report into Rotherham's child-grooming scandal reinforced the town's growing reputation an emblem of post-industrial neglect.

There has always been a divide between the west London 'haves' and the South Yorkshire 'have-nots'. And yet, even before Johnson's arrival, the gap between the two had been potentially bridgeable. In the utopian sixties both Rotherham and Chelsea had reached League Cup finals and had even been managed by the same man, the flamboyant Tommy Docherty, whose largely homegrown young Chelsea side won promotion to the top flight. After he resigned in 1967 – the core of 'Docherty's Diamonds' going on to win the FA Cup and European Cup Winners' Cup and thrill the young Breckin – the Doc arrived at Rotherham promising to do the same thing for the Millers. Striding onto the Millmoor pitch before his first match in charge, he announced to a packed stadium that his aim was to take the team out of the Second Division. True to his word, they made their exit – but down to the third tier. At least the equally boastful Johnson delivered, in his first couple of years, on his cocksure promises, treating fans to a fast-paced, no-holds-barred, rollercoaster ride, showing the world that, if everything was more or less equal, even a small, unfashionable, decaying Yorkshire town could, as Breckin put it, 'go toe to toe with the big boys'.

By the time ill-health had forced him to retire, at the end of the 1984–5 season, John Neal had stopped the rot at Chelsea. Indeed, as the coal closures were bringing Rotherham to its knees, the tough but warm-hearted old-school gaffer had begun to pave the way for a revival at Stamford Bridge, guiding a team of bargain buys – Kerry Dixon, Joey Jones, Mickey Thomas, Nigel Spackman, David Speedie and Pat Nevin – to a Second Division title and then sixth place in the First Division. In the 1990s, under Glenn Hoddle, Ruud Gullit and Gianluca Vialli, Chelsea began to accumulate trophies and impressive Premier League finishes but, once again, a massive debt left them close to financial ruin. In 2003, with the club facing insolvency, Roman Abramovich turned up in the nick of time to bail them out and usher in a new era of unprecedented riches, world-class players and countless baubles. Since the oil tycoon bought Chelsea for £140 million, they have consistently charted in the top ten of Deloitte's Money League, which ranks international clubs on the amount of revenue generated each season. In the Abramovich era, they have won fifteen trophies, four more than they did in the ninety-eight years prior to the billionaire's arrival.

Back in the seventies, when London was a drab, depressing city, a place that had never quite recovered from losing an empire – and before the panic about its falling population triggered a government-backed expansion of banking and financial services – the East Stand was the folly of the pre-commercial age, a warning of the price clubs would soon be paying for 'living the dream' during a recession. Hampered by debt, they had been unable to buy players for four years. Four-figure crowds had become commonplace. Two months after their 4-1 home defeat to Rotherham, only 6,009 people had turned up to a clash with Leyton Orient. This remains their lowest-ever home attendance.

During Chelsea's extraordinary ascent, which has seen the European Cup, four league titles and a glittering array of superstars arrive at the Bridge, the divergence between the north and the south has grown considerably. Under New Labour, the economic divide was further widened: Yorkshire went from being 10 per cent behind the UK's employment average in 1997 to 17 per cent behind. Today, for every twelve new jobs created in the south, only one is created anywhere else. A couple of developments prompted the capital's rise to total dominance: the establishment of the London Docklands Development Corporation in 1981, followed a year later by the London International Financial Futures Exchange. Until the early eighties, its banks and financial services had been kept in check by national and international controls on currency and investment flows.

At the same time, as regional broadcasting declined, the ever-ballooning capital expanded its media base. A fourth TV station, Channel 4, was established there in 1982 and, seven years later, the London-based Sky TV was launched.

With foreign money flowing in like never before, the previously grey, down-at-heel capital began to swing again. It became the global magnet for wealth, an international tax haven. During the recession that followed the 2008 global credit crunch, the government saw it as the engine room of recovery, showering money on its infrastructure in a dash for metropolitan growth that further unbalanced the economy. 'It is the hyper-capitalist version of George Orwell's Airstrip One,' wrote the *Guardian*'s Jonathan Freedland, 'the landing pad for global capital.' With a population that just keeps on growing, it has become a global hub, sucking in the top talent from the rest of the country, the centre of the nation's political, cultural, entrepreneurial, artistic, financial and sporting activity. 'It is to the billionaire,' boasted its former mayor Boris Johnson, 'as the jungles of Sumatra are to the orangutans.' In much the same way, the Premier League, which broke away from the Football League in 1992, has become a rich man's playground, the natural habitat of oligarchs, sheikhs, corporate raiders and sports consortiums.

As the capital boomed – it now has a quarter of the nation's economic activity – there was a reshaping of the sporting landscape, a pronounced southward shift in the balance of power. Football, indeed sport in general, became as lopsided as the economy. The inaugural Premiership boasted four sides from the broad acres: Leeds, Sheffield United, Sheffield Wednesday and Middlesbrough. And yet in 2015, like the Ashes, the world's most lucrative league became a Yorkshire-free zone. During the long boom between the recession of the early nineties and the financial crash of 2008, London's sporting base, like its economy, underwent a profound change, becoming a place where oversees investors could park their wealth. The richest city in the world began to provide some of its richest football teams, attracting the interest of oligarchs, sheikhs and American venture capitalists. With the exception of Manchester, the balance of footballing power has shifted away from the big-city northern clubs who dominated post-war football, towards Arsenal and Chelsea. 'This is a sport geared around money,' argued sportswriter Barney Ronay, an environment in which London's extreme, disproportionate wealth – one-tenth of the world's billionaires live in London; average household wealth in the south-east is more than twice that of the north-east – can't help but begin to exert its own gravity . . . The measure of how much English football is a London game is not in the number of clubs near the top of the money list, the fact that West Ham are richer than Roma. It is instead present in the way a league that was always a business is run entirely on London principles . . . London looks like football: football looks like London. Looking from one to the other, it is already impossible to say which is which.

THE FIRST OF THE NEW BREED

It would be something of a stretch to claim that, in the early eighties, football looked like Rotherham. But their cigar-smoking, puffy-coated owner was, for a while, the coming man. Brash, ego-driven and hungry for success, and publicity, Anton Johnson was the personification of the Essex Man so assiduously courted by Thatcher's Conservatives. He was the first of the new breed of football directors – opportunistic businessmen who saw clubs as speculative investment opportunities rather than sporting organisations – to challenge the old guard. During the four years of Thatcher's first term, the Millers were taken on an exhilarating ride by a sharp-suited, sharp-elbowed entrepreneur straight out of TV comedy's Central Casting: Del Boy meets Arthur Daley with *The Long Good Friday*'s Harold Shand thrown in for good measure. A forgotten figure today, he was also the first of the new breed to be pursued around the world by a *World in*

Action investigative team. Indeed, his memoir, *King of Clubs*, which promises to give the 'amazing tales' of his life as both a nightclub and football club owner, opens with Johnson in a holding cell in Chelmsford Crown Court awaiting a verdict.

Two and a half years before his side's unprecedented double over Chelsea, he had paid a peppercorn fee of £62,000 for a modestly profitable club that, since the sixties, had been run by the Purshouses, a local, philanthropic, quintessentially Old Yorkshire family. When Johnson took over, Rotherham were £250,000 in the black and boasted a financial base that was the envy of most other teams. At an awards ceremony in the seventies, Liverpool manager Bill Shankly, to many in the game then – as now – a kind of secular saint, made a point of congratulating Lewis Purshouse on his integrity. 'How nice,' Shanks greeted the Millers' vice-chairman, 'to see an honest man.' A vocal minority of United fans, however, had become fed up with the family's apparent lack of ambition and, following some vicious personal abuse, the Purshouses decided to sell up. After watching TV presenter Jimmy Hill announce this news on *Match of the Day*, Johnson immediately rang Lewis' dad Eric and flew into Millmoor to close the deal. During half-time he was furious to be told that Eric had changed his mind after a private detective had discovered a notorious East End gangster was staying in Johnson's house. 'I was absolutely raving,' wrote the businessman. '"You could have told me that over the phone," I said as I put my hands around his throat.'

After sealing the deal he drove his Rolls-Royce down to London to buy a big fur coat and a box of Churchill cigars. 'I felt I had the right image,' he recounted. 'The amount of money spent by Rotherham on transfers was unheard of for a Third Division team; at the next chairman's meeting they all asked if I was mad – spending that sort of money for an untried manager [Porterfield] ... in 1979 it was quite unusual for anybody to buy a football club, so I was in demand for all types of interviews on radio and television. I was on the Russell Harty show twice.' The fans were delighted as his speculate-to-accumulate approach began to pay off and the club embarked upon, in Breckin's words, 'an amazing, fantastic two-and-a-half-year adventure'. The untried Porterfield, renowned for scoring the 1973 FA Cup final winner for underdogs Sunderland against Don Revie's great Leeds side, saved them from relegation to the Fourth Division and then went on to build one of the best teams in Rotherham's history. Ronnie Moore was signed from Cardiff and banged in forty-five goals in two seasons. 'He was six-foot something,' recalled the future World Cup referee Howard Webb, then a young Rotherham fan. 'He had blond hair, was a centre-forward, a goal-scorer and full of character, charisma and personality.' Big Ron was joined by winger Tony Towner, who cost the club a record £150,000. When Porterfield jumped ship a year later, Johnson managed to lure Liverpool and England defender Hughes, who immediately erected a 'This is Millmoor' board at the top of the players' tunnel, mimicking Shankly's famous Anfield sign. The exuberant Hughes then proceeded to win nine games on the spin, increasing crowds by over 50 per cent. The only way, it appeared, was up.

There was one slight problem. In the space of almost three years, Rotherham had gone from having plenty of cash in the bank – mainly thanks to the prudence of the Purshouse family – to being £285,000 in the red. This was the cue for Johnson to disappear almost as quickly as he had appeared. Accused by a Bradford City director of 'using club money for [his] own personal business', he left behind a mountain of debt and myriad stories of dodgy dealings. In 1987, now £500,000 in arrears, the club were only saved from extinction by a council loan. Local journalist Paul Rickett remembered Johnson arriving

in his fur coat, in a helicopter, a big minder with him. Eric and Lewis Purshouse had built the club on solid foundations. Then Anton rocks up, promises them the earth and the fans buy into it massively. He's promising everybody this and that. But there was no substance to what he was promising. His name is still debated in pubs and clubs, whether he was good or bad for the club. True, people had a good time, but they were duped to an extent. There was a bit of success, it was party time, but Rotherham have been paying the price ever since. Johnson took the club to the brink of financial ruin. When he left, *World in Action* were chasing him all over the country. He became involved with other clubs. The year Rotherham were relegated to Division Three he was involved at Derby and he was paying the wages there with United's money. Derby survived and Rotherham went down. Nobody found out about that for years afterwards. It ruined United.

'Today British football is in a sad financial state,' the *World in Action* documentary, which was broadcast in 1984, began. 'Higher wages, hooliganism and shrinking attendances have undermined the game's commercial foundations.' Johnson was described as 'a typical football showman [but] there's more to him than that. He boasts of association with a convicted criminal and speaks of crime and violence. He blurs the line between football club money and his own pocket.' The narrator acknowledged the showman's flair for publicity and celebrity networking – a pop song he recorded with Elton John was played frequently at Millmoor, adding 'to the aura of money and glamour' – and his popularity with many fans. Some supporters clearly regarded him as a messiah, or at least a benevolent wealthy figure prepared to spend freely on players. By late 1983, however, the game was up. The club fell back into the Third Division and, with their annual loss rising to more than £1 million, Johnson was suddenly nowhere to be found. Two years later, the FA banned him from football. In 1988, after private detectives finally caught up with him in the United States, he was declared bankrupt.

'Football clubs never came on the market,' he told an Essex newspaper many years later while promoting his self-serving memoir. 'But suddenly, a lot of football clubs were going on the market and so many were going into receivership.' This was at a time when, as *When Saturday Comes* reported, crowds 'were in freefall [and] many owners no longer had the means to prop up their local club, no matter how philanthropic their intentions. As a result smaller clubs in particular became vulnerable.' From the end of the Second World War until the end of the seventies, financially prudent local businessmen had tended to run these outfits out of a sense of civic duty, believing themselves to be providers of a public good that was, or at least should seek to be, universally affordable. A football ground, as the sports historian Simon Inglis put it, was 'as much part of a burgeoning corporation as a public library, town hall and law courts and was certainly used by more people'.

Although it wasn't until 1992 that the Premier League, created out of the top clubs' desire to keep Rupert Murdoch's millions for themselves, would revolutionise the game's finances, the direction of the football economy was already being transformed in the eighties by piecemeal deregulation which, slowly but surely, allowed clubs to mutate into profit-making concerns. Family dynasties, like the Purshouses, the Cobbolds at Ipswich and the Hill-Woods at Arsenal, were on the wane. As the decade progressed, and the paternalist spirit evaporated, the old guard was gradually ousted by directors whose business careers had been forged in the deregulated climate of New Britain. Property developers, embezzlers, asset strippers and crooks began to dabble in the game. Perhaps the most notorious of the new breed was *Mirror* pensions robber Robert Maxwell, who was allowed to invest in both Oxford United and Derby County.

Rules introduced a century earlier to limit commercial activity, and prevent the wealthiest teams dominating football, were relaxed. In 1981, the FA loosened its restrictions on dividend payments and directors' pay, hoping that full-time directors would bring more rigour to the game's economic governance. In 1983 the agreement to give the away team a share of the home gate was revoked; ending a 100-year-old practice that had benefited smaller clubs with smaller grounds (and weaker gate receipts). In the same year, Irving Scholar, a thirty-something, Monaco-based property developer, announced that Spurs would become a plc; nine years later, Manchester United would follow suit, with majority shareholder Martin Edwards as one of the first football club chief executives to be paid, making £6 million out of the flotation. By then, several other top-flight clubs had been floated on the stock exchange and become very lucrative for share-holders. In 1984, the Football League abolished a rule that prevented directors paying themselves: board members' salaries quickly shot up.

In the first half of the decade, Scholar and Edwards, together with their counterparts at Arsenal, Liverpool and Everton, were continually pushing for their clubs to keep more of the league's TV income. 'The smaller clubs are bleeding the game dry,' said Edwards. 'For the sake of the game they should be put to sleep.' In 1985, the Big Five's threats to secede forced smaller clubs into accepting a new split in the TV money: 50 per cent of a new £44 million four-year deal with ITV went to First Division teams, 25 per cent to Second Division ones and 25 per cent to the Third and Fourth. 'The Premier League,' wrote Nick Varley, 'was where the game had been heading throughout the 1980s.'

THE SCRAPYARD YEARS

Johnson's vanishing act had left Rotherham £250,000 in arrears. Local businessman Graham Humphries stepped in but a year later his company folded – he blamed the miners' strike – and the debt increased by a further £100,000. In 1987 United went into administration. In a move that delighted the headline writers, a local scrap dealer decided to ride to the rescue. Rotherham were 'saved from the scrapyard' by Ken Booth, a no-nonsense, penny-pinching, old-school industrialist, who immediately wiped off burgeoning liabilities of almost £800,000. The 65-year-old, who also brought onto the board a car-dealing acquaintance, had taken over the family business from his father and built it up into a massive recycling empire that, for seventeen years, bankrolled the Millers. Frequently criticised by fans for failing to invest in Millmoor, by the end of his reign he cut an isolated, almost parodic, Dickensian figure, seemingly out of step with the modern world – and certainly with the new football order.

Booth was often compared to Bill 'I love scrap' Fraser of *Ripping Yarns* fame. Breckin took a more benign view. 'Mr Booth did a great job for the club,' he insisted. 'Things were going a little bit pear-shaped, but then this knight in shining armour comes along and takes us over. He did get a lot of stick but the old man did it his way and he needs a lot of credit for that. He did a lot for the town. His company still does. It employs a lot of people. He's part of the club's history. He was a great character and a very powerful man. I'll never forget the way he'd spit on his hand and seal a deal with a handshake. We knew the club was safe. He didn't splash the cash. That was frustrating for me and Ronnie of course, and the supporters, but he had his way of doing it. He kept us afloat.'

Booth was a throwback to the old Rotherham, which had developed in the nineteenth century from a small market town into a major industrial centre based on coal and steel; its furnaces and mills had made the cannon that armed Nelson's HMS *Victory* at Trafalgar. Much of the steel needed in both world wars was produced at the Templeborough steelworks that, in the seventies, employed over 10,000 workers and produced 18 million tones of steel every year. In the mid-seventies, before de-industrialisation began to devastate South Yorkshire, deep coal production thrived in the borough: around 10,000 people worked in in the local pits. Booth owned the biggest independent scrap venture in the country, its yards surrounding Millmoor on three sides. Rotherham's main industries might have been hit hard by the eighties recession but the scrap metal business thrived. Despite making a fortune, however, the old man was obsessed with being prudent. British Rail trains would often appear behind the ground's away end, waiting to be dismembered. Whenever a player was sold, word would get around that 'Boothy' had needed a new crane. 'Ken didn't want to spend his family fortune on Rotherham United,' said Rickett. 'He put a lot of money into the club over the years but he was never going to redevelop the ground or spend a million on a star. If Moore and Breckin fancied someone, they had to play things down.' On one occasion, when the pair had wanted to buy a player for £50,000, they told Booth the player's club had asked for £75,000. 'We made out if he offered £50,000 we'd get him,' said Breckin. 'And Ken says "Let me just think about this".' And we knew very well he'd be going around his scrapyard asking the Rotherham fans: "Does tha know this player, lad?" So we got word to them. "If he asks you about this player put your thumbs up." So Ken goes into his scrapyard and says to one or two of them: "Have you heard of this player? What's he like?" "He's all right him, Ken," they says, "he's a good player." And we got a phone call a few hours later saying: "I think we'll take a flyer on that. Aye, offer them 50 grand."'

Rickett also recalled the time the Rotherham team coach returned to the town centre late at night after a long-distance trek back from the south-west coast. 'They came back over the flyover that passes Ken's building, next to the ground,' he said.

His office light was still on. He was in the office with his flask and sandwiches. He had just sacked his nightwatchman for fiddling so he was doing the books himself. A week after his wife died, Ken told the commercial manager to put a rack up in the club shop. 'Want to put our lass' clothes on it.' But he was talked out of it. The workforce at CF Booths were treated as serfs at times, but he would always sort them out. They were fiercely loyal to him. If one of them got locked up, his wife went to Mr Booth. He would pay his mortgage. Ken belongs to another century. Fans didn't realise the size of the cheques he paid just to keep them afloat. His money kept them above water. If he found a fiver he was as happy as Larry. He didn't want to spend half a million pounds on a football club. He just wanted to sit there, put his red and white scarf on during a Saturday afternoon and go in the boardroom afterwards and have a glass of whisky, lord it and be happy. He couldn't get it in his head that footballers were being paid what they were for what they did – and this is in the 1980s.

With little money being spent on the team, the club yo-yoed between the bottom two divisions until Moore was appointed manager in 1997. With Breckin as his assistant, the former striker, who was reportedly the worst-paid boss in the league, masterminded back-to-back promotions. This latest meteoric rise, unlike the one financed by Johnson, was achieved on a shoestring budget. Like the previous ascent, however, it also proved to be a costly adventure and United, once again, came close to extinction. In 2005, they crashed out of the Championship after a woeful campaign that produced only five wins. Booth, now well into his eighties and struggling to cope with a high wage bill, low crowds and the implosion of ITV Digital – the lower league transfer market collapsed after the broadcaster failed to honour its £315 million contract – sold the club to a fans' consortium, writing off a debt of £3 million in exchange for keeping ownership of Millmoor. Two years later, the club were relegated to the third tier and went into administration for a third time in twenty-one years.

Many fans blamed the old man's Old Yorkshire prudence, resenting his tight control of the purse strings. As a youngster following Rotherham at the time, Jonathan Veal, now a Press Association journalist, remembered constant 'Booth out' chants during games. 'He saved the club from extinction in the mid-eighties and kept them going for seventeen years,' said Veal. 'But he didn't move the club forward. There were several opportunities to invest some money into the club. For our Auto Windscreens win at Wembley in 1996, 20,000 people from Rotherham went. It was a massive opportunity to invest money, buy players, but the season after that we had one of our worst-ever seasons.' Reflecting on the Booth era many years later, however, *When Saturday Comes* writer Tom Davies praised the scrapman's careful husbandry, especially in the light of the overspending that had imperilled the existence of several other small (and big) Yorkshire teams. 'The inability of smaller clubs to compete in the Premier League has become such a commonplace complaint as to have become almost a cliché,' wrote Davies. 'The worry now is that chasing even the Championship dream is proving just as perilous for so many clubs.'

WELCOME TO EVERYTOWN

Towards the end of the scrapyard years, the philosopher Julian Baggini decided to embark upon a 'cultural tour' of Rotherham. In *Welcome to Everytown*, his attempt to understand the English mind, the academic's six-month residency in one of its districts coincided with a period when the club's existence was under threat. Collection buckets rattled outside Millmoor, the Save The Millers campaign organised endless fundraising events, there was constant talk of liquidation and, to rub salt into the wounds, the team went seventeen matches without a win. Despite this, noted Baggini, the fans still loyally sung 'I'm Rotherham till I die.' The philosopher was impressed. 'Perhaps the greatest symbol of the centrality of working-class culture to English life is football,' he declared. The fans' emotional commitment to the team, Baggini went on to explain, came from 'a strong sense of tribal loyalty and attachment to place'. He concluded by praising the defiant spirit of a town he believed 'was more representative of the nation than others': its S66 postcode had the closest match of household types to the country as a whole. 'The way of life here is much like it is in any English town [but] this world is rarely written about, because people in the national media and the arts don't live here and don't come here.'

Ten years later, when he returned to Everytown, it was being written about, and visited, a great deal. Indeed, you couldn't move for state-of-the-nation philosophers, cultural tourists and celebrity do-gooders. With its high unemployment, economic deprivation and social divisions, Rotherham had become a symbol for the decline of Old Yorkshire, 'slashed and burned', as Owen Hatherley put it, 'by 30-plus years of Thatcherism'. In the mid-seventies, around 10,000 people had been employed in the mining industry. By the end of the eighties, that figure had halved and today no deep-mined coal is extracted from the area. In 1981, from an employment base of 82,000, the town lost over 8,000 jobs in metal manufacturing and engineering. In the next six years, there was an overall decrease of 8.7 per cent in the number of jobs. The highest levels of unemployment were recorded in January 1986, when 24,580 people were registered as unemployed.

This scorched earth policy had been played out against a national transfer of assets from the public sector to the private sector, and the state's withdrawal from public housing, income maintenance and other forms of social provision and welfare. As the frontiers of the local state had been rolled back, various self-help organisations, celebrity charity crusaders and media personalities had stepped in to 'rescue' Rotherham. The first high-profile do-gooder to invade Everytown was Jamie Oliver. Outraged that some mothers had sneaked high-fat, high-salt burgers and fish and chips into a local school through its fence, the Essex multimillionaire established a network of worthy shops called the Ministry of Food. Accompanied by the obligatory book and TV series, Oliver set up the flagship outlet in the town centre, which taught basic cooking skills and encouraged children to eat their greens. The restaurateur's main concern, wrote Hatherley, was 'to take "good food" – locally sourced, cooked from scratch – from being a preserve of the middle classes and bring it to the "disadvantaged" and "socially excluded" . . . one could argue that he was the latest in a long line of people lecturing the lower orders on their choice of nutrition.'

Next to arrive was country music legend Dolly Parton, who established a scheme to give deprived children free books. The £2 million 'personal vanity project', as one opponent described it, was instigated by Rotherham council leader Roger Stone amid massive fanfare. Stone, a lifelong fan of the platinum-bouffanted singer, invited hundreds of businessmen and civic leaders to a slap-up lunch in which she sang various hits including the inevitable 'Jolene'. Finally, television retail guru Mary Portas, hired by the government to improve the nation's high streets, rode into town. Rotherham, she gravely informed *Daily Telegraph* readers, was 'on the brink of despair'.

All three high-profile projects eventually ran into difficulties. Oliver's army was forced to withdraw following health and safety concerns, although its outpost reopened in 2014. Portas bemoaned the lack of government support for struggling shopkeepers. And the Parton reading scheme was axed to save £400,000 – with Stone forced to step down after a report into the child-sex grooming scandal had criticised the council for failing to put the community's interests first. When Baggini revisited Everytown, a decade after his original tour, he noted that 'the poor white working class' – the core of Rotherham United's support base – had become an 'increasingly disenfranchised group. Coal and steel used to supply work for pretty much any local man who wanted it . . . The children of miners laid off in the 1980s now have kids of their own and in some cases these children live in households that have never had a wage-earner.'

The sight of three generations of Millers fans attending a game on a Saturday afternoon, remarked veteran supporter Geoff Needham in his football blog, was 'now a rarity rather than commonplace' – a trend he attributed to the disappearance of 'the family tradition of following your father and his father into the foundry or down the mine'. Needham, like Baggini, was nostalgic for an Old Yorkshire golden age – roughly, the late 1940s and 50s – when the steelworks and pitheads thrived and the local community had been at its most cohesive. In a post-war period regarded by many as the high point of British social democracy, with communitarian values entrenched in the new welfare state, manufacturing was still the bedrock of British industry; in 1952, it produced a third of the national output and employed 40 per cent of the workforce, whereas today it accounts for 11 per cent of GDP and employs only 8 per cent of workers. At the same time, Football League attendances boomed, reaching record levels, and the maximum wage brought down player costs, reducing the wealthier clubs' bargaining power and creating more equal competition. The exciting, if short-lived, adventures of the Johnson and Moore–Breckin eras might stand out in living memory, but the two decades immediately after the Second World War remain the club's most successful period of all time. The town was bustling, vibrant and forward-looking and its upwardly mobile, all-out-attacking team reflected this newfound confidence.

In the post-war years, as Yorkshire football expert Cameron Fleming has pointed out, the Millers 'brimmed over with working-class heroes who supplemented their low football wages by boiling away in the pits during the week.' Most of the players worked in the coal industry, which had been a reserved wartime occupation. Alarm bells had rung in government circles when the industry's workforce dropped from 784,000 to 690,000 in the first eighteen months of the conflict. The subsequent legislation, which prevented miners leaving their employment without the permission of the National Service office, allowed Reg Freeman's youthful side to stay together during the war, giving them a huge advantage when the Football League restarted. While most of their rivals were rebuilding, Rotherham galloped through the 1946–7 season, winning all their Division Three home games except the last, a 3-3 draw at Rochdale. They then finished third three times in a row before being promoted to the Second Division. In 1953 they knocked the then mighty New-castle, winners of the previous two FA Cups, out of the competition at St. James' Park to reach the fifth round for the first time. After finishing fifth the following year, they excelled themselves in the 1954–5 season; agonisingly missing promotion to the top flight on goal average, their third-placed finish remains their highest-ever league position. And in 1961 they played in the inaugural League Cup final, against Aston Villa, winning the first leg at home 2-0, but eventually losing 3-2 on aggregate.

'I thought playing for Rotherham was something out of this world,' explained Danny Williams, whose League Cup final appearance was one of a record 462 for his hometown side. 'We were very hungry to play. I don't think today's players are, really.' A one-club man, Williams had been seventeen when he broke into the team just after the war. 'I used to go to the mine at six in the morning and come away at eleven,' he recalled. 'Then I'd have a light lunch and go and play for Rotherham. The demise of the coal industry took thousands of jobs out of the community. In fact, the steel industry was the first to go – after that everything changed. It kicked in later on in the decade and the team suffered for years to come.' As a young Rotherham fan, Breckin idolised Williams. He remembered the early sixties as a time when town and club were united, still both riding high on a wave of post-war optimism. Williams had a sports shop in the thriving town centre and, recalled Breckin, 'you could just walk in and say hello. You would just walk up to your great hero in his town-centre shop. The town now has its work cut out to entice people back into the centre. It was unbelievable what happened in the mid-eighties. It affected families, especially mining families. The steel closures were bad enough, but the mining collapse was the thing that really crippled us as a town. The strikes were horrendous. Families fell out. I had friends who were working in the pits. We went through hell in this area – we closed seven pits in a short time. But at least we had Millmoor to go to. Attendances fell. I knew a hell of a lot of people who couldn't afford to go to matches. But that ground – it kept our spirits up.'

THE GHOST OF OLD YORKSHIRE

Built in the middle of the Edwardian era, on the site of a flour mill, Millmoor was football's version of the Boulevard. It was always a bit tight for space, and in constant need of a lick of paint, but for United's old faithful it had been the theatre of their greatest memories. It drew its strength from the town's plucky, underdog, backwater status: seeing off Aston Villa in the first leg of the 1960 League Cup final, twice crushing Chelsea in the early eighties and, in the Moore–Breckin era, holding Kevin Keegan's Manchester City to a draw. Before the City game, a furious Keegan, disgusted with the state of the away changing room, had redirected the team coach to a nearby hotel. The snub gave the Millers, battling for Second Division survival at the time, even more of an incentive to bring King Kev down a peg or two. After the match, the enraged former European Player of the Year accused Moore of moving the touchlines in to narrow the pitch. 'People like Keegan, and others who were at that kind of level, wouldn't give us any respect,' said Moore. 'They didn't know us. Me and Breck were two lads from a council estate who got a team together and they thought they should be twatting us because they'd done this and that.' Another group of Big Time Charlies, West Ham United, were also cut down to size after refusing to get changed in the visitors' dressing room. Not long after the Hammers' shock defeat at Rotherham, their defender Scott Minto joined Moore's side on loan. 'It was back to the old school,' he said. 'It was almost how it was back in the 1980s when I started. Real down-to-earth people, down-to-earth facilities and it kind of made me laugh that there was no gym at the training ground. Sometimes the showers weren't always hot, but also the fact that you had to take your kit home and wash it yourself . . . it made me realise how lucky I was playing in the Premier League for so long because at Rotherham you had a set of working lads working just as hard, if not harder, to look after their families on two-year contracts.'

When Millmoor celebrated its centenary in 2007 – with a 1-1 draw against Notts County – supporters gathered for the last time at the ground to pay their respects to a civic symbol as important as any church or town hall. Its industrial rhythm, camaraderie and architecture had once mimicked the town's steel factories and mines, providing a rich store of local myths and folk wisdoms. The match-day programme, which carried a host of nostalgic articles, was adorned with a commemorative cover and 100 balloons were released bearing the club badge, a representation of the flour mills and windmill that used to stand near the ground. The end-of-an-era feel was emphasised by the scarves specially designed for the occasion: 'Rotherham United F.C.' on one side, '1907–2007' on the other. For all its blemishes, wrote Needham – particularly 'its leaking roof, crumbling cement and ancient timbers' – Millmoor represented the town's last link with a dying era. He contrasted the match-day experience of 'queuing in the rain for a cup of Bovril and a meat and potato pie from a hut at the back of the terrace' with the modern stadiums' 'quality carpeted, chandeliered restaurants with smartly-clad waiters and waitresses in attendance. It was home, our home, our ground. It was where we met our pals . . . it was where we supported our team. Win or lose, rain or shine.'

Long before Booth entered the fray, the ground had been an extension of his scrap business. In his classic tome *Football Grounds of England and Wales*, Inglis described it as standing 'in the three-sided grip of a collection of scrap yards, whose walls on two sides form the backs of the stands. There is literally no room for manoeuvre, as cranes swing backward and forward almost over the ground itself . . . Millmoor is quite a mixture of oddities in odd surroundings, but as a result of good maintenance and lots of red paint, is actually a compact, cosy, cheerful island in the midst of a clanking and rather noisome sea of debris.' Two players from the golden age, Roy Ironside and Barry Webster, were interviewed about their unorthodox training sessions for the community history project 'Coal to Goal', which was studded with photographs of old folk heroes and mufflered, flat-capped men waving rattles. 'We had five-a-sides playing on the concrete,' said Ironside. 'We used to train on the shale behind Booth's yard. We used to have to duck when they dropped the crane on steel.' Webster would never forget the 'flying missiles coming round the scrapyard when we were running round the track.' To lifelong fan Dave Rawson, Millmoor embodied 'identity, that indefinable quality that drew together individuals over the years to the place a few hundred yards down the road, and an almost incalculable distance away. It's inherent in supporting a football team that you impress the qualities that you value onto the club you follow . . . Standing in the shadows of the home end at Millmoor, straining to hear the echoes of a century's cheers and cries, you can sense something of it . . . Millmoor will never be forgotten.'

A year after celebrating the crumbling stadium's centenary, and two years after United's insolvency, lighting salesman Tony Stewart bought the club off the fans' consortium. Booth still owned the ground and, refusing to be held to ransom by the old man's hefty rent demand, Stewart upset many locals by moving the Millers out of their spiritual home. Like Rotherham's shoppers, fans were now expected to 'consume their product' at an out-of-town centre, the Don Valley Stadium, which was never more than a third full during the club's four-year tenure. At the end of this exile, however, the New York Stadium was ready, complete with executive lounges, conference centres and banqueting facilities. 'You can't talk big and act small,' said Stewart.

> To me, if you think big you've got to get your wallet out. Money makes and ruins football. Football is a bit like show business. The stadium has become an iconic feature of the town. I have put the Eiffel Tower into Rotherham. You drive into Rotherham and what do you see? This fantastic stadium. And I'm proud of that. It creates a favourable impression for any new visitors and that has to be a good thing. Manchester City pulled up outside Millmoor, took one look and drove off to a hotel near the M1 for their overnight stop. I never want that to happen again. I want it to be something that turns heads and makes people stand up and realise where we are going as a football club and a town. It's a statement.

Millmoor's pitch is still in use, but only Booth's grandchildren are allowed to play on it. It, too, is a statement – of Everytown's disappearing industrial identity. Like the derelict steelworks, silent cranes and colliery headgear dotted around Rotherham, it is a monument to abandonment, a tomb from which the treasure has long ago been plundered, a time capsule where asbestos roofs, floodlight pylons and rusting terrace barriers have been preserved in the collective memory. The ghosts of Booth's scrapyards still inhabit the town, not only as figments of the imagination. They remain a going concern but, since he cut off his connection with the club, Millmoor has become a piece of neglected, fenced-off land, closed to the public. While countless old-era stadiums lie buried under housing estates, supermarkets and car parks, or have been abandoned to let nature take its course, Millmoor's crumbling remains are a reproach to Stewart's gleaming new edifice. For more than a hundred years it was indelibly connected to the local area, surrounded by the Midland Railway to the west, tramlines to the east, the Guest & Chrimes industrial brassworks to the south and Masbrough, a working-class village with its own industry, shops and pubs, to the north. 'The Booths still own all the area around the ground,' explained Rickett. 'Sooner or later Millmoor will end up being absorbed into the scrapyard. It's going to die and it's going to go to dust, which is a shame.'

Like the KC Stadium, the New York Stadium is a beacon for football's new era. It remains haunted, however, by the ghosts of Old Yorkshire's ruinous grandeur, unable to escape the dim shadows of its immediate, backward-looking surroundings. Its name is a nod to its Victorian heritage: the local area is known as New York because Guest & Chrimes made the red fire hydrants which can still be found on the streets of the Big Apple. In his economic history of Glasgow, Sydney Checkland told the legend of the upas tree, whose exhalations ensured that no living thing could exist within a fifteen-mile radius. The metaphor neatly illustrated how an ailing industrial sector, its limbs gradually falling away, managed to infect everything that sought to grow under its branches. Erected in the middle of the nineteenth century, and closed at the end of the twentieth century, the Guest & Chrimes façade, described by Stewart as 'an eyesore', is in a state of rapid deterioration. Protected by English Heritage's commitment to preserve industrial buildings, its demolition would increase the stadium's capacity from 12,000 to 16,000, possibly 20,000, and open up new revenue streams for the club. 'As a businessman it's my job to make sure that we maximise the attendances we are going to get moving forward,' said Stewart. 'You look at our lovely stadium but it's still a building site. It's ready to be redeveloped and I'm gagging to do it. All around the stadium and ground are revenue streams waiting to kick in and move forward: banqueting, weddings, conference suites, a gym, a hotel and a pub.'

Lying dormant in its lavish successor's shadow, it is Millmoor's empty husk, not the state-of-the-art stadium, that really stands out on the skyline. It is a reminder of Old Yorkshire's doomed attempt to modernise, its failure to transcend its industrial past, to soar above the dilapidated post-war estates with their boarded-up houses and shops. Despite Portas' best efforts, Rotherham's high street remains dominated by betting parlours, pawn shops and pound stores. The decimated town centre gives off an air of neglect, reeking of stolen childhoods and broken lives. Shoppers, or at least the more affluent ones, continue to flock to out-of-town complexes such as Parkgate and Meadowhall. In an age of mass consumption, these malls – like the Magna Science and Adventure Centre, once home to a great industrial cathedral – are acknowledged, by some, to be successful attempts at post-industrial reinvention. But a few miles away, on a small patch of land just off the M1, the fault lines dividing the dilapidated, communitarian shell of Old Yorkshire from the trapped, soulless ambition of New Britain remain clear for all to see.

Act Two:

Defeat

'We are becoming a more private society, abandoning
the cinema for the home video, the football terrace for
Match of the Day, constituency meetings for the jousting
of party leaders on *Panorama*. The result is a society with
a strange new kind of unhappiness: better fed, clothed and
housed than ever before, yet progressively impoverished
in its capacity to provide collective belonging – a sense
of community'

Michael Ignatieff, *The Great British Dream Factory*, 1983

*9 June 1983. The Conservatives are re-elected; the euphoria cre-
ated by the Falklands War, and the bonanza of North Sea oil, has
brought Thatcher another landslide victory. Her 144-seat majority
ensures the Tories are likely to last at least two more terms in
government and triggers a decisive shift towards the free-market
economy. Low inflation is prioritised over full employment. Fourteen industries, including gas, electricity, telephones and British*

Airways, are taken out of public ownership. Thatcher believes that by breaking the monopoly of coal, and then privatising it, the power of the NUM, and the trade union movement, will be broken. She had been a minister almost a decade earlier when the NUM had brought down Edward Heath's government. 'The last Conservative government was destroyed by the miners' strike,' she says. 'We'll have another and we'll win.' The 1984–5 strike is triggered by the announcement that Cortonwood pit, near Barnsley, is to close. Yorkshire's 56,000 miners are called out on strike by the NUM, who then learn of the government's plan to shut twenty pits and shed 20,000 jobs. A year later, the miners' defeat cements Thatcher's authority; according to her loyal ally Norman Tebbit it breaks 'not just a strike, but a spell', re-establishing the government's authority over organised labour. Free-market fundamentalism is now, unquestionably, the new orthodoxy. In his epic poem 'V', written in the midst of the miners' strike, Yorkshire poet Tony Harrison, part of the post-war, upwardly mobile generation of working-class writers, laments the self-destructive conflicts of the New Britain. The poem, a howl of rage against the waste of human potential, berates the southern-centric Conservatives for fighting a civil war against the north – and the police for becoming a brutal, quasi-military arm of a heartless government.

4

The Knights of Fev

'What shift is thy on, on Monday?'
'Nights. Can tha' do owt about it?'
Exchange between former NUM president
Lord Gormley and Featherstone captain
Terry Hudson during the presentation
of the 1983 Challenge Cup

7 May, 1983. Wembley. Featherstone vs Hull. The Challenge Cup final. Rovers take an early lead through a David Hobbs try. Hull draw level following a hotly contested penalty try by Lee Crooks and a conversion – and a James Leuluai try and further goals by Crooks give them a 12-5 lead. Hull lose Kevin Harkin after a collision with Terry Hudson and John Gilbert is carried off when, in retaliation, Paul Rose tackles him high. Rose's crude tackle earns him a sin-binning – and then Hudson, the Rovers captain, is also banished to the bench for ten minutes. Allan Agar's team stick to their game plan and a Steve Quinn penalty goal and then another Hobbs try, which is converted by Quinn, level the score. With two minutes to go, Quinn lands a twenty-yard penalty shot at goal and Featherstone run out as shock 14-12 winners.

Having played a key role in Hull KR's Challenge Cup win three years earlier, Allan Agar knew what it was like to taste victory at Wembley. He had already experienced the feeling of an embattled industrial community decamping to London and enjoying their Big Day Out. But this was different. This was a tiny pit town, synonymous with rugby league. *His* tiny pit town, his hometown team, whom he had supported as a boy and played for as a young man. 'Nobody gave Fev a chance,' he says. 'In fact the bookies stopped taking bets on Hull. We'd been near the bottom of the league all year, and only escaped the drop by one place. But the attitude for the cup ties was different. Many of our lads worked, or had worked, down the pit and two or three of them were knocking on a bit. So they knew this was their last chance to win something.' Agar is sitting, unrecognised, in a darkened, sparsely populated pub in Castleford, Featherstone's neighbouring town. He flicks through the pages of a scrapbook lovingly stuffed with yellowing newspaper cuttings and alliterative posters: *Agar's Amazing Army, Follow Fearless Fantastic Featherstone, Rocking Rolling Rovers*. Not owning any videos of the 1983 final, and ill acquainted with the ways of social media, these are his only mementoes of a match many regard as the biggest upset in rugby league history. To the millions watching on the box, Featherstone represented the soul of the oval-ball game. The very appearance in a Challenge Cup final of these no-hopers from a small Yorkshire village was, as the BBC commentator Ray French put it, a minor miracle. The word 'miracle' appears frequently in Agar's album. As does the phrase 'mining village', with many column inches devoted to Featherstone's paradigmatic status as a gritty pit area. Such words and phrases are absent from today's rugby league match reports. 'It was the biggest-ever shock at Wembley in my opinion,' says Agar, 'and I don't think it will ever be beaten. That's because of the way the game is now and how money dominates rugby. Well, all sport really. Today, you only have the rich clubs who have a hope of getting there. I hope I'm wrong. It would be great if one of the lesser clubs could go to Wembley and turn over one of the rich clubs. But money governs this sport now, just like it does every other sport.'

JUST A SET OF TRAFFIC LIGHTS

Eight of the 1983 team dug coal for a living. In fact, most Featherstone officials and supporters were miners, ex-miners or the children of miners. But the town's characterisation, constantly alluded to by French, as 'just a set of traffic lights between Wakefield and Ponte-fract' – 'easy to miss,' as one wag wrote, 'if you are in anything but bottom gear' – was some distance from the truth. Although not listed in either the AA or RAC guides, and meriting only a one-line entry in *Bartholomew's Gazetteer*, Featherstone hadn't been a village since around 1868, when the first shaft was sunk at its main colliery. Virtually overnight, a medieval manor village of a few hundred people was transformed into a nineteenth-century boom town, all its inhabitants suddenly dependent for their existence on coal. The 1881 census, taken four years after the opening of a second colliery, Ackton Hall, recorded a population of 5,900 and by 1983 there were around 14,500 people living in the town – a tiny number when compared to the half-a-million-strong conurbation of Hull.

The resentment towards the BBC's, and some of the press's, patron-ising coverage fed into a more deep-seated objection to the media's refusal to take the sport seriously. A hard core of its fans blamed Eddie Waring, who had retired the previous year after an unbroken, four-decade stint as Mr Rugby League. In the seventies, 12,000 oval ball purists had signed a petition calling on Auntie to sack a commentator whose perceived levity supposedly undermined the game's sense of itself as an icon of northern vibrancy. His celebrity status, it was argued, especially his lucrative star turns on popular comedy programmes such as *It's A Knockout*, *The Goodies* and *The Morecambe & Wise Show*, completely overshadowed the action on the pitch. Rugby league's popularity had subsided during the late seventies and early eighties, whereas Waring's, which owed a great deal to a bizarre, and often unintelligible, Yorkshire accent, had continued to grow. The BBC's condescending attitude towards 'the little mining village' was viewed as symptomatic of the channel's stereotyping of northern working-class culture; Waring's nationally revered catchphrases, such as 'early bath' and 'up and under', instantly conjured up an unchanging, parallel *Coronation Street* universe of slag heaps, ale and back-to-backs.

Featherstone had its own personal myth. It saw itself as an overlooked mining town with a penchant for punching above its weight; through its exploits with the oval ball, it had repeatedly put itself on the sporting map. 'It's a communal, collectivist thing,' said Ian Clayton, author of numerous books on both the town and the club.

It goes to the very essence of what sport is. The players had muscle and build but, to me, they were like knights because they represented their town, going into battle for us on the playing fields every week. It's a romantic vision, I suppose. In Featherstone, instead of the knights, they had the Rovers players, the big, rough men who didn't fight for the nobility, they fought for those who, for generations, had been disadvantaged up here in the north of England and yet hadn't lost their pride.

The club's 1983 win was no fluke – and certainly not to be confused, as some metropolitan columnists had patronisingly suggested, with that classic fictional account of a sporting fairy tale, *How Steeple Sinderby Wanderers Won the FA Cup*. Since joining the Northern Union in 1907, money had always been tight but, despite their meagre resources, Rovers had consistently produced a wealth of local talent. All but one of the cup-winning team lived within five miles of their Post Office Road ground. In the previous sixteen years they had come top of the First Division, reached four Wembley finals and won three Challenge Cups. Good cup runs were the rule not the exception: they had appeared in ten semi-finals in the previous twenty-five years. Their sides were tough and uncompromising but also skilful and entertaining. Like their supporters they enjoyed getting one over self-important opponents, pompous referees and all self-regarding members of the game's establishment. The team's success meant more to Featherstone than just sporting achievement. A year before a strike that would devastate the town, and with the fear of job losses looming on the horizon, the Wembley triumph galvanised the community. 'It gives the village a much-needed boost in these hard economic times,' the club's official cup final brochure reflected. 'Let us all hope that this appearance is the start of a new era for Rovers.' It marked, in fact, the end of an era: for the club, the town and the sport.

THE INVISIBLE BOND

If Hull were the fish dock team, then Rovers, to an even greater extent, were the pitmen's team. During the final, Hull fans, somewhat ironically given the collapse of the fishing industry, could be heard taunting their opponents with the refrain: 'We all agree, dockers are better than miners.' Even a year before the miners' strike, this sounded like a hymn to a disappearing industrial age. Andy Smith, who played for Rovers' great rivals Wakefield Trinity and watched the final as a neutral, remembered how brutal the rivalry could be. 'If you wanted to see a rough match, you'd go to a Yorkshire Cup tie between the Hull National Dock Labour Board team and Feather-stone Miners Welfare,' he said. 'That were a proper rugby league match, I can assure you. All twenty-six players ended up with plenty of bruises. That were dockers versus miners. Instead of a war, there was a rugby match. Each team wanted to win to show that their industry produced better rugby players than the other lot.'

Formed in 1902, Featherstone were nicknamed 'The Colliers' because every single one of their players worked down the pit. For many years, the community's umbilical attachment to the team was neatly symbolised by a row of miners' houses on Post Office Road whose washing lines seemed permanently tied to the ground's outer walls. On match days, those walls and bedroom windows would be used as grandstands. 'I noticed over a hundred lads perched rather precariously on one wall,' a reporter at Featherstone, marvelling at the ingenuity of the club's supporters, noted in one inter-war match report. 'They simply didn't get excited or they would have clattered down into the passage. Some of the old colliery houses had trap-doors on the roof and from each tiny trap-door there peeped forth a pair of eyes intently watching the game. It was, for all the world, like one of Heath Robinson's sketches.'

Mining gave birth to the collectivist culture that, over many generations, shaped the team's character, bringing it self-confidence, a sense of identity and financial clout. Pit workers automatically paid the club a small subscription from their wage packets – for many decades it remained a penny – and, at times of crisis, volunteered to build new stands and raise extra cash: in 1955, for example, the miners' welfare club spent £2,300 on new dressing rooms and improved terracing. 'It was generally accepted,' wrote Tony Collins, 'that miners represented the [game's] moral core.'

With the exception of Hull's fish docks, the sport has traditionally been confined to the former pit and mill towns of Yorkshire and Lancashire. The first teams of coalminers were formed in these counties in the 1880s and, for over a century, they emphasised such pit-life qualities as strength, endurance and skill. Hacking coal from cavernous seams, blasting and drilling, hour after hour, day after day, was extremely dangerous work: at least 164,000 miners had lost their lives in the pits since the 1700s. Lung disease, blindness and deformity were occupational hazards in the dark tunnels. Miners risked their lives every day and watched each other's backs. The repetitive hard work toughened them up, both physically and mentally; it proved to be the perfect training for the hard labour of rugby league. By the time of the great split of 1895, it was commonplace for sides like Featherstone, Castleford, Wakefield Trinity, Dewsbury and Hunslet to be composed entirely of colliers. These towns, and others across Yorkshire, Durham and South Wales, had been the engines of the industrial revolution, the foundation of the modern British economy, their tight local societies based on shared endeavour, social clubs and sport. The dust, heat and mutual dependence had engendered a solidarity that propelled their endeavours on the field. 'I used to think of rugby league as an extension of the coalmining industry,' wrote *This Sporting Life* author David Storey, who was born in Wakefield. 'It has the same mechanical, repetitive process. Tackle, play-the-ball, tackle – it has a similar rhythm to chipping away at rocks.'

'If you were in mining you were suited to being a rugby league player,' explained Smith, who worked down Sharlston pit with 'Tex' Hudson, the Featherstone captain. He is now manager of the National Coal Mining Museum for England, near Wakefield, which features exhibits ranging from a small diesel locomotive to a rope-hauled railway running for 300 metres above ground. It begins in the 1800s but stops, abruptly and pointedly, in the 1980s. Smith pointed out that the spirit of the '83 team had been forged down the pit. 'Professional rugby league players now go to gyms,' he said. 'But a bloke who was used to physical work, dangerous work, didn't need to go to a gym.' For Clayton, being the miners' team explained why such a small, isolated town consistently overachieved in the sport. 'People round here knew how to play rugby league,' he said. 'Yes, the players had strength and stamina – of course. Jimmy Thompson did his own weight training at a blacksmith's shop at Ackton Hall pit; they were home-made weights. Harold Box ran around with weights fastened to his ankles. They were very keen trainers. It was an industrial, muscular game made by men who were used to moving weight about. But it was also camaraderie. Like all miners, they washed each other's backs. And that sense of camaraderie spilled over to the dressing room and on to the field.'

Before a game, according to legend, if Rovers needed a prop forward, an official would go to the top of the nearest mineshaft and whistle. This may have been apocryphal, but Smith confirmed the story's essential truth by recalling a desperate outing in the 1970s. 'I were playing for Wakefield A team,' he explained. 'We were playing at Hull and we were two men short. So we drove through Featherstone and stopped at a pub and we got two players. We played Hull with two straight out of the pub. No matter how good a miner you are, you're relying on your mates to keep you safe, to help you. It builds this invisible bond between you. That 1983 Featherstone team had that bond. They'd taken it from the pit to the rugby. One to thirteen, you were treated exactly the same. You were expected to do your job, in rugby and mining. After the strike were over, Acton Hall pit shut down and they dispersed all the men and some of them came to Sharlston. And that invisible bond went.'

Ever since the Industrial Revolution, the coal industry had been one of the foundation stones of British prosperity, fuelling the rise of both modern football and rugby. Before the great strike, Rovers' fortunes had intertwined with those of King Coal. The team began to establish itself as a force during the arms race before the First World War, when more than a million miners produced 292 million tonnes of coal a year. At that time, the town's livelihood was completely dependent on the black stuff and it was unsurprising that in the 1920s and 30s the team was weakened to the point of near-collapse by the double whammy of a doomed General Strike, which had been called to oppose wage cuts and deteriorating conditions in the coal industry, and the Great Depression. Conversely, they were boosted – like Rotherham United – by the wartime policy of protecting mining as a reserved occupation; Ernest Bevin, the minister of labour, conscripted 48,000 'Bevin Boys' to keep the industry going and many rugby and football players were kept back from the army. From the industry's nationalisation in 1947, when the 958 largest pits were taken into public ownership and Labour propaganda celebrated the place of the miner in the engine room of post-war reconstruction, to Harold Wilson's 'white heat' technological revolution of the sixties, rugby league revelled in its new sense of national importance. National Coal Board (NCB) publications carried regular paeans to miners who played the sport and stressed the importance of the game to the mining districts. Post Office Road was often full. A record 17,531 turned out for Rovers' 1957 cup game against St Helens.

It was during the 1950s, not long after the club's first-ever Wembley appearance, that Norman Dennis and two other pioneering sociologists visited Featherstone to observe the local trinity of home, work and leisure. In *Coal Is Our Life*, a classic social scientific account of a vanished mining community, the academics discovered that Rovers were the central topic of conversation down the pit, as well as in the pubs and clubs, fulfilling the sociological function of maintaining the town's prestige. The authors contended that 'Ashton', as it was renamed in the study, derived its self-worth from the success of the rugby team, going so far as to produce a table to demonstrate the correlation between a good run of results and increased productivity. To understand why miners worked harder, they stated, 'one had to bypass productivity appeals and inquire more into the miners' way of life as a community ... with regard to the importance which the defeat or victory in these matches assumes for the supporters, it is a joke in Ashton that when the Ashton team is defeated "two thousand teas are thrown at t' back o' t' fire". The men are said to be too distressed to eat.'

A disproportionate number of rugby league stars have emerged, over the years, from the mining triad of Featherstone, Castleford and Wakefield, an area that used to be known as West Yorkshire's golden triangle. Featherstone, in particular, was renowned for being a hotbed of talent. 'When I was playing,' recalled Paul Coventry, a regular fixture in the three-quarter line throughout the seventies, Rovers' most successful decade, 'there was a man from Featherstone playing in every team in the championship. In my childhood they were all coalmining towns and I came from a secondary modern school and your destiny was the coal mine. And to get above the crap you had to be good at sport. And because we're circled by three great rugby teams – Castleford, Featherstone and Wakefield – that was the avenue you took. And I played for Featherstone and became a kind of a hero.'

Like Frank Machin, Storey's protagonist in *This Sporting Life*, Agar is uncomfortable with the notion of individual heroism. ('There's no such thing as stars,' says Machin, 'just men like me.') Being part-time miners kept his players' feet on the ground. 'Rugby's always been a stronghold in this area, an outlet for the guys,' he said. 'Mining was a good grounding for them. You couldn't go to Ackton Hall colliery and be a prima donna. You were soon brought down to earth. You were just one of the lads.' As David Hobbs, who won the Lance Todd man-of-the-match trophy at the 1983 final, reflected: 'Featherstone were massive underdogs and we beat the massive favourites. [But] when I went back to work on the Monday morning I were back in the mines, amongst all the critics.'

Clayton, who went to school with Hobbs, once saw one of his favourite players, a tall, bullying, loose forward who played for Great Britain, walking down Station Lane in his slippers. 'This old banger pulled up mid-afternoon in downtown Featherstone,' he remembered.

To my astonishment, the man at the wheel was Vince Farrar. He went into the off-licence and emerged with a bottle of milk in each hand. As he talked to two pensioners who had known him from childhood, I noticed his footwear: battered carpet slippers. I saw him again, once, as I was going to school. I ripped a piece of blotting paper out of my exercise book and rushed over to him for an autograph. 'I haven't got a pen on me, cock,' he said. I mean, why would you if you were emptying people's dustbins for the council? I had one in my pencil case. He put 'V Farrar'. Not 'best wishes', 'love from', nothing. It was a glorious moment: a particular Featherstone story.

A YORKSHIRE TRAGEDY

A month after Fearless Fantastic Featherstone's famous Wembley win, the Conservatives, in spite of doubling unemployment to 3 million, were returned to office. 'Winning the cup was a golden moment,' said Agar, 'but things didn't get easier because we'd won it. On the contrary. We'd no money. I bought a couple of players, but it didn't come off. The town never had money, really, but it got particularly bad during the strike.' After the miners' defeat, Ackton Hall colliery, Featherstone's last operating pit, was razed to the ground with indecent haste; it was like 'knocking the crown off the king's head', a woman told a local newspaper reporter after watching its winding towers being destroyed. 'It might make players hungrier,' said Agar, 'which is what everyone always says, but being skint doesn't make them better players. Money, or lack of it even, can't motivate a player. My step-dad was at Ackton but I worked in an office so I bought pints for friends who were on strike. Friendship gets you through those things. And that's what got the rugby team through, the friendship amongst the players. The strike was vast in this area. It made life difficult. It made playing rugby difficult. I couldn't get the side to win, so I left.'

Although the strike was 100 per cent solid at Ackton Hall, there had been turmoil at the nearby Sharlston pit, where some of the cup final heroes had been employed. As Greg Chalkley, one of Rovers' many former amateur internationals, put it: 'It were family against family. The most difficult part about it was when we played other teams with a scab in. He would come in for some serious treatment.' Throughout the M62 corridor, that semi-mythical ribbon of tarmac between junctions 7 and 38 that defines the scope of rugby league's heartland, blacklegs were jeered by their own supporters. The scars of the dispute lingered for a long time: even eighteen years later, at the Great Britain–Australia World Cup final, thousands of fans angrily defaced the British Coal logos that had been provocatively printed on the front of their replica shirts.

Some club directors supported the strike and sanctioned collections at their grounds. Rovers allowed season ticket holders in for free during the 1984–5 season on a watch-now-pay-later scheme which allowed strikers to pay back the money at the end of the dispute. Ironically, amateur clubs like Sharlston were fleetingly reinvigorated by the strike, suddenly finding themselves able to recruit out-of-work miners. 'They played as a release following the stress of what they were going through,' Smith explained.

When it got to the summer of 1984, a few months into the strike, I thought I'd get myself fit again. I hadn't time when I was working at the pit. I went on strike at Sharlston and I was twenty-nine. I played for a Pennine League team, Swan Bees. But Rovers struggled because people just didn't have the money to watch them. It wasn't a fight against the mining industry but against the government. They wanted to destroy the union movement altogether. And to do that they had to destroy the strongest union, which happened to be the NUM. And that happened. When the pit went it was the beginning of the end for Featherstone.

'It affected our attendances,' said Terry Jones, who had been the Featherstone secretary during the strike. People couldn't afford to come. The club used to generate an income from the pit. Miners used to pay subscriptions. The whole place fell apart.' As Smith pointed out: 'Support for professional teams went down because there was not enough money. Mining created wealth. People had money, a well-paid job. Miners were people who spent money. So miners' welfare clubs thrived. Every pit had a football pitch, a rugby pitch, a bowls green, a cricket pitch. The miners' museum I run is now the only place you can go down the shaft and go underground. If you'd have told me that before the 80s I wouldn't have believed you. The slogan used to be "Join the NCB and have a job for life," and people did. So taking away the mines took away the miners' strength. We lost our industrial muscle. It was like Popeye without his spinach.'

At the height of the dispute, Customs and Excise officers threatened to close Rovers down and take away the Post Office Road goal posts. To ease their financial worries, the social club was sold – as was Hobbs, whose father was deputy manager at Ackton.

'The strike knocked the hell out of the town,' said Kenny Greatorex, a star of Featherstone's 1967 Challenge Cup-winning side, who returned to mining after retiring from the game.

People were down. Until the home match came – and then they would get a lift again, just going to the ground like. You couldn't get a brown halfpenny from nowhere. Me daughter wanted to join a music festival and it were £1.80 and I said we haven't got it. She's a musician now. Somebody told me the manager at pit I were a gardener. 'Come and start work,' he said, but the strike wasn't over yet so I said no. If men got to know about that sort of thing you'd have no windows in. It broke marriages up. And friendships: some who you thought were your friends were sneaking into work. But what do you do when you've no food coming in? Lad I know lost his wife and all his kids.

Clayton was shocked by Thatcher's television interview in which she accused the miners of being the 'enemy within', a treacherous fifth column chipping away at freedom and free-market capitalism. In the First World War, pitmen had been used to tunnel under German lines and blow them up. In the 1939–45 conflict they were deemed vital to the war effort. 'She said: "We had to fight the enemy without in the Falklands. We always have to be aware of the enemy within, which is much more difficult to fight and more dangerous to liberty." I was watching with my granddad and he was disgusted and hurt by that. He had fought in the desert for his country and mined coal for near-on fifty years.' Eleven months into the strike, travelling back to the town after a game at Oldham, Clayton's best friend suddenly announced he was returning to work. He worked at the Prince of Wales pit. Before I closed the car door to let him out I said "Don't go back." He did and after that I didn't speak to him for nearly twenty-two years. I feel ashamed now to have let so many years go by without talking to a man who was my friend. This was a man I'd arm-wrestled with, supped pints with, told jokes to, a man whose shoulder I'd leaned on. We'd gone to see Rovers together.'

Every Sunday evening during the strike, as Clayton recalled in his moving memoir *Our Billie*, a ritual would be played out.

Droves of police from all over the country descended on the coalfields, coppers on double time and more, drafted into villages and towns they'd never heard of to form uniformed barriers, break up pickets and stop people walking down streets they'd walked down all their lives. Those were the men who waved their overtime ten-pound notes at folk who hadn't seen a wage packet since last March. Those were the ones who arrested my mate Phil under a medieval law called 'Following and Besetting' after he'd walked alongside somebody in his own home town and told him he ought to be ashamed of himself for blacklegging. Those were the men who formed lines on the roads to pits to make sure that people who had decided to go back to work could get there unbruised. One of the big tensions in the strike was caused by the 'visits' of police units from well outside the coalfields. These were men who knew nothing of the local culture and motivations of the people who lived there.

The use of a militarised police force to break the NUM created a bitter rift between the police and Yorkshire's industrial communities. In preparation for the strike, the government had built up coal stocks and provided the police with the training and equipment they needed to defeat the mass picketing of the Heath years. Chancellor Nigel Lawson compared this to 're-arming to face the threat of Hitler' and the Cabinet, as its minutes reveal, pressured the force to get tough on the pickets. The violent clashes between police and miners resurrected Featherstone's strongest, and most painful, folk memory: the 1893 massacre. Following a lock-out* instituted because the workers refused a wage cut, Liberal home secretary Herbert Asquith had allowed mine owners to send in the

---

* The exclusion of employees by their employer from their place of work until certain terms are agreed to.

police and then the South Staffordshire Regiment. After reading the Riot Act to pickets at Ackton Hall gates, the troops shot dead two men and wounded twelve innocent bystanders. The aristocratic Scottish adventurer Robert Cunninghame Graham penned a short story about the massacre called 'A Yorkshire Tragedy'. 'In the drear town the blinds were all drawn down,' he wrote. 'Police and soldiers stood about the corners of the streets, and children played in a subdued and melancholy way at reading T'riot Act. "Government didn't oughter shoot men dawn like that," a scarred old miner muttered.' The MP John Burns accused the press of giving the impression that 'the death of a collier here and there, amongst a surplus population, was of no great moment in England.'

AFTER THE STRIKE

When the sociologist Royce Turner decided to find out what had happened to 'Ashton' forty years after the publication of *Coal Is Our Life*, he discovered a town Dennis et al. would have failed to recognise. Call-centres had been set up on shiny new industrial estates and enterprise zones had sprouted a collection of small businesses that made everything from first-aid kits to plastic fabrications. At the end of the strike, a plague of advisers and consultants had descended on Station Road in a bid to persuade redundant miners to turn their redundancy 'windfalls' into daydreams, fantasies and half-baked whims. For a few years in the mid-to-late eighties, the high street leading to the pit boasted more financial-advice agencies than bakeries. The number of banks in Featherstone dropped from four to one. The working-men's club where Scargill had rallied the troops was boarded up. When a Morrisons supermarket was built in 1990, 2,300 people were interviewed for 350 jobs. According to Turner, Featherstone, at the beginning of the twenty-first century, was a microcosm of national industrial decline. Before the strike, there had been nearly sixty mining communities in Yorkshire; in 2000, when *Coal Was Our Life* was published, only seventeen pits remained, with a total employment of just under 8,500. 'In those forty years the pattern of life has changed dramatically,' Turner concluded.

> The end of the coal industry has meant that full employment – at least for men – has turned into far more insecure employment at best and, for many, benefit dependence. Hard drug abuse has, in some places, reached epidemic proportions. Crime has rocketed. Famed once for their social cohesion, former pit towns and villages are now afflicted by social pathologies that were once the exclusive preserve of the inner-cities . . . A spirit [had] developed over generations, based on collectivism, kinship, advancement by co-operation rather than individuality. The social institutions that characterised the places were all symbolic of that: the Co-op; the miners' welfare; the club trip; the union. [This] is the story of a working class community which suddenly has its world destroyed.

During a walk down Station Lane, the academic spotted two separate groups of men smoking cannabis. 'It's something you would see occasionally in part of a run-down city,' he wrote. 'It's not something you would ever have seen in a small mining town . . . now it's a way of life. The growth of heroin abuse in former mining towns has been phenomenal.' Clayton had never seen any hint of a drug or crime culture before the eighties. 'Lads in their teens and twenties died too soon,' he wrote,

> because they got hooked on the drugs that washed through the pit villages in the hard times after the miners' strike. After the pit shut, the local pubs and clubs were full of redundancy money. A mate of mine called Johnny went on more holidays to Spain in four years than he'd had in the rest of his life. He started to drink every day, afternoon and night. He started with £27,000 but it didn't last long. After a while Johnny started to turn a peculiar shade of yellow. The doctor told him he was ruining his liver. Johnny carried on drinking – he couldn't stop. I'd always associated him before with the smell of wintergreen and liniment, the smell of the rugby-league player. Johnny had been a great rugby player in his youth. Now he smelled of stale booze. He died with a liver twice its natural size before he reached fifty. Dick, another lad who'd worked at the pit and who I'd played rugby alongside, told me that his lad was a smackhead and that he couldn't do anything with him. He told me you could buy a wrap of heroin in Station Lane as easy as ice-cream. After the redundancies and the financial advisers, the hard-drugs dealers had ridden into town.

AFTER THE GOLD RUSH

If there was hope, then surely it lay in the People's Game. 'What would Fev be without rugby?' Clayton wrote in *When Push Comes to Shove*, his 1993 encomium to the beguiling, residual allure of the thirteen-a-side code. 'Or Cas [Castleford], or Leigh or anywhere? Small, grey towns that had their day, that were born from coal and died with it, like so many up here in the north. At the end of such sombre thoughts there is always a Sunday when a cheeky scrum-half outflanks three opponents, dives over the line and triumphantly plants the rugby ball on the ground. That's victory. The fans cheer their champions and their faith will hold fast to the next Seventh day.' Three years after Clayton's book was published, he was organising a campaign to stop his beloved team being erased from existence. After joining forces with English football's elite clubs to create the Premier League, Rupert Murdoch had hijacked Australian rugby league and its lucrative television rights to fill BSkyB's pay-TV programming. He had then turned his sights on English rugby league, proposing an £87 million summer competition that would not only ensure its survival but make it more attractive to a global television audience. The game was in a state of financial ruin – the result of the social and economic blight that had desolated its northern heartlands – and this appeared to be an offer that couldn't be refused. One of the many strings attached to the five-year deal, however, was a series of mergers, including one amalgamating the golden triangle clubs – Rovers, Castleford and Wakefield Trinity; the new super-club would be called Calder, after the polluted river that ran through the West Yorkshire coalfield, and be based at an out-of-town stadium. The storm that greeted this proposal, and other mooted mergers involving eight more northern towns, was, wrote Collins, 'perhaps unprece-dented in British sport. As an expression of popular discontent and opposition to authority, nothing like it had been seen in the north since the end of the 1984–5 miners' strike.'

Murdoch warned the league's thirty-two clubs that unless there was a quick and positive response to his offer, it would be withdrawn. Featherstone's militant resistance – protesters invaded the pitch during one game and then blocked Station Lane with traffic – once again put it in the national spotlight. The anti-Murdoch campaign even became an international cause celebre. Clayton told *Baltimore Sun* readers that 'a media tycoon with no sense of community is going against the authentic voice of the people' and the newspaper compared the scenario to 'the Dodgers leaving Brooklyn or the Colts fleeing Baltimore under cover of darkness'. As Steve Wagner, the club's chairman at the time, explained: 'Now that coalmining is gone, and there's no heavy industry here, Featherstone Rovers is the last remaining part of the town's tradition, a tradition that we are steeped in. I was sure the people would fight for it in the same way as they fought to keep the pits open. The only thing in Featherstone to warm the hearts of the people is Rovers. Our success down the years has put Featherstone on the map, and whatever the financial sense of a merger, the common view was that it would be a disaster for the town.' A hundred fans gathered at the Railway Hotel, the pub where, ninety-three years earlier, the first-ever Featherstone team had been formed, and a book was published, *Merging on the Ridiculous*, which accused the game's rulers of selling its soul to global corporate interests. 'They've taken our jobs,' one protester told the hotel meeting, 'now they want to take away our leisure.' Another campaigner called on everyone who had Sky TV to send back their dishes.

Murdoch's ham-fisted attempt to impose a Super League from above was successfully resisted. In an era of increasing homogeneity, this small victory showed how important clubs like Featherstone still were in preserving the identity of their towns. (By pooling their resources with Castleford and Wakefield, they might indeed have enjoyed more success.) The *Baltimore Sun* summarised the original Murdoch offer as: 'Here's a pile of money and go form a Super League – a league without room for the Featherstone Rovers.' This turned out to be a prophetic statement: since the 1996 revolution (or, as some would have it, *coup d'état*), when a new top flight was created and televised exclusively by Sky, the league has not had room for one of the game's most important clubs. Rovers came close to promotion in 1998 but, during the past two decades, they have struggled to stay afloat, going into administration in 2002 and 2006. Despite a salary cap, the richer clubs – the big five of Leeds, Wigan, St Helens, Warrington and Hull FC – have dominated Super League since its inception. During a 220-mile charity walk across the M62 corridor, amusingly documented in his book *Up and Over*, Dave Hadfield mused that Featherstone 'would probably be the best place on our entire route [to] start a riot by standing in the main street and shouting out what a good thing the Super League has been. The belief here that they have been done down by marketing men and administrators in shiny suits, for whom rugby in pit villages was not the object of the exercise, is stronger than anywhere in Rugby League Land . . . it is an article of faith [which] taps into a deep seam of local militancy.'

Rugby's second great split, which took place 100 years after the rebel Northern League had broken away from the clutches of its 'southern oppressors', reinforced the new sporting fault lines that had emerged during the eighties. Critics of the elite competition were, like Hull City's old faithful, caricatured in some sections of the media as sporting Luddites. Rugby league, it was argued, had always embraced modifications and innovations; over the course of a century it had evolved into a fluid, open game, reducing teams from fifteen to thirteen, dropping line-outs, phasing out rucks and mauls and, to a large extent, scrums, and introducing 'play the ball', in which the tackled player heels the ball back to a teammate. But this latest mutation appeared to have presented it with a Faustian choice: become a rich 'global' brand funded by satellite television, or stick to its roots and die a slow death. There is no doubt that Super League has developed into a commercially dynamic sport with high levels of athleticism, commitment and entertainment. And, although restricted to a narrow pay-per-view rather than a much bigger mainstream terrestrial TV audience, it has widened the game's appeal. And yet it has also widened the gap between the big clubs and the small ones.

Rugby league was built in the mines, docks and textile factories of the Industrial Revolution. As a result of the de-industrial revolution of the eighties, the great majority of those mines, docks and textile factories disappeared. 'The industries that formed the physique of the players either at semi-professional or amateur level are no more,' rugby league journalist Phil Caplan pointed out. 'Our raw material is in increasingly short supply.' It is one of the oldest clichés to say that sport mirrors life. Yet the demise of northern manufacturing, particularly in the mining communities of Featherstone, Castleford and Wakefield, the heavy woollen areas of Dewsbury and Batley and the railway engineering hub of Hoggart's Hunslet, has severely depleted the gene pool of many small-town clubs. 'The cotton mills have long since closed down,' noted Simon Kelner in his 1995 book *To Jerusalem and Back*. 'The pit winding gear is now silent. The quality of life has suffered repeated erosions. We are right to fear the loss of the greatest game.' Reflecting, almost twenty years later, on the game's Murdochengineered metamorphosis, Kelner admitted it was 'more professional and more popular than at any point in my lifetime'. He also argued, however, that 'an authentic, genuine sport became superficial. And, unsurprisingly given Murdoch's involvement, the rich got richer, and the poor got poorer. My club [Swinton] like a good few others, was left behind in this gold rush and is now clinging on to life.'

Featherstone narrowly missed the initial Super League twelve-team cut in 1996 – Post Office Road being deemed too small and outdated – and have struggled to survive in the new, Murdochised economy. 'The commercial modernisation of rugby league has crushed [Rovers'] ambitions,' a 2010 *Guardian* editorial lamented, but 'it can't crush the pride.' The paper's unlikely panegyric was written in praise of an economically depressed 'small and unprepossessing mining town' that had just won the Second Division championship. Not that finishing top of the table had been enough to propel Rovers into the top flight; three years earlier, promotion and relegation had been sealed off in favour of a licensing system which guaranteed the chosen top-flight clubs three years in the elite.

The small-town, never-say-die spirit was again demonstrated a year later when a team of volunteers, led by Paul Coventry, a former Rovers player, transported Scarborough Football Club's entire stadium, girder by girder, to Post Office Road, adding an extra 2,000 to the ground's capacity. This was a throwback to the *Coal Is Our Life* era when miners' welfare clubs were able to fund new dressing rooms and stands. Coventry recognised that attendances were falling. 'That could be down to austerity,' he said. 'But Leeds Rhinos get £1.6 million from Sky TV. If we're lucky enough to win the championship, we'd get half a million. They get three times as much as we've got. The game is going nowhere. It's stagnated.'

Already, in the late 1990s, Turner had noted that while rugby was still important in Featherstone 'it is no longer so dominant . . . It is still an outlet for a fair number of people that way inclined . . . but I never came across anybody in a pub or a club talking about Featherstone Rovers. For many, it was no longer important at all.' The former deputy at Ackton Hall admitted that 'the interest has gone. When we were down the pit, Featherstone Rovers were the conversation from Monday to Friday. You *had* to be a Rovers man.' Clayton, after a lifetime's devoted support, no longer attends games. 'Rugby league has moved away from me, from us,' he explained. 'I'm one of a lot of people who got fed up with it. It's not the same game. I don't think they should even dignify it by calling it rugby league any more. Its modern, new and shiny, has massive television exposure and players get better money. But that doesn't mean it's a better game. It's not. Nothing keeps still. Rivers are born new every day. But I want to enjoy something I feel a part of.'

Sammy Lloyd disagrees. 'There had to be change,' said the former Castleford and Hull goal-kicker. Lloyd reveres rugby league history but thinks Super League saved the sport: 'The people who were marketing it said: "Hey look, you've got to get over yesterday. It's now all about these lads, full-time professionals, with videos from all angles, Sky, the money, the imports."' Physically, you could get away with a lot more in his day, like flying elbows and spear tackles. 'The game was different. In my day, people were taking each other's heads off. There were clothes-line tackles, elbows everywhere, but not any more. Now these guys run 100 miles an hour into each other. Occasionally, accidentally, they might clash heads. The science now is brilliant. We never even mentioned hydration but I always wondered why we were running out of gas early in a game that was played in hot conditions. If a coach saw a player attempting to get a drink, he'd tell them not to. There were just two oranges on a table at half-time. Today, the fitness levels are extraordinary.'

Agar lives half a mile away from the Rovers ground. It has been through a succession of re-namings – including the Chris Moyles Stadium, named after a Yorkshire-born national radio personality – and is now known as the Big Fellas Stadium, following a sponsorship deal with a Pontefract nightclub. But it will always be Post Office Road to him. 'I can see it from my window,' he said, 'it brings back great memories. Especially of 1983. But my interest has waned. I'm not being funny but I wouldn't pay £22 to watch a match. And yet, when I was a kid, all I wanted to do was grow up and play for the Rovers. Which is what I ended up doing. It might be me that's lost touch with the game. But the game has changed. When Sky came, they said it was going to be the making of the sport. I said it would be the ruination of some clubs as well. Well, we've seen some clubs go under. There's something wrong in sport if that happens. In rugby now, you've got to be in a city to be a big success. The days of small-town romance have gone. What we did, in 1983, you'll never see happen again.'

5

Casper's Last Stand

'They rather enjoy the sense of isolation, a two-fingers-to-the-world stance. Not for them the broad, bland church of a Manchester United or Chelsea. This is about a district, a town, a community, a family, and everyone else can get lost. Or, get chuffing lost, as they say around here.'

Mark Hodkinson, *Life at the Top*, 1998

YORKSHIRE'S HERE, YORKSHIRE'S HERE

18 June 1984. Orgreave. The police vs the miners. On a hot summer's day, around 8,000 striking pitmen respond to a call by the NUM for a mass picket of the South Yorkshire coking plant. The government ship in thousands of officers from around the country to guard the plant workers. Some coppers – without numbers on their chests – wave their overtime-swelled pay packets at the miners who have assembled in a nearby field to block lorries carrying the coke to steel mills. A group of pickets chant: 'Bring out your riot gear, Yorkshire's here, Yorkshire's here.' Stones are thrown. Dogs chase the miners. The police lines, barricaded behind long riot shields, suddenly open and the picket lines are charged by baton-wielding police on horses and snatch squads. Fifty-one pickets and seventy-two police are injured and there are ninety-three arrests.

'There was no holding back,' says Sean Fitzpatrick. 'The horses were at full tilt when they went in to us.' Fitzpatrick and his friend Paul Darlow are telling me their 'war stories' in The Old Number 7 pub, the traditional haunt of Barnsley fans. Before we met up I'd read his vivid account of one of the most violent few hours in the coal industry's history. In an article commissioned by *West Stand Bogs*, a Barnsley FC fanzine, he'd compared being at Orgreave to standing on the terraces at Oakwell, the club's football ground. 'Like a surge on the old Ponty End that greeted a goal,' he wrote, 'my body was fixed in position by many hundreds more. As the wagons got closer the urge to break the blue line grew and we worked it down towards the opening gate. Graft was something we miners knew all about. Then they appeared, coming in at full canter and supported by the snatch squads, the police Trojans drove through our lines scattering bodies, me among them.' There are two versions of the set-piece battle that shocked millions of TV viewers. In the official one, faithfully reproduced in the evening's news bulletins, the miners launched a violent assault on a thin blue line, provoking the police to unleash their horses. The unofficial version, put forward by the NUM, is that the pickets were ushered into a nearby field, a departure from the normal practice of blocking access routes, and led into a prepared trap. In Yvette Vanson's seminal 1985 documentary, *The Battle for Orgreave*, miners are shown being dragged, throttled, kicked and punched – with one policeman mercilessly hitting a picket about the head with a truncheon. Fitzpatrick claims that the industry, historically wedded to working-class struggle, was shut down for political reasons. 'Orgreave,' he says, 'was the last stand of the working class.' For Darlow, the strike was a defensive battle for jobs, livelihoods and communities. 'We lost, but our culture didn't go overnight,' he adds. 'It wasn't the town finished, like. It took about five years for it to go gradually down. Football, in my opinion, is now just part of the service industry. People are making fortunes out of it. The working class shaped football, developed football, brought it on. That's all gone now, because the working class has been squeezed out of football. I see the miners' strike as part of that squeezing out.' I leave the pub to visit a football exhibition at the nearby town hall entitled 'It's Just Like Watching Brazil'. On entering the building I am greeted by the familiar tones of Brian Blessed, who grew up in the nearby village of Goldthorpe. Back in the day, his recorded voice tells visitors, Barnsley used to be an important centre of mining. In the

1920s, miners at dances had their 'eyes emphasised by the deliberate leaving on of coal dust on the rims' and experts compared coals from different pits 'in the way that winemakers discuss grapes'. The queen, apparently, used coal from an esteemed seam called Barnsley Bed. 'Built on iron and coal and the toil of its people,' booms Blessed, 'it was a wealthy industrial town standing on rich seams of coal.' The football exhibition is a celebration of all the local lads who became internationals. Pride of place goes to Mick McCarthy, the 'hard man of Oakwell', who captained Allan Clarke's early-eighties side before moving on to Manchester City and playing for Ireland in the World Cup. 'I haven't changed since I left Barnsley,' he says. 'But Barnsley has. Before the closures, fellas worked hard, had a beer at the club, dinner on the table. That's how we were brought up. Then the pits shut and there's regeneration and new people are coming in. When I was growing up, the majority of people worked in the mines. That was the primary source of jobs and income. I'd left for Man City when the 1984–5 strike took place. But in the seventies, when the miners were out on strike, those of us from non-mining families would stand alongside them. I was a fifteen-year-old, not a shop steward, but they were my peers, my friends, my family. Back then, it was all about the community.'

BATTLING BARNSLEY

Despite shedding most of its mines and attempting, at one stage, an unlikely Tuscan-esque reinvention, Barnsley remains a byword for an old, industrial, communitarian Yorkshire that largely survives only in the popular imagination. Like Featherstone, its coalmining ancestry had created a sense of clanship that moulded a tough, tireless, physical sporting culture. Unlike that much smaller town, however, it had been converted to the round ball game in the late nineteenth century, with the Rev. Tiverton Preedy determined to 'start an association club such as the rugbyites will not crush out'.

As an integral part of Britain's industrial heartland, the town tended to achieve sporting success during periods of socio-economic advance. In Edwardian times, the immediate post-war era, the seventies and the late nineties, Oakwell produced a series of battling, often memorable, football teams. For the first half of the twentieth century their game, wrote the TV presenter Michael Parkinson – their most famous fan – 'was founded rock solid on two basic principles best summed up by the exhortation of their supporters to "Get stuck in" or, alternatively, "Get rid."' Their pre-war status as a top club was enhanced by the 1909 signing of Wilfred Bartrop for an undisclosed 'substantial sum'; during another great FA Cup run in 1910, which ended with Newcastle beating them in the final, 25,574 people packed into Oakwell to see Bartrop score what one journalist called 'the greatest goal ever'.

Sports historian Richard Holt described 'the pleasure that the Barnsley crowd took in seeing Swindon's amateur forward and ex-theological student Harold Fleming ... being kicked out of a cup tie in 1912.' According to Holt, he 'compounded the crime of coming from the south by being middle class'. This was the year 'battling Barnsley', renowned for their attrition, fierce tackling and never-say-die spirit, beat West Bromwich Albion to win the FA Cup.

The 1912 cup campaign coincided with the high tidemark of industrial unionism, a month after almost a million miners had taken part in their first-ever national strike. As in 1984, there was widespread civil unrest, but in this dispute the government capitulated, rushing a minimum wage bill through Parliament. The quarter-final defeat of Bradford took place in the middle of what *The Times*, somewhat hysterically, called 'the greatest catastrophe that has threatened the country since the Spanish Armada'. The train service to Bramall Lane, where the tie was played, was disrupted by the strike; the *Barnsley Independent* correspondent reported that many 'pit lads' forced to walk to the ground during a snowstorm looked 'wretched but resolute . . . some more active spirits tried to rouse the spirits by singing for "good old Bairnsla!" . . . The Barnsley enthusiasts came from places as widely apart as Hemsworth, Ryhill, Staincross, Dodworth, Barnsley, Worsbro', Hoyland and Wombwell. Several hundred colliers in clogs must have passed me on the road during the four hours. Often they looked limp and stiff, and suggested a problem of "what about the return journey?"'

Angus Seed's post-war team were similarly renowned for their menacing toughness. Their intimidator-in-chief was 'Skinner' Normanton, a local legend immortalised in a series of well-known essays by Parkinson, whose sport-obsessed father had been a miner at Grimethorpe colliery. 'Sydney Albert Normanton was a local legend when he played at Barnsley in the 50s,' wrote Parkinson,

He was the hard man of the side, the minder for ball-playing colleagues of delicate disposition. There wasn't much of him but every ounce counted. He was destructive in the tackle, as unrelenting as a heat-seeking missile in pursuit of the enemy.

If I close my eyes I see a replay of Skinner taking a penalty in a Cup-tie and running from the halfway line before toe-ending the sodden football, which became a blur as it passed the motionless goalkeeper, crashing into the underside of the crossbar and rebounded on to the back of the goalkeeper's head and into the net. The goalkeeper was pole-axed and took several minutes to recover and it wasn't until much later that the iron crossbar stopped quivering from the impact of the shot. For a while it hummed like a male voice choir.

He was a local celebrity. Mothers would tell their children to stop mucking about or they would send for Skinner. He gained a wider audience many years after he retired when I first wrote about him. I don't know what it was about the article that captured the imagination. I think it might have been the name. If you wanted to invent a local football hero of the time, someone who worked in the pits during the week and spent Saturday afternoons kicking lumps off the opposition, you'd invent a man called something like Skinner Normanton.

Whatever the reason may have been, his fame extended far beyond his beloved Oakwell. There used to be a Skinner Normanton Appreciation Society in Kuala Lumpur, and I have been asked about him during all my travels throughout the world. There was something in the name that was irresistible to Brits living abroad, particularly when they were feeling homesick for Saturday afternoons and kick-off time.

Many people believed him to be a mythical character like The Great Wilson of the Wizard. I remember Yorkshire Television producing him as a surprise guest on a programme I was doing in Leeds. They brought him into the studio and announced him in a triumphant fashion as if they had found Lord Lucan or were about to produce the Loch Ness monster on the end of a lead.

He was smaller than I remembered and was wearing a blue suit with a nipped-in waist. The hair was as immaculate as ever and he looked like he was going to church. I had never seen him in his Sunday best. When he spoke his voice was soft, the manner modest, even shy. It was difficult to convince people that this gentle and diffident man had at one time put the fear of God up any member of the human race who didn't wear a Barnsley shirt.

He played at a time when the game drank deep from its tap roots and although there were many more skilled and talented than he, there was no one who better represented what you were up against if you took on a collier from Barnsley.

I was thinking that they ought to name a stand at Barnsley after him. The Skinner Normanton stand would be a constant reminder that no matter how much we merchandise the modern game we must always remember what it is we are really selling. Nowadays they talk of image. There was a time, when Skinner was a lad, when it had a soul.

Seed's team were infused with the optimism and idealism of an era that created the modern welfare state, achieved full employment and nationalised hundreds of privately owned mines. In Richard Benson's family memoir *The Valley*, the author's mother and father join a large crowd gathered in Barnsley's Locke Park to hear prime minister Clement Attlee's speech to the Yorkshire Miners' Gala. It was shortly after the 1946 Nationalisation Act, when Labour had taken the 958 largest pits into public ownership. Coal was the primary source for 90 per cent of the country's energy and over 700,000 men worked in the industry. 'No one of us can carry on without depending on the work of other members of the community,' Attlee said. 'You in the mining industry are now working not for private profit but for the nation. You have the incentive of your earnings, but you have besides another powerful motive. You are at the forefront of the new society which we are building.' Benson's mother remembered 'standing with her father as he listened to a brass band shortly after the speech that day, and glancing at his face to see him weeping'.

The post-war football boom, which saw a huge increase in attendances – greatly benefited Seed's team. 'The impact of economic conditions on sport was perhaps clearest in the late 1940s and early 1950s,' wrote Martin Johnes. 'Full employment and a desire to forget the horrors of war created a high demand for entertainment but material shortages and the government's need to export manufactured goods meant there was little for people to actually spend their money on. Spectator sport however was both cheap and easily accessible and attendances thus reached an all-time high in this period.' In the 1947–8 campaign, Barnsley averaged home crowds of 21,050. According to *Barnsley: A Study In Football*, Ian Alister and Andrew Ward's account of the club's resurgence in the 1950s, by the end of that season fans 'clung tightly as buses rolled in from mining villages, perhaps eight or ten hanging on the platform. They tumbled from trains at Bunkers Hill and toppled down the embankment to walk along Oakwell Lane. They cycled through the throng and paid two pence to store bicycles in front gardens while they watched the game. Others had to walk.'

Alister and Ward revealed that, under the maximum wage, Barnsley players – most of whom tended to live within the community – were not much better off than miners. Quite a few, in fact, were worse off – and a football career was shorter than a miner's. Being an important centre of mining gave the Tykes the edge over bigger clubs when it came to recruitment. The book opens with Seed trying to persuade a young Scot, Jimmy Baxter, who is standing 'slight and slouched, dusty and dirty from a Monday's work at the pit', to move south of the border. Liverpool and Arsenal were not in mining communities, reasoned Seed, and therefore less able to accommodate a pit worker. 'There's a position at Wharncliffe Woodmoor Colliery waiting for you, Jimmy,' he added, playing his trump card.

In the twentieth century, football – and, in parts of Yorkshire and Lancashire, rugby league – replaced traditional village sports like cockfighting, fox hunting, coursing and shooting, potshare bowling, handball and quoits. With the raising of the school leaving age, from nine to fifteen, children were exposed to the game for a much longer period of time, playing with anything they could lay their hands on: rags, cans, tennis balls and even pigs' bladders. By the time they went down the mine, the game was already dominating their lives.

Although they failed to match the success of the pre-war years, and even imported the occasional Scot like Baxter, Seed's squad was renowned for being built on young, local, mining talent. 'At the bottom of the steep slope stood Oakwell,' noted *A Study In Football*, 'a resplendent red and white in contrast to the darker colours of Barnsley Main Colliery behind'. Nine local lads, most of them miners, played in a 1957 fifth-round cup tie watched by England manager Walter Winterbottom. Since the club's formation in 1887, the area had churned out many players – and managers, like George Raynor, a miner's son who led Sweden into a World Cup final and semi-final – but Seed's pioneering youth policy more than doubled the proportion of Barnsleyites in the squad. 'The high number of local players,' observed Alister and Ward, 'meant they kept their nicknames from school or even earlier: "Cabby" Swift, "Skinner" Normanton, "Chippie" Rowe, "Chuckie" Jackson and "Tich" Edgar.'

For the great part of the twentieth century, Barnsley, and the South Yorkshire coalfield in general, rivalled the north-east as a hotbed of sporting talent, supplying sons of miners to both the First Division and the England team as well as driving professional football in the region. Mining was, as we have seen, uniquely dangerous work. Explosions killed 361 men and boys at the Oaks pit near Barnsley in 1866; deaths did not fall below a thousand a year until well into the twentieth century. And yet the industry, as in rugby league, swelled the gene pool of many small-town Yorkshire clubs. Even big-city clubs from outside the region drew upon the area's 'raw material' for their success. None more so than Wolverhampton Wanderers, the dominant English side of the fifties, who were particularly dependent on Cortonwood miners. This important colliery, whose closure sparked the 1984–5 strike, not only produced the Barnsley pair Malcolm Graham and Henry Walters but, as a result of hiring out its football ground every Saturday morning to Wolves juniors, developed future top-flight stars such as Ron Flowers, Cyril and Peter Knowles and Terry Cooper. The Robledo brothers, who were brought up in a village near Cortonwood, went on to play for Newcastle after leaving Oakwell. The most famous product of Seed's youth system was Tommy Taylor, who, according to John Roberts, author of a book on Manchester United's 'Busby Babes', learned his skills in Barnsley on 'the bog, a rock-hard piece of ground where local boys played in clogs, pit boots or bare feet'. When he signed Taylor for United in 1953, Matt Busby wrote a cheque for £29,999, giving the other pound to an Oakwell tea lady, so as not to burden the youngster with a £30,000 price tag. Taylor went on to win two league titles, and score sixteen goals in nineteen England games, before losing his life, along with another Barnsley-born youngster Mark Jones, in the Munich air disaster.

Steve Bruce's question in the opening chapter – 'where have all the young footballers gone?' – is even more pertinent when applied to South Yorkshire's once-legendary youth football scene. Hull, a former rugby league stronghold, never really produced professional footballers in great numbers. The South Yorkshire region, however, was renowned for being one of English football's most productive nurseries – and yet it did not feature at all in a 2011 survey of the Premier League's top ten catchment areas. The last Barnsley team to have a sniff of success – Simon Davey's 2008 Championship side, who reached the FA Cup semi-final after beating Liverpool and Chelsea – contained ten overseas imports.

BILLY CASPER IN A SUIT

Before the seventies, the Battling Barnsley mentality tended to be evoked every time a Tykes side embarked on a cup run or earned a promotion. But since the release of *Kes* at the beginning of that decade, the Ken Loach classic has become the go-to reference point. The first post-*Kes* Barnsley team to tell the world to get chuffing lost made their mark during 1978–9's 'winter of discontent' – a rash of public sector strikes against the Labour government's incomes policy. This coincided with a halcyon period both for the town, and a belligerent trade union movement that thought nothing of turning out the lights, switching off the power and bringing down the government of the day. Wage levels were high, jobs were plentiful and, as the economist Thomas Piketty has demonstrated, the gap between the highest and lowest paid workers was the smallest in history. 'People had the money, particularly in the second half of the 70s when the economy was better, to become interested in buying their own home, having a bigger car,' said Andy Beckett, one of the decade's many chroniclers. 'Living standards for most Britons in the 1970s were probably growing more than they had done in the previous 60 or 70 years.'

'There was that working-class confidence,' wrote Benson. 'We felt as if we had power in our hands.' In 1972, the NUM's first national strike for forty-six years won a massive pay increase from Heath's government; 30,000 Birmingham factory engineers had been persuaded to force the closure of Saltley Gate coke plant. 'Here was the living proof,' boasted Arthur Scargill, who at the time led the Yorkshire NUM, 'that the working class had only to flex its muscles and it could bring governments, employers, society to a total standstill.' Two years later, after Wilson replaced Heath as prime minister, the miners were awarded a 35 per cent pay rise, making them the best-paid industrial workers in the country. In Benson's book *The Valley*, his cousin, a miner at Houghton Main, argued 'there was almost a sort of destiny to [the militancy]. Our parents and grandparents had struggled, and now that struggle had reached a point where it was our time. It was a question of us getting fairness for everyone at last.'

'The seventies were a boom period for miners,' recalled Fitzpatrick.

We had lots of local lads made good, like Michael Parkinson, Geoff Boycott and Charlie Williams [a footballer turned comedian] and Dickie Bird, the most famous umpire in the world. They were on the telly all the time. The town of Barnsley had a decent brand, if you want to use the current football parlance. And there was Arthur. If you spoke to the blokes in the coalfield Scargill had done a great job in terms of securing proper compensation for men who were injured underground, and that's how his star began to rise. He started his mining career at my pit, Woolley. Allan Clarke once brought his Barnsley footballers to our pit on a visit. That told you a lot about Clarkey. They got loads of stick as they went through the face. Miners don't pull any punches. We brought them down to earth, to our base level. A few pranks were played on them.

'I loved Clarkey,' said McCarthy, who was one of the players Fitzpatrick bantered with the Monday after the team had been hammered 7-0 at Reading. 'After that thumping, he decided he was going to take us down a pit and show us what a real job was like. I was from the area. I knew some of the lads who were there. Like always with a group of footballers, there was a bit of piss-taking. "Here's a pick and a shovel" – all that bravado nonsense. But we were all moved by it. We couldn't believe how bloody far we had to go down and then we had to walk for what seemed like miles. It was great to see what I'd missed out on.' As the young, tough-as-nails skipper of Clarke's Fourth Division side, he was frequently compared to Normanton. 'Skinner was from a different era when people were harder,' he said. 'I played against him once in a charity match. I was only eighteen and I was running around, you know, being a professional footballer. The king is dead long live the king, that sort of thing. He got a little bit cheesed off and put me on my arse. He was just letting me know. Which is fair enough.'

Clarke, a scrawny, whippet-like goal-getter for Don Revie's Leeds side, was Billy Casper in a suit. Norman Rimmington, his assistant, remembered the impression the cocksure player-manager made on his first day at Oakwell. 'We were all in the changing room and we could hear him approaching, his Italian shoes echoing down the corridor,' said Rimmington. 'And then Sniffer walks in wearing this amazing white suit.' The players were told to smarten up, improve their time-keeping and act like professionals. 'He was like a breath of fresh air blowing through the club,' remembered McCarthy. 'We were on our uppers when he came. We were really down. He captured everybody's imagination. We played some really good football. We got promoted, we had full houses, it was an amazing time. We no longer washed our own kit. We got massages. He was hot on a dress code. The old white slacks, blue blazer, red shirt: all that. He was an iconic figure.'

The sixties had seen a slump in fortunes following the break-up of Seed's team – Taylor was sold to Manchester United, Blanchflower to Aston Villa – and the abolition of the maximum wage, which created huge financial problems for smaller clubs. Following relegation to the Third Division in 1957, Barnsley's squad had been slashed from thirty-six to nineteen professionals, with only twelve of those full-time. Ten years later they dropped into the Fourth Division for the first time in their history and the following season finished sixteenth, which remains their lowest-ever league position. For one game, against Notts County, they were too hard up to print any programmes. In 1970 and 1975 they suffered humiliating FA Cup defeats to non-league clubs and in 1973 only 1,428 people turned up at Oakwell for a match against Exeter. Journalist John Sadler recalled a hilarious moment during this dark period when a fellow hack, while playing on a fruit machine outside the boardroom during yet another crisis meeting, won the jackpot. This triggered, according to the *Sun*'s football correspondent, 'a clattering avalanche of cash [and] a stampede from the boardroom. The proceeds of the win were handed over and my friend insisted for years that he was the one who kept Barnsley solvent. There were times when there was no milk for the tea and when the few light bulbs allowed to be lit had to be of the lowest wattage.'

Clarke's arrival, in 1978, transformed Oakwell, replicating the galvanising effect Hughes' appointment had on Millmoor. The flashily-suited-and-expensively-booted former England striker brought a sense of purpose and professionalism, and even a touch of glamour, to the unfashionable, struggling, lower-league side. He created, said Fitzpatrick, 'a buzz around the place. It was a great era. Oakwell was such a brilliant place to go. I remember 30,000 being there on a Tuesday night against Liverpool. Lots of us miners used to wear our donkey jackets at the games at that time. It was about identity. If you were playing away, say, at Reading, you walked into the pub and you knew it was an okay pub because of the lads with donkey jackets on. There were no miners in Reading. Back then, you always got that sense of community.' In *The Who's Who of Barnsley FC*, club historian Grenville Firth argued that Clarke, despite his short tenure, 'made as big an impact on Barnsley Football Club as anyone in its history'. Firth described the appointment as 'a football bombshell, shattering doubters' complaints that the club lacked ambition. Even regular supporters were dazed . . . the town fizzed with excitement . . . His celebrity aura . . . gave an instant fillip to the players . . . He brought the discipline and standards of a successful First Division background to Oakwell, and expectations that had not been poisoned by the futility of life at the lower ends of the

Football League . . . His higher expectations rubbed off.' Thanks to a newly introduced club lottery scheme, he was also able to bring in a group of good players, and average home attendances almost doubled from the previous season, rising from 5,700 to just over 11,000. His revivified side, in which McCarthy was an ever-present, went up to Division Three at the first attempt. Although he left to manage Leeds in 1980, the team Sniffer built was then promoted, under Norman Hunter's guidance, to the Second Division.

Eric Winstanley, who captained the club in the 1960s and spent a total of thirty-four years at Oakwell, worked in the commercial department during Clarke's time. 'Clarkey did a brilliant job,' he said. 'There was a more confident mood in the town. Arthur [Scargill] did well for them in the 1970s. I saw a big difference in the mining communities. I had some mates who worked down the pits who, because of the strikes, got good pay rises. They came in the pubs and had money to spend. We were one of the first clubs in the Football League to have a lottery. They could pay fees out for players because the money was there.'

Darlow, unlike Fitzpatrick, still goes to Oakwell but feels the game has become gentrified. He pines for a more egalitarian football era when every club had the potential to have its day. 'For me, the Allan Clarke era was the last working-class involvement with football,' he declared. 'People were employed,' said Fitzpatrick.

> We did a hard job but we got a decent coin for it. There were opportunities for people. You could leave school and earn some cash. You always had that disposable income. The football club benefited from that. The town was vibrant. We produced some good footballers. Everything came together. We had pride

because we were from the Barnsley coalfield. There were the Yorkshire, Nottinghamshire, Scottish, Welsh coalfields, but we had our own Barnsley coalfield. There were that many pits here, over sixty I think. If you fell out with someone at a pit, you kept your cards and went to another pit. You'd finish on Thursday at one and start Friday morning at another. The football club fitted beautifully into that sense of community, particularly when it had success. There were no need to get educated. It were good money. I earned more in my final years at the pit than I earn now as a librarian.

When Clarke returned for his second spell, a few months after the end of the strike, things had changed. It was as if he had arrived on a different planet. After peaking at 17,000 in the second tier, crowds had slumped to around 6,000. 'By the time Clarkey came back in 1985,' said Fitzpatrick, 'the town was mentally defeated.' Despite having no money to spend, low gates, and being forced to sell up-and-coming young players such as David Hirst and John Beresford, he twice led Barnsley to the FA Cup fifth round and they finished the 1988–9 season only two points away from a Second Division play-off place. The following season, however, with the club third from bottom, he was sacked. The miners' strike had left Barnsley on the brink of extinction, with only a heavy round of cost-cutting keeping the bailiffs at bay. Clarke had even resorted to thinking up his own schemes to raise money, including one where fans paid the club £100 to sit next to him on a match day. In one reserve game, against Manchester United, he had fielded most of his first-team players, attracting a crowd that was five times bigger than normal. The directors sent an open letter to supporters expressing their fear that the club, who were losing £4,000 per week, would fold unless extra revenue could be found. The Oakwell Centenary Society was launched, aiming for a 1,500-strong membership that would reap an income of £80,000, but only 300 fans subscribed.

'It was difficult for the town,' said Winstanley. 'People had no money. Football in the past had been a great uplift to get them out of despair, but this was hard. Some had to bring a family up with no money.' Winstanley persuaded some former Barnsley players to join him in a miners' fund-raising match at Darfield. 'I would have done anything to support them,' he said.

I scored a goal. It was a bit of a joke goal. It shouldn't have been allowed, but it was only a laugh, a fun game. The goalkeeper was bouncing the ball and I pinched it away from him as he dropped it and put it in the net. And the referee gave it. They all complained it shouldn't be a goal. I got a lot of ribbing locally in the Darfield village. 'We're going to beat you and we're going to do this and that.' Everyone in a village thinks they're better than the players in their local football club. Clubs are not the same as they used to be. Now it's people with briefcases being much more serious. The camaraderie between players in the dressing room was fantastic. And the jokes. I went into pubs and had pints with people, swapped jokes. It were the same down the mines. Now all the players talk about is how much money they've got. And they can't get away from the ground quick enough because they've got some business things or whatever. When we were playing, even if you could have got home early there weren't many who wanted to get away from it because of the atmosphere. The football club was a great place to be.

The connection between the local community and the club is still there. But it's not as strong as it once was. That's because the pits have closed. On Monday morning, going down the pit, that's what people talked about: 'How did Barnsley get on?'

Fitzpatrick no longer goes to Oakwell. The final straw came during a 2014 home match against Nottingham Forest, on the thirtieth anniversary of the miners' strike, when stewards ordered him to take down a 'Coal Not Dole' banner. 'The club has lost its way,' he said. 'We've not got that *Kes* spirit now. That film started it, back in the seventies, making us famous. It had so much influence when you think about it. People had pride in the town. We weren't the "grubby little shithole" any more. We were punching above us weight.' *Kes* also had a huge influence on Mick McCarthy, who was only a few years older than David Bradley. 'I've still got the film on DVD,' he said. 'I think it's fabulous. I showed it to the lads at Wolves when I was manager there. I could identify with Billy Casper completely. I even had a kestrel, although it flew off in the end. After the film we all wanted kestrels. We didn't have much when I was growing up, but all the pits were open.'

Kes was a career-defining role for Bradley. Like Casper, he was from a mining family, although he was a lot keener on football than Billy. 'Towards the end of the shoot,' he remembered,

the football season started and I said I couldn't work past midday Saturday as I sold football programmes at Barnsley. They asked how much I earned and agreed to pay my wages. From the age of seven or eight my aunt and I would walk down to Oakwell and watch the team. When I was ten or eleven, in the summer holidays, I would go down to the football ground and offer my services to get the ground ready. In the summer I'd be pulling grass sods up off the standing terraces, shifting dirt around, doing a bit of painting. They'd give you a meal and a drink and I'd feel part of the club. We'd get to play football, not on the pitch but close by. And then later, I started going to the matches without my auntie. I didn't have any cash but there was nothing that would stop me watching my team. If you were careful you could climb up at the back wall on the East Stand, and it was quite a wall, make sure no-one was looking and just jump down. And there you go, you were in for free. It was a very tight-knit, working-class community and I think we've lost a lot of that, to tell you the truth. I live back in Barnsley now, have done for a few years, and I know my immediate neighbours around me, but when I was a nipper I used to know the entire street. The desecration of the coal-mining industries certainly affected the Yorkshire communities. They destroyed the industry and we're now reaping the consequences. There were a lot of divorces, a lot of physical domestic abuse. That was brought about by Margaret Thatcher. I wonder if the coal mining communities of England and Wales have ever recovered. It was just so brutal.

JUST LIKE WATCHING BRAZIL

The last time Casper appeared as a footballing reference point came during 'the cherished season' as Barnsley fans now refer to it. The 1997–8 campaign remains the only season the club have played in the top flight. 'The Reds going up is two fingers to the fat cats,' declared the fanzine *Better Red Than Dead* after Danny Wilson's side had clinched a Premier League place with a 2-0 win against Bradford City. '[It's] like crashing the posh knobs' cheese and wine gathering with a party-sized can of Watney's Red Barrel and spraying it in their faces.' A home defeat against Liverpool, which was distinguished by a notoriously poor refereeing display, was presented as a re-enactment of Casper's teacher Brian Glover's bullying antics on the hill overlooking the windswept Yorkshire Moors. The official, according to *The Times* football writer Mark Hodkinson, was denounced as 'a vindictive agent of the Premiership that wanted to relegate Barnsley and maintain its closed shop'.

Despite this us-against-the-world mindset, Barnsley, like other northern 'minnows' who have enjoyed short stays in the top flight – Oldham Athletic, Burnley, Bradford City, Blackpool and Hull City – became everyone's second-favourite team. They were relentlessly portrayed as down-at-heel underdogs cocking a snook at the big-city clubs: a powerless and dispossessed post-industrial town having one last crack at the moneyed elite. 'Fans were deeply moved by the support from around the country,' wrote Richard Darn in *When Saturday Comes*. 'It seemed whether the club wanted it or not, they were carrying a banner for the bulk of the league and saying something about the way finance is consuming the game.' Appearances on *Match of the Day* were invariably soundtracked by brass music and accompanied by the obligatory images of Casper's kestrel and Barnsley's cobbled streets. The club programme had some fun with such London-centric condescension, publishing a spoof column by 'Tommy Tyke'. Tommy wore a cloth cap, a scarf and a bemused expression and kept harping on about whippets, pigeons and back-to-backs.

There was a more serious point, however, as Hodkinson explained to his readers: 'Barnsley does not suffer fools and it has a historical mistrust of authority . . . the football club has become a focus for regional pride and naked passion; a two-fingered wave back to a country that they believe has consigned them to afternoon television and twice-weekly trips to the job club.' Wilson, their ambitious young coach, appeared on the cover of the *Times* columnist's *Life at the Top* paperback – a bracingly honest account of The Cherished Season – in the guise of a classic, black-and-white, kitchen-sink, working-class hero. He represented, declared the writer, 'Barnsley, in human form: gritty, unfancied, determined, efficient, a small man prepared to meet the big world head-on.' Some sections of the media seemed amused by the idea of this grimy, unrefined town, populated by Normantons, Glovers and McCarthys, trapped in this old-fashioned social-realist mindset, embracing the modernised, monetised and internationalised world of the Premiership. And yet Barnsley's playing style, based on technique, tempo and skill, was more Billy Elliot than Billy Casper, closer to the sweet, samba-style passing of the great Brazilian sides than Skinner's thuggery or Glover's grandstanding. Which is why, as a tongue-in-cheek tribute to their team's fluid pass-and-move football – and yellow away shirts – the fans adopted 'It's just like watching Brazil' as their theme tune.

Wilson's 1996–7-promotion-winning side had been, mostly, local heroes – down-to-earth lads like David Watson, Nicky Eaden, Andy Liddell and Adrian Moses. Their most expensive recruit was John Hendrie, who cost £250,000. 'We've done it the right way,' said Wilson, 'working hard and honestly and playing good football. These fans have seen a lot of hard times here, they deserve this.' In a forward to Hodkinson's book, Barry Hines wrote: 'I was touched by their pride and loyalty for at last, following years of hardship after the miners' strike and wholesale pit closures, the town and its football club had something to shout about.' Once they had joined the moneyed elite, however, Wilson, like the town planners, attempted to reinvent his team as a sophisticated, cosmopolitan concern. To try and keep up with the 'fat cats', he paid £1.5 million for Macedonia's Gjorgji Hristov – a club record fee – and added an assortment of foreign stars: South African Eric Tinkler, Trinidadian Clint Marcelle and Dutch defender Arjan de Zeeuw.

This brought to the fore the underlying tensions between the old and new Barnsley, especially when it came to ticket pricing. Following the Hillsborough disaster, the club, although at first baulking at the expense of ground improvements, gradually began to benefit from lucrative Football Trust grants and higher admission prices. And, with Premier League riches adding to their bounty, they felt able to invest in a new academy. Yet even before the season began, loyal, long-time supporters were complaining about being 'shafted' – as several of them put it in letters to the *Barnsley Chronicle* – by a money-obsessed season ticket scheme. 'As in the strike of 1984, it has turned friend against friend and father against son,' wrote P. Woodhall. 'Why has the club which prides itself on integrity betrayed its true supporters in favour of those who merely wish to see established Premiership clubs play?' asked Frank Beevers of Mexborough.

Fourteen years after the strike, Oakwell embodied all the contradictions of a post-industrial northern town split down the middle between New Britain modernisers and Old Yorkshire traditionalists. Hodkinson argued that while one part of the ground had become embourgeoisised – 'serviettes supplied with the pies, toilets that flush, fans that applaud David Seaman because he is the England goalkeeper' – the other remained fiercely parochial. 'They are ex-miners, and sons of ex-miners,' he wrote. 'Back in the 1970s, they saw through the smoke and mirrors and detected that the National Coal Board had a secret agenda. They were patronised, told that too much time underground had made them over-fond of baseless conspiracy theories. In the 1980s, the pits duly closed and their frustration was played out against lines of policemen.' There were several cultural conflicts, both on and off the pitch. Although they beat Liverpool 1-0 at Anfield, and knocked Manchester United out of the FA Cup in a fifth-round replay at Oakwell, Wilson's stubborn insistence on playing stylish, attacking football was blamed for the shipping of eighty-two goals. 'I'd shut up shop if I were you,' Rimmington, Clarke's one-time right-hand man, advised his 'naïve' boss. 'Keep kicking the ball into Row Z. You can't go out and play against them lot, they're just too good.' Wilson stuck to his principles and the heavy defeats kept on coming: a 5-0 loss at Arsenal, 6-0 thrashings by West Ham and Chelsea and a 7-0 hammering at Old Trafford.

The 'signing' of a poet-in-residence, rather than a defender in the Normanton–McCarthy mould, left many fans underwhelmed. 'I was walking through Wombwell and this fella wound his window down,' recalled McMillan. "You're the Bard of Barnsley." "Yes." "You're on the telly." "I am." "On the radio." "Yes." "You write poems." "Yes." "You're shite," he said, and drove off.' In the dressing room, as the German journalist Ronald Reng discovered, an 'invisible dividing line' had emerged between the Brits and the foreigners. 'Barnsley was always a monocultural town,' said McMillan. 'And all of a sudden these players from around the world were coming here.' For the telly poet it was 'exotic and exciting' but, as Hodkinson noted, others at the club remained, 'suspicious of outsiders and slow to trust'.

BRASSED OFF

'In the golden summer of 1997,' wrote Reng, 'Barnsley, both club and town, was a bastion of loveable romanticism.' New Labour's election victory, ending eighteen years of Conservative rule, had raised hopes of a northern resurgence and the Barnsley story seemed in tune with a country bursting to change. After watching *Brassed Off*, released the year before Tony Blair's landslide victory, future environment secretary John Prescott was inspired to adopt a regeneration policy for the former coalfield communities. Set in the fictional village of Grimley, the film was loosely based on the celebrated, century-old Grimethorpe Colliery Band's attempt to sustain morale in the face of Michael Heseltine's 1992 pit closure programme, which shut thirty-one of the fifty remaining mines and resulted in the loss of 31,000 jobs. When the village wins a national brass band competition at the Royal Albert Hall, its leader, played by Pete Postlethwaite, declines to accept the trophy, stating that human beings are more important than either music or prizes. This now legendary scene was an homage to the famous denouement of *The Loneliness of the Long Distance Runner*, when Courtenay's class-conscious borstal boy refuses to claim victory in a cross-country race; his governor had been desperate for him to win but, despite being way ahead of the field, Courtenay suddenly stops, just before the finishing line, and looks at the officer, as if to say: 'You don't own me.' It chimed with the purism of those Barnsley fans who had always been sceptical of participating in a league dominated by global mega-brands; like Casper, they'd rather swing from the goalposts than take part in a contest dominated by vindictive bully-boys. A section of supporters, noted Darn, had never been convinced that 'the Premiership is where you want to be.' Darn himself wondered whether the Barnsley chairman should have written to the Premier League after the 1996-7 promotion thanking them for their kind offer of joining the elite but adding that 'on the whole we'd rather stick with our mates lower down. Send the cash anyway.'

For most fans, however, the club were defiantly carrying a banner for the town's downtrodden. They had put Barnsley back on the sporting map and won thousands of new admirers. The Chumbawamba song 'Tubthumping', with its defiant mantra 'I get knocked down, but I get up again', became a regular part of the players' pre-match ritual. This created a powerful negative energy, echoing the fans' sense of injustice, a belligerence based on the feeling that, despite once being the cradle of the industrial revolution, the former mining citadel had never got its due. 'The narrative,' explained McMillan, 'was that, in the end, a place like Barnsley, despite its good kicking, will somehow triumph 3-0 against the forces of capitalism. We've always had this *Kes*-like thing about being aggressively stubborn, or "brussen", which means a bit oppositional, curmudgeonly.' Their year-long adventure in the richest sports franchise in the country, competing against clubs owned by wealthy businessmen who paid their players hundreds of millions of pounds, had been, as captain Neil Redfearn put it, 'a shot in the arm for the working man'. In the face of the Tories' 'managed decline' of the north they had demonstrated a *Kes*-like determination to survive.

And yet there was no escaping the fact that the mine closures had plunged their community into long-term decline. In 1994, a European Union study announced that Grimethorpe was the poorest village in England. Since the strike, unemployment and crime had both soared – the latter rising from 30 per cent below the national average to 20 per cent above – a fifth of the local population had left to find work elsewhere and property prices had plummeted. The coal board's sports facilities – it had provided funding for everything, from the bowling green to the football and cricket fields – had fallen into disrepair. When Thatcher died in 2013, her effigy was burned in several former pit villages, described by *New Statesman* writer Martin Fletcher as 'mostly depressed, run-down places with shuttered shops, closed pubs and neglected colliery sports grounds. The camaraderie and community spirit born of shared danger and hardship have largely gone. Where the 'stute – the Miners' Institute – once stood in Grimethorpe, now there is just a rubble-strewn wasteland next to an overgrown field that used to be the bowling green . . . younger miners who lost their jobs in the 1990s mostly found work elsewhere, but not the older ones. They live on their pensions or benefits. You find them on their allotments, walking dogs, standing on street corners, or drinking, perhaps, in the Rusty Dudley pub on Grimethorpe's high street on weekday mornings.'

Rather than reverse the decline of team and town, the Premier League adventure had, in fact, proven to be counter-productive. After relegation, the board took a punt on a swift return to the summit, sanctioning a spending spree that increased their wage bill to around £6 million. They nearly got there at the turn of the millennium when the veteran coach Dave Bassett, who had masterminded Wimbledon's unprecedented rise up the divisions, guided them to the play-off final. However, two years later, losing £50,000 a week and carrying debts of £3.5 million, they entered into administration and teetered on the very lip of extinction. As chairman John Dennis admitted in his autobiography, success had turned their heads; like several other living-the-dream Yorkshire clubs, including Leeds, Bradford City and the two Sheffield teams, they had overreached themselves.

Four managers in succession were hired and fired – Hendrie, Bassett, Nigel Spackman and Steve Parkin – and attendances fell to half their Premiership average of 18,600.

While the team were paying the price for such a reckless reinvention, the town, financed by the Australian company Developer Multiplex, was also attempting to remodel itself, somewhat improbably, as a walled hill village. The brainchild of architect Will Alsop, its much-mocked attempt to become the 'Tuscany of the north' was one of a slew of grandiose New Labour schemes, including a futuristic 'super city' running the length of the M62, devised to breathe new life into, and even create new identities for, Old Yorkshire's former industrial towns. 'We were talking about creating a living wall,' explained council leader Steve Houghton, 'a series of landmark buildings.' The remodelling was intended to eradicate the dereliction left by de-industrialisation and introduce a New Britain-type entrepreneurialism into the area. 'To change public perceptions of the place,' Houghton explained, 'we had to break the mould. Sometimes, you have got to be outrageous to make people sit up and take notice. We've got to raise aspirations, to move from what was very much a dependency-based culture into a more enterprising, can-do culture.'

McMillan, one of the few Barnsleyites to welcome the project, thought it would 'examine the way that expectations have shifted since the miners' strike and the Blairite dawn' and hoped that 'sport and art and regeneration could all be part of some human endeavour that would lift us out of some kind of slough'. Alsop's high-concept project was, however, left in tatters after its funder pulled the plug, citing problems with the design. This flop seemed to typify New Labour's failed attempt to recast declining northern areas as glowing monuments to the new leisure economy. During the Blair–Brown years, as the manufacturing sector continued to shrink – between 1997 and 2010 its workforce halved from 4.5 million to 2.5 million – the north–south gap widened.

Not far from Grimethorpe lies the Dearne Valley, where *Kes* was filmed. All eight of its pits have now been razed, their shafts and labyrinthine tunnels sealed up. The mine-shaft headgears, muck heaps, winding wheels and pithead buildings that once dominated the landscape have been grassed over, replaced by retail parks and leisure centres. At The Keel Inn at Stairfoot, a couple of miles away from Oakwell, Beryl Hodgson remembers how, in the seventies, Barnsley-supporting miners would play dominoes and cards before setting off for the match. The pub, once surrounded by red-brick terraces, had been a vital component of the local social fabric. But after the main colliery closed, people moved away and the houses were demolished. It remains a shrine to Barnsley's battling past, with framed photographs and signed shirts decorating the walls. 'It was always very busy,' said Beryl. 'All the miners and their families would come in. We knew all their names.' There used to be a unifying bond, generated by a local community which drank together, played sport on their day off and rallied round to help if anyone was in trouble. 'People don't mix like they used to,' said Kevin, Beryl's son.

This pub has been in our family for nearly fifty years. Some of the fans would come in here before a game. Then they'd come back in afterwards. When I was younger a lot more people went to the match. Today a match-day ticket is £24. It's just too much money. A lot of these miners who were at the pits, they struggled to find employment after the strike. If you're not earning, you can't afford to go to games. The younger generation are into computers, video games. You don't see a lot of kids out playing football or cricket. We were always kicking a ball in the street, stopping the traffic or kicking it into somebody's garden. It's not the same culture. The drug situation is a major problem. If I catch anyone with drugs here they're out and they never come back again. But you hear about places where they can get hold of drugs so easily.

Back in the early seventies, cinema audiences had been deeply moved by Hines' ode to working-class struggle. Old Yorkshire got knocked down, but it got up again. The miners in *Brassed Off*, however, put up little resistance, seemingly resigned to the fact that coal, and indeed community life, has had its day. Before the strike, there had been 170 mines employing 148,000 workers and producing 120 million tonnes of coal. After the 1992 Heseltine closures there were only thirty pits left, employing 7,000 workers and producing 50 million tonnes. The Casper generation had come of age in a decade of long-term unemployment, economic dispossession and political subjugation. Their wings had been clipped. A displacement had taken place, leaving them feeling useless, trapped and emasculated. 'Over the last ten years this bloody government has systematically destroyed an entire industry,' Postlethwaite tells the Royal Albert Hall audience at the end of *Brassed Off*. 'And not just an industry: our communities, our homes, our lives, all in the name of progress and for a few lousy bob. If this lot was seals or whales, you'd all be up in bloody arms. But they're not, are they? No, they're not. They're just common or garden, honest, decent human beings. And not one of them with an ounce of bloody hope left.'

Act Three:

Disaster

'There was a definite feeling that something new was happening, something old was dying. It was a defining moment in the battle between old and new Britain. Torvill and Dean's perfect pirouettes on the ice were being re-enacted on the streets of Britain's pit villages, as police and pickets, scabs and striking miners mimicked the pair's fluid dance, this time in violent confrontation. The coal industry, loss-making and dominated by the NUM, a union that had the power to bring down the government, represented everything about the old Britain that dogged the new, blossoming ethos of free enterprise . . . After years of economic gloom, a new Britain with a new attitude was finding its voice.'

Olga Craig, Daily Telegraph, 2004

5 March 1985. The last day of the miners' strike. Almost a year after they'd walked out of the pits, the miners return to work.

It is the beginning of the end for the coal industry, for defiant trade unionism and for sport's collective, working-class culture. The strike was fought, and lost, mainly in Old Yorkshire. The NUM's defeat enables a New Britain, rooted in free enterprise, to emerge. Citing the disasters at Bradford and Heysel, Thatcher demonises football fans, like the miners, as the 'enemy within' and announces the introduction of compulsory identity cards. To the prime minister, both the coal and football industries are now lame ducks; backward-looking, reluctant to entertain change, part of a doomed proletarian culture. They are symptoms of the Old Britain: an embittered, run-down country, resigned to failure. The culture of financial deregulation, which began with Howe abolishing exchange controls, is confirmed by the Big Bang, which ends the age-old restrictive practices of the Stock Exchange and transforms the City of London. The direction of history is reversed. Thatcher imposes curbs on union power and local government. Caps are imposed on local taxation. Metropolitan and GLC councils are abolished. 'Popular capitalism,' proclaims the prime minister, after winning another landslide victory, 'is on the march.'

6

The Bradford Hole

'It's a deserted cemetery, a decayed graveyard.'
J. B. Priestley on Bradford, *Lost City*, 1958

THE FIRE

11 May 1985. Valley Parade. Bradford City vs Lincoln City.
11,076 people, the biggest crowd of the season, are packed into
the stadium to watch the final game of the campaign. There is a
pre-match carnival atmosphere as a group of majorettes perform
and City players bring out placards with messages of thanks
to supporters. Peter Jackson, who at twenty-three is the club's
youngest-ever captain, collects the Third Division championship
trophy. Towards the end of the first half, a small fire breaks out
in the main wooden stand. Just over four minutes later the stand
is engulfed in flames. Some of the 3,000 people inside manage to
escape by climbing over walls on to the pitch or dashing through
exit gates. But fifty-six spectators, including two Lincoln fans, are
killed and more than 250 injured.

'Let me show you something,' says Peter Jackson, running upstairs
to fetch his Bradford City top. 'It's the first time I've had it out for
twenty years.' When he returns he is holding the shirt he was wearing
the day he watched a bushy flame explode into a roaring inferno,
speeding in the wind along Valley Parade's old wooden stand. He
can still vividly remember climbing into the stand to rescue his
wife Alison and young daughter Charlotte and then rushing out
of the stadium to the pub at the top of the hill. On the pub TV,
standing alongside teammates who had gathered for a head count,
he watched the nightmare unfold. An hour later, returning to the
dressing room to retrieve his belongings, he saw the body bags.
'That's when it hit home,' he says softly. He decided, there and then,

to drive to Bradford Royal Infirmary to console fans. 'Apart from the shoes and blazer, I was still wearing this City shirt and my shorts. I walked into the accident and emergency unit. It was horrendous. The smell of the hospital, the smell of burnt flesh. People with 60 or 70 per cent burns were lying there. But all they wanted to talk to me about was Bradford City, our fantastic season, about playing teams like Leeds, Huddersfield and Sheffield United next season. Sadly, some of them didn't make it to those games.' When he got home at 10.30 p.m. he was still wearing the shirt he tightly clutches. 'I will never forget it,' he says. 'You just don't. People being pulled out of the stand and people trying to get back in to help. People's coats melting on their heads. I will never get over it.' During his two years as a City apprentice, one of his jobs had been to clean the old, dilapidated stand. 'There were holes in the floor, under the rows of seats and on the stairways,' he recalls. 'And when we were clearing up, we'd just brush everything down those holes. For years, generations of apprentices had done exactly the same thing so you can imagine how much rubbish had piled up down there. It was a tinderbox. All it needed was a stray cigarette to be dropped down a hole. Everybody knew it was a hazard.'

Before I set off for a whistle-stop tour of Manningham, the inner-city district on Valley Parade's doorstep, Alison tells me that many local Asian families had opened their doors, that day, to distressed fans, offering comfort, food and the use of their house phones. My tour guide, Jerry Ashraf, a community organiser and ardent City fan, was studying at his mosque at the time. 'I ran out to see what was happening,' he says. 'It was like an emotional flooding of people from the ground going towards the city centre. Lots of Asian residents were out on the streets, trying to support people.' On our way back to the railway station, we drive past a row of empty shops, a clutch of neglected Victorian buildings – built on the back of wool trade profits – and a gaping 23-acre void in the town centre known to one and all, Jerry tells me, as 'the Bradford hole'.

A MEAN OLD SCENE

Despite litigation for damages establishing the club was two-thirds to blame, the coroner considering a charge of manslaughter and one of the survivors, thirty years later, raising serious concerns about the role of the club's then chairman, Stafford Heginbotham, the vast majority of City fans have always refused to blame the board for the fire. Many continue to view it as a tragic accident, a blow from fate – an act of God even. There was an understandable need to close ranks, to grieve collectively as a city and to come together in a time of great trauma. 'We didn't have the mindset of a city looking for a scapegoat,' explained John Helm, the Bradford-born TV presenter who was commentating on the game when the fire broke out.

Besides, we wanted to support each other. It seemed, at that time, that we were the focal point of all the bad things in the world. The decline of the wool trade, the Yorkshire Ripper and a few other things had put Bradford on the map for all the wrong reasons. And a number of sporting shocks: Bradford City going into administration, Bradford Park Avenue falling out of the Football League and the speedway and the greyhound racing stopping in the city. And there was a lot of economic hardship. And on top of all that came the fire.

In the mid-eighties, around 5,000 of the city's 16–19 year olds were on the dole. More than a third of its families received state benefits because their income was below the poverty line. Two thirds of council tenants were on housing benefit. In the wake of the Donald Neilson killings (the so-called Black Panther murdered heiress Lesley Whittle and three sub-postmasters), the thirteen gruesome murders by Yorkshire Ripper Peter Sutcliffe and four random knife killings by Mark Rowntree (all three men hailed from Bradford) the Valley Parade Kop had morbidly taken to chanting: 'This is the valley, the valley of death.' In a hard-hitting book about the period, the veteran local journalist Jim Greenhalf wrote: 'Bradford, which had once made cloth, marine engines, cars, televisions, tractors and much else, was now shedding its skilled labour. It is no exaggeration to say that the fabric and pattern of working life was torn apart.'

And yet there had been a huge amount of optimism on the morning of the Bradford–Lincoln match. For the first time in almost half a century, the Bantams had been promoted to Division Two. Valley Parade's notoriously decrepit, 77-year-old timber structure was due to be demolished and replaced by a brand new stand; 'City stand work starts on Monday,' the local paper had reported on its back page. Promotion had given the depressed city a bit of hope: a new league, a new stand, a new era. 'We thought we were unbeatable,' said Jackson. 'That year we only used sixteen players. We loved going into work. We socialised together. We had nights out together. We were just a group of young lads coming through but, come Saturday, we thought we were invincible.'

As with Barnsley, Rotherham United and Hull's two rugby teams, there had been a surge of energy in the early eighties. City had enthusiastically started to embrace the commercial opportunities opening up in New Britain. Two revenue streams had proved to be particularly lucrative: the club lottery and advertising on the players' shirts. One of football's first fanzines, *City Gent*, had been launched by supporters disillusioned with the inanities of the match-day programme. In 1985, in the seemingly safe hands of Heginbotham and his multi-millionaire partner Jack Tordoff, who had both saved the club from extinction two years earlier, the only way was up.

The year, instead, turned out to be Bradford's – and indeed football's – *annus horribilis*. The sense of anomie was summed up by the graffiti 'It's a Mean Old Scene' which suddenly appeared overnight on a blackened brick wall in the town centre and quickly achieved folkloric status. In the first half of the year, football's reputation sunk to an all-time low. In February, its leaders were accused of being grasping and short-sighted after rejecting a £19 million deal, which took the game off the TV screens for the whole of the following season. The next month, during a Luton vs Millwall game, Kenilworth Road witnessed one of football hooliganism's worst-ever incidents as police fought running battles with hundreds of fans and were bombarded with coins, bottles, cans and seats ripped out from the stands. On the same day as the fire, a teenage boy was killed when Birmingham City and Leeds United fans rioted. Eighteen days later came the Heysel disaster. Thirty-nine fans died and 600 were injured when a stadium wall collapsed during the European Cup final between Liverpool and Juventus. The *Sunday Times* denounced football as 'a slum game watched in slum stadiums by slum people', suggesting it was now the preserve of the undeserving poor. Crowds dwindled: the 1984–5 campaign recorded the first-ever aggregate attendance of under 18 million. Newspapers devoted far more column inches to events off the pitch than on it. 'We have far too many football clubs,' complained Thatcher. 'In any other industry the inefficient would have gone to the wall years ago.'

Her government, seeing the game entirely through a law-and-order prism, proposed an Orwellian Football Supporter Act, which demanded that all fans carry some form of identity card. One of the prime minister's closest allies, Luton chairman and Tory MP David Evans, went even further, proposing to ban all away supporters from his club's games at Kenilworth Road. After Heysel all English clubs were kicked out of Europe for five years, a move which produced a 20 per cent loss of income from sponsorship deals and TV and gate money. This prompted the big five – the directors of Liverpool, Everton, Manchester United, Arsenal and Tottenham Hotspur – to give serious consideration to an ITV proposal for a lucrative break-away league. 'By 1985, football was further from being the "people's game" than it had been at any time since the 1870s,' noted the social historian Dave Russell. 'It was obvious that clubs needed the support of individuals with considerable disposable wealth if they were to prosper. Moreover, the game's altering business culture represented another force tending to take power away from fans.'

A CULTURE OF NEGLECT

In its influential editorial, *The Sunday Times* had urged a new breed of entrepreneur to step into the void. This, as we have seen, was already starting to happen; Tottenham Hotspur's Irving Scholar, Manchester United's Martin Edwards and Arsenal's David Dein were already transforming the business cultures of their clubs. Although first surfacing at City back in the sixties, Heginbotham was cut from the same cloth as these dynamic eighties businessmen, his drive and showmanship breathing new life into an ailing institution. 'There are three types of people,' a sign in his office explained. 'Those who make things happen, those who watch things happen and those who wonder what happened.' Heginbotham clearly fell into the first category. Even his admirers referred to him as a loveable rogue who enjoyed flying by the seat of his pants. He grew up in Oldham, left school at fifteen and borrowed money to open a sandwich shop. Following a short spell as a successful foam-cushion salesman, he established his own soft furnishing firm, which he then sold off to set up Tebro Toys. After acquiring licences to produce the 1980 Olympics mascot Rupert the Bear, as well as children's entertainer Keith Harris' nationally famous puppets, Tebro's turnover increased to £1.8 million. At the beginning of 1985, however, it dropped by 50 per cent after Heginbotham lost a key licence. Three years later he sold his City shares to Tordoff for a £370,000 profit.

In *Fifty-Six: The Story of the Bradford Fire*, Martin Fletcher – whose father, brother, uncle and grandfather all died in the tragedy – revealed that previous blazes in the city could be linked to Heginbotham. Members of other bereaved families found it hard to countenance any foul play, pointing out that the chairman's family had been in the stand that day. Still, Heginbotham was clearly guilty of ignoring warnings about the flammable rubbish that had accumulated underneath the main stand's wooden seating. Fletcher remembered his dad telling him off, during a previous game, for dropping a Kit Kat wrapper though a hole under his seat, explaining it was a fire risk. Amongst the piles of uncleared debris discovered after the fire was a charred copy of the Bradford *Telegraph & Argus* dated Monday 4 November 1968 and a bag of peanuts costing six old pennies (decimalisation had been introduced in 1971). In his 1983 tome on football grounds, Simon Inglis had described the view from Valley Parade's antiquated main stand as 'like watching football from the cockpit of a Sopwith Camel', noting that 'underneath the seats are flaps which open to reveal piles of accumulated litter.' There had been two warnings from the Health and Safety Executive, a non-departmental public body, in 1981. One of them had stated: 'The timber construction is a fire hazard and in particular there is a build-up of combustible materials in the voids beneath the seats. A carelessly discarded cigarette could give rise to a fire risk.' Three years later the West Yorkshire metropolitan county council issued another warning about 'the void'.

While Valley Parade's decline had been apparent for fifty years – the main stand had not been upgraded since 1911 – the ground began to decay at an alarming rate at the beginning of the eighties. In 1981, a League Cup replay was postponed after television engineers discovered structural faults in both the main stand's pylons. In 1983, all evening games were cancelled after a vicious gale snapped one floodlight pylon in half and dismantled another. As at countless other clubs, supporters were expected to uncomplainingly put up with such terrible conditions. This was an era when crowd control and cost-cutting took precedence over fan safety. On the day of the fire, the pre-match police briefing to the 144 officers on duty, who were clearly expecting public disorder rather than an inferno, made no mention of evacuating the stand. There was no dedicated person in charge. Fire extinguishers, seen as potential missiles, had been hidden away.

'The Bradford fire can be said to have highlighted football's dysfunctional priorities,' wrote David Conn. 'The accumulation of rubbish itself became a symbol of football's widespread mis-management.' The holes in the stand also appeared to be symptomatic of a more widespread culture of neglect; on boats, rigs and railways, the disease of sloppiness was rampant. In 1980, the MV *Derbyshire*, a merchant ship with forty-two crew members, two of their wives and 157,000 tonnes of iron ore on board, disappeared in the Pacific Ocean, south of Japan. In the four years after the fire, a series of high-profile disasters caused the loss of almost 700 lives, an epidemic of catastrophe that exposed a scandalous disregard for public safety. They included the sinking of the *Herald of Free Enterprise* ferry outside Zeebrugge Harbour, the fire in King's Cross Underground Station, the explosion on the Piper Alpha oil rig and the Southern Region rail crashes at Clapham Junction and Purley. Inglis blamed the Bradford fire on complacency, neglect and 'the systemic failure of an industry that had lost its way'. As David Pendleton, City's official historian and a former editor of the *City Gent*, noted: 'The need to make ends meet and keep the club in business has more often taken precedence over ground improvement. Decades of neglect, allied to a lack of regulation, were responsible for one of the worst tragedies in British sporting history.'

Such blatant disregard for safety predated the eighties. The Ibrox disaster, in which sixty-six supporters died, had taken place at the beginning of the previous decade and led to the introduction of the 1975 Safety of Sports Grounds Act. The act's Green Guide insisted that wooden stands be capable of evacuation in two and a half min-utes, that all combustible material be removed from beneath them, that all voids be sealed and that no one be more than 30 metres from the nearest manned exit. Because these stringent safety guidelines only applied to designated grounds – those in the top two divisions

– Bradford City had not been obliged to comply with them. The Labour government's intention was to have all Third Division clubs designated by 1981, and the rest by 1983. The first Thatcher government, however, indefinitely postponed further designation, claiming that lower league grounds were not attended in sufficient numbers. According to Fletcher, 'the Thatcher regime was more interested in deregulating free enterprise, looking to lift restrictions, not impose further regulations or obligatory costs, even in the name of safety.' It was the Conservative's government's 'failure to fully implement the recommendations of the original 1975 Act that had laid the groundwork for the Bradford fire'.

A GRAND NEW WORLD

In its Victorian heyday, Bradford had been one of the richest cities in the country. Boasting a plentiful supply of soft water, it was known as the wool capital of the world. An indication of its past prosperity can be gleaned from a series of grandiose civic buildings located in the warehouse district known as Little Germany. From being a small market town of 16,000 on the eastern slopes of the Pennines it had, by the turn of the twentieth century, morphed into a booming textile capital, an industrial powerhouse of 280,000, one in five of its workforce employed in higher-wage occupations. In Edwardian times, it remained a place of wealth and modernity, boasting more Rolls-Royces per head than any town in the world. The Bradford Exhibition of 1904 had been the perfect illustration of its growing self-confidence. Opened by the Prince and Princess of Wales, it presented to the outside world a view of the vibrant, trading city as industrious, prosperous and internationalist. Jacob Behrens' knighthood in 1882 had recognised the importance of its German, largely Jewish, community. In *The Waste Land*, T. S. Eliot referred to those on whom assurance sits 'as a silk hat on a Bradford millionaire'.

The city's businessmen were renowned for their paternalism: Sir Henry Whitehead left £100,000 to local charities, Lord Masham gave £40,000 towards the construction of Cartwright Hall, the city's art museum, and Sir James Hill devoted his year as mayor to raising £100,000 towards a new Royal Infirmary, personally donating £30,000. The most philanthropic manufacturer of all was Titus Salt, who built a utopian village for the workers in his mill. 'The Bradford I knew so well then satisfied – no, delighted me,' wrote Priestley, who, with the artist David Hockney, the composer Frederick Delius and the Nobel laureate Sir Edward Appleton, heads a long list of eminent Bradfordians. The vibrant Bradford of his childhood was the product of a Victorian boom and an Edwardian augmentation. It offered 'three daily papers, and a weekly; the subscription concerts on Fridays, the Bradford Permanent series on Saturdays and superb choral singing almost any night; two theatres, two music halls, two or three professional concert parties; an Arts Club, a playgoers society; one football team that had won the FA Cup not long before; several fine old pubs ... [one] easily reached from the band concerts in Lister Park.' It also offered an oppositional attitude towards authority. In 1890, workers at Samuel Lister's mill, after striking against a 25 per cent pay cut, set up the Bradford Labour Union, a move that eventually led to the formation of the Labour Party. Forty-three years later, at Odsal rugby league ground, a Bradford crowd underlined this rebellious tradition by singing the Yorkshire anthem 'On Ilkley Moor' rather than 'God Save the Queen' before a Great Britain match against Australia.

The success of Priestley's beloved Bradford City – he had trials with them before the First World War and the team are thinly disguised in his books as 't'United' – mirrored the city's social and economic progress, and was as much an indication of its late Victorian and Edwardian civic pre-eminence as its majestic buildings, friendly societies and muscular trade unions. In his 1929 novel *The Good Companions*, which opens with a long description of a football match, Priestley pays tribute to the lifelong bond between a football team and its supporters: 'To say that these men paid their shillings to watch twenty-two hirelings kick a ball is merely to say that a violin is wood and catgut, that *Hamlet* is so much paper and ink. For a shilling the Bruddersford United AFC offered you Conflict and Art.'

City were the first West Riding team to be elected to the Football League, becoming members of the Second Division before they had even kicked a ball in anger. Within five years they had been promoted to the First Division, and they remained in the top flight for ten successive seasons. In 1911 they won the FA Cup, beating the then mighty Newcastle United in a replay, and finished fifth, their best-ever position. As John Dewhirst wrote in *A History of Bradford City AFC in Objects*, the club's 'can-do-mentality' epitomised the 'self-made man who had the balls to drive the Roller and the big house and the big mouth – and he had the confidence to do it in sport'. During their golden age, between 1908 and 1915 – an era of entepreneurial spirit, affluence and upward social swing – the Bantams became a fixture in the national sports pages. In his meticulous trawl through hundreds of artefacts, Dewhirst managed to unearth a French magazine match report from 1911. Such foreign interest in the club would not be repeated until the fire.

There was a spectacular growth of association football at the turn of the twentieth century, resulting in the emergence of two soccer teams in Bradford: City and Park Avenue. At the outbreak of the First World War, both graced the top flight. The latter's rise was financed by Arthur Briggs, an early investor in Rolls-Royce and a very wealthy man. Park Avenue served the working-class communities of Horton in the west of the city while City drew its support from the Manningham district, a mile or so to the east. The city's pre-war affluence, in fact, managed to sustain three big sporting teams; Bradford Northern, the rugby league side, also had wealthy benefactors. Cricket was also hugely popular, with Yorkshire playing regularly at Park Avenue. 'The rugby club had money and rich people behind them,' said Pendleton. 'And there were rich wool men behind Bradford City. They refused to go a couple of miles across town and merge with Avenue, who were the "posh boys" who gave ivory passes to their members. They were seen as a threat.' Two world wars and the Great Depression took its toll on both soccer clubs and in 1950 the Bradford *Telegraph & Argus* carried a front-page article on their seemingly irreversible decline. By 1958, they were firmly entrenched in the Third Division. Since the 1960s, when City were relegated to the Fourth Division for the first time in their history, their decline has coincided with the textile sector's plunge down the production cycle, the result of overseas competition and trade tariffs.

And yet, as Bradford-based, social realist films like *Billy Liar* and *Room at the Top* showed, the urban renewal of the fifties and sixties gave the image of old industrial towns and cities a huge boost. The working class was on the move. *Room at the Top*'s upwardly mobile hero Joe Lampton, mimicking the dynamic, can-do mentality of an Edwardian entrepreneur, was a one-man northern powerhouse. Like Casper's bird of prey, he soared to the top of his valley. Even in the mid-seventies, as Greenhalf wrote, 'it was possible to look proudly at Bradford's new city centre: the Interchange, Magistrates' Court, Police HQ, Library . . . and see in them the promise of a grand new world delivered.' In an interview with Priestley in the sixties, *Room at the Top* author John Braine praised his home town for being 'dominated more than any other in England . . . by a success ethos'.

GAMBLING MEN

Throughout the twentieth century, from Rolls-Royce-driving mill owners to white-heat-of-technology social-climbers, Bradford had been driven by ambitious trailblazers. In the first decade of that century, these pioneers had brought great sporting success to the city. Their early twenty-first-century equivalents were also responsible for an exhilarating ascent, providing top-flight football for the first time in seventy-seven years. The result of this surge, however, would be a humiliating freefall from which the club has yet to recover.

At the turn of the millennium the Bantams appeared to be the last hope for a city that had almost been brought to its knees by de-industrialisation, civic decline and racial tension. Like Barnsley, after taking a big hit in the eighties, the team had ridden the wave of the nineties credit boom. As a result – also like Barnsley and several other Yorkshire teams – they had overreached themselves and plunged into the abyss. Bradford's rise-and-fall cameo, the result of a notorious spending splurge its instigator would later describe as 'six weeks of madness', stands out in particular as a cautionary tale.

City's flirtation with bankruptcy at the beginning of the eighties was a precursor of the implosion to come. Although 1981 was a recessionary year, the club were relatively well off, reaping the rewards of a successful lottery. Chairman Bob Martin, a supermarket owner and would-be developer, and director John Garside appointed Roy McFarland as player-manager; like Hughes and Clarke, he was a big England star of the seventies. In his first season, the former Derby captain steered them into the Third Division, equalling a club record of nine successive wins. But as lottery receipts fell and expenses rose, short-term debt reached unprecedented levels. Midway through the following campaign, McFarland returned to the Midlands to manage his old club. Another ex-England defender, Trevor Cherry, took over and managed to stave off relegation, but in 1983, with mounting debts of almost £400,000, City went bust. The 1908 company ceased trading after its (very few) assets were transferred to a new company, Bradford City 1983 Limited, now run by Heginbotham and Tordoff. 'I can't say why the club ran for so long,' the Official Receiver reported. 'For a number of years its accounts have shown it to be insolvent.' According to Heginbotham, City had 'gambled for far too long. That is why they went into debt and almost lost league football for this city.'

The finances had collapsed, according to the then *Telegraph & Argus* football reporter David Markham, as a result of Martin and Garside's greed and mismanagement. 'Martin's board found the day-to-day efficient management of the club very boring in the extreme,' said Markham.

Like a lot of football directors, a lot of these people run their businesses Monday to Friday and leave the business principles to one side when they come to manage a football club on the Saturday. They attempt things they would never attempt in their own business. Bob Martin was chairman for ten years. It ended in disaster with the fall into receivership. They simply ignored all the tax demands. If it wasn't for the 12-month strike at the Inland Revenue, they would have gone into receivership earlier. Garside and Martin were possibly part of a new breed, like Anton Johnson at Rotherham. They weren't the solid businessmen we'd had at City before. They were young people at the time, they had quite a few fanciful ideas that had little chance of succeeding at Bradford. Garside was very flash. He gave everybody the impression he was an architect. I remember reporting one of his schemes and describing him as the club's architect. The following morning I had a call from local secretary of the Royal Institute of British Architects. I was told that on no account should I refer to him as that again. He was not a qualified architect.

Markham discovered that large sums of money had been taken out of the club to pay for ground improvements which had never been carried out. The laying of drains under the pitch by a company called Shanmace cost them £40,000 – but the drainage was never put in. 'Martin and Garside formed a company and applied for grants from the Football League,' he explained.

They claimed for £21,000 and the breezeblock wall cost about £1500. They pocketed the rest. They got no more grants after that. They applied for far more than it cost. The fire was an accident waiting to happen. I think there is an element of culpability because Martin's board were just not interested in basic maintenance. There was a wall that collapsed at the back of the Kop. The terraces on the Kop were crumbling. I remember City and Sheffield United fans picking up lumps of concrete from a fence during a big game in the early eighites and throwing them at each other. Valley Parade was in a bad way.

In his book *Paraders*, Pendleton echoes Markham's argument – that the board's grandiose, delusional plans took precedence over the boring, day-to-day matters of ground maintenance. 'There was very little development at Valley Parade in the 1970s and early 80s,' he wrote, 'but a number of plans. These plans were over-ambitious for a club that had been languishing in the lower reaches of the Football League for a generation, with average gates of around five thousand.'

When Geoffrey Richmond arrived on the scene in 1994 he was seen, at first, as a breath of fresh air. Like Johnson, he was a flamboyant, cigar-smoking businessman – but he also had a reputation for shrewdness, having guided the struggling Conference club Scarborough into the Football League. Richmond had bought the Ronson cigarette lighter business when they were insolvent before selling up for £10 million. He immediately paid off City's debts and began to turn the club into a profitable concern. Crowds shot up to 15,500. As Pendleton wrote in *When Saturday Comes* a year before they were promoted to the top flight, 'a few years ago you would have been laughed out of town had you mentioned the words "City" and "Premiership" in the same sentence.' Eight years after Richmond's arrival, however, the Bantams were £36 million in debt and on the brink of liquidation.

What went wrong? Richmond, as he would later admit, lost the plot. After City had dramatically avoided relegation to the second tier on the last day of the 1999–2000 season with a 1-0 win over Liverpool, he should have thanked his bright young manager Paul Jewell for confounding expectations by keeping a bunch of hard-grafting journeymen in the Premiership. Instead he berated Jewell for presiding over a poor season. 'Why,' asked the chairman, 'can't we be like Manchester United?' Jewell promptly called time on his tenure at Valley Parade and dropped down a division to manage Sheffield Wednesday. After installing assistant Chris Hutchings as the new coach, Richmond then embarked on an extravagant bout of spending, borrowing heavily to bring in a series of big-name Fancy Dans on big wages. The arrival of these superstars undermined what remained of the team's fighting spirit. City finished bottom of the league on 26 points, having won only five games. Suddenly finding themselves with a wage bill they couldn't afford, and with a First Division income, they proceeded to drop like a stone. 'The march to glory had been done on tick,' wrote Conn. 'Everything was rented: the floodlights, furniture, kitchen fittings, CCTV, the shop tills, everything . . .'

The six weeks of madness were to produce six years of suffering. Between 2000 and 2006 City were relegated three times and had two spells in administration as they nose-dived into the fourth tier. 'For a region that had previously traded on its miserliness,' wrote David Goldblatt, 'Yorkshire football has proved particularly prey to the temptations of overspending and overindulging. Leeds United and Bradford City "lived the dream" and, in a pyrotechnic display of hubris, exploded.' Deluded to the end, Richmond reflected: 'We saw the bright lights. Looking back, staying up [in the 1999–2000 season] was the worst thing which could have happened to the club. Had we gone down, I'd still be a hero in Bradford; they'd have put up a statue to me.'

FILLING THE HOLE

Since the end of the Second World War, Bradford has made various attempts to fill a Woolopolis-shaped hole. For almost a decade there was an actual void, a vast empty crater in the heart of the city centre – the result of a £260 million Westfield shopping centre being mothballed after the 2008 financial crisis. To the chagrin of conservationists, earlier regeneration schemes had also created holes in the old wool city's Victorian edifice, ripping out magnificent buildings and replacing them with high-speed flyovers, inner-city ring roads and other manifestations of the bland, concrete, utilitarian future. Such vandalism was singled out for particular criticism by the architectural historian Gavin Stamp. In his book *Britain's Lost Cities: A Chronicle of Architectural Destruction*, Stamp declared the city's post-war regeneration to be 'a criminal waste of money, energy and materials'.

In 1980, the council's marketing department decided to take a new approach to its hole-filling. Re-branding the metropolitan district as a tourist mecca, a place of rolling hills, minarets and mills, it adopted the slogan 'A Surprising Place' and, to the bemusement of most Bradfordians, and the amusement of the national media, promoted the city of riots, racism and poverty as the ideal destination for a weekend break or package holiday. Its first package tourist, Sussex pensioner Ted Adams, was greeted at the railway station by a brass band and a smiling mayor, brandishing a two-foot stick of Bradford rock. 'The sparrows woke up coughing, the pigeons flew backwards to keep the dirt out of their eyes and the dayshift down the legendary "treacle mine" was hard at it,' mocked the *Guardian*'s Simon Hoggart. 'But everyday life in industrial Bradford was halted for a few hilarious minutes when a 71-year-old pensioner stepped from a train.'

By the end of the eighties, it was clear that this *Wuthering Heights* rebrand had been a huge flop. So much so that the council felt obliged to put out a statement reassuring sceptics that its tourism officer's time had not been spent 'guiding coach parties around tripe mines, black pudding co-operatives or potential sites for the Whippet Winter Olympics'. It admitted, however, that the idea of 'Brontëland' had failed to stick. In 2015, it finally admitted defeat, announcing plans to close many of its visitor centres. Its National Media Museum, a key tourist attraction which had opened back in 1983, lost its world-famous photography collection to London's Victoria and Albert museum, prompting a Conservative council leader to denounce 'an appalling act of cultural vandalism'; Sam Jordison, the co-editor of the 'Crap Towns' series of books, argued it had 'significance not just for a once great and now struggling city, but for anyone who cares about the United Kingdom functioning as an entire nation, rather than allowing it to subside into a series of wastelands around the inaccessible citadel of London'. The museum had basked in an industrial landscape which inspired cinema's first black-and-white film screenings – in 1897, some thirteen years ahead of Hollywood – as well as *Billy Liar*, *Room at the Top* and *Rita*,

Sue and Bob Too. Like Brontëland, however, those sixties kitchen sink films now seemed like ancient history. For, in the two decades since they had first appeared, Bradford had undergone another reinvention: as a multicultural melting pot.

THE RISE AND FALL OF
SHOUTY BRADFORD WOMAN

Racial harmony, or the lack of it, had been as much a motif of eighties Bradford as industrial decline. In 1981 the 'Bradford 12', members of a militant organisation who had marched against the National Front, were arrested; despite admitting making petrol bombs, they were acquitted by a jury who agreed they had acted in self-defence. Three years later, Ray Honeyford, a Bradford headmaster, became a cause célèbre after publishing an article pointing out the adverse effects of multiculturalism on British education. Honeyford made some valid points about segregation in schools but he was accused of racism – he ridiculed a parent speaking English 'like a Peter Sellers' Indian doctor on an off-day' and blamed heroin addiction in northern cities on Pakistani migration – and was eventually forced to take early retirement. And, most notoriously of all, at the beginning of 1989, around 1,000 Muslim protesters marched through the town centre to protest against Salman Rushdie's novel *The Satanic Verses.* The public burning of Rushdie's book became an instant emblem of Islamic rage. It was followed up, a month later, by a fatwa against the author issued by Iran's supreme religious leader Ayatollah Khamenei. Bradford's growing reputation as a crucible of ethnic tension was reinforced by the 2001 riots, when racial violence erupted on the streets and Manningham was turned into a battleground. Two years later, with the club in the middle of its Moorhouse-triggered slide into obscurity, the council announced yet another makeover. Will Alsop, fresh from 'Tuscanising' Barnsley, came up with the brilliant idea of dividing the city into four new neighbourhoods: 'the bowl', 'the channel', 'the market' and 'the valley'. The emergence of 'the hole', however – a direct result of the 2008 crash – eventually put paid to the architect's latest grand plan.

Once again, if there was hope, it lay in Bradford City. During an unprecedented League Cup run in 2013, which ended with a 5-0 defeat to Swansea in the final, the Bantams, then a League Two side, began to appear on the front, as well as the back, pages of the national press. As in the eighties, they were international news. This time, however, they were an uplifting, feel-good story. 'If ever something in sports could be a metaphor for life and the human spirit,' declared the *New York Times*, 'it would be named Bradford City A.F.C.' The club's reversal of fortune – after a six-year struggle in the league's bottom division, they had swept aside Arsenal and Aston Villa to become the first fourth-tier team to reach a major cup final at Wembley – was heralded as a great advertisement for modern, diverse Britain. Publishing a photograph of a young female fan wearing a hijab and a City scarf, a *Daily Mail* headline praised 'Bradford's fantasy Cup run [which was] helping unite multicultural society on the terraces'. During the League Cup semi-final, as Villa's Barry Bannan had run over to take a corner, the midfielder had been harangued by an overexcited Asian woman. 'What is more,' wrote the *Daily Telegraph*'s Jim White, 'she was with a couple of female Asian friends, in a section of the Valley Parade crowd dotted with Asian faces. If it is possible that someone yelling at a footballer represents evidence of social progress, then this was the most encouraging image of the season . . . The good news is that shouty Bradford woman is not alone. For years it was to the game's shame that Asian people felt excluded from immersing themselves in its glories. Such was the sense of isolation, British Asian men largely preferred to follow cricket, while young Asian females would never have felt comfortable at a match.'

This was less a reinvention, perhaps, than a return to the city's cosmopolitan otherness. In the mid-nineteenth century, its huge woollen industry had been developed by entrepreneurial German Jews. 'Bradford was probably one of the most international cities of the pre-war era,' said Pendleton. 'It traded with the world. In 1911, the Lord Mayor gets on the train to give the team an impromptu reception. He talks about "Yorkshire" grit, teamwork and the values that won the Cup. Eight of the team were Scottish. One was Irish. The Lord Mayor himself was a German Jew. So it was obviously a bit tongue in cheek.' Immigrants from India and Pakistan had begun to arrive from the mid-1950s onwards, cheap labour drafted in from India, Pakistan and Bangladesh to facilitate Britain's post-war national recovery. Yorkshire was a popular settling place for diasporic communities. 'I like the fact that Bradford is completely different to everywhere else, that it's a bit of an odd city,' continued Pendleton.

It's struggling to find a sense of its own value. In 2013, a quarter of the crowd at Valley Parade were Asian and a lot were women. That's very reflective of the city of Bradford. We're from a different planet. I don't know what planet we are on. We are completely different though. We look different, our colours are a bit bizarre and our ground is still one of the few remaining old-fashioned ones. And after a game, it's beer and curry. That's modern Bradford, which most of the supporters have embraced. The big cup matches galvanised everybody. The old divisions were suspended. It all began, I suppose, with Zesh Rehman.

Rehman's arrival at the club, in 2009, was a turning point. Five years earlier, at Fulham, the Pakistan international had become the first British South Asian footballer to play in the Premier League. His appointment as captain enticed hordes of new, mainly young supporters to Valley Parade. City appointed an 'Asian ambassador', the local entrepreneur Omar Khan, and reduced ticket prices for young Asian fans. Proclaiming himself to be a role model for ethnic minorities, Rehman set up a community foundation with his brother Riz, persuading City to hold inner-city football trials. 'When Zesh came to Bradford it was like, wow, a Pakistani captain, what a brilliant capture,' said Jerry Ashraf.

Not only because he was Pakistani but he was a half-decent footballer who had played at Premiership level. You want bragging rights over your friends who support Leeds, especially if they're not from Leeds. There was an explosion when Zesh arrived. A lot of young kids could finally identify with an Asian who'd made it. We had 5,000 Asians supporting Manningham All Stars, a local semi-professional team, against Bradford Park Avenue. It was at Valley Parade and I managed that team. I'd dreamed, ever since I was a kid, of standing in the dugout at the ground. One year we even played City. We invited local semi-pro lads to the ground. We had this mad idea about taking local kids to the ground and we persuaded the club. We took nearly 300 tickets, boys and girls, to watch Bradford City.

By the time of Rehman's departure in 2010, however, City co-chairman Mark Lawn was admitting there had been a dropping off of Asian support. In fact, Rehman is one of only a handful of British Asians to have enjoyed any kind of success in the English game. (The others are Michael Chopra, Neil Taylor, the brothers Adil and Samir Nabi, and Permi Jhooti). Born to Pakistani parents in Birmingham's Aston district, he was told by a scout when he was only ten years old that 'your lot' wouldn't make it. This 'negative mindset', claimed Riz, was the product of English football's institutional racism. After his rejection, said Zesh,

I went home in tears. But you have to roll your sleeves up and prove them wrong. More importantly, you've got to prove yourself right. As a minority player, you had to be two or three times better than the others. At the time, the scouts, and the people who took the decisions, took your background into account. But things are improving. The first generation that came over had no love for football. The second generation got involved in the game a little bit. Now, obviously, the third generation – like me – can hopefully inspire the next generation. I believe they will be the real difference-makers: the kids who are born here to parents who were born here.

During their FA Cup run in 2015, which included a 4-2 win at Chelsea, the club were criticised in the media for failing to inspire that generation. Whatever happened to shouty Bradford woman?

'Of the 14,000 people who regularly attend Bradford's home games, only a handful watching Phil Parkinson's team at Valley Parade are of Asian origin,' observed the *Daily Mail*'s Neil Ashton. 'Why aren't more Asian families attending matches at Bradford City and beyond?' But it is too much to expect one club, by themselves, to challenge the social, cultural and historical barriers that have restricted Asian involvement. And it's asking a great deal to expect the Bantams to reinvent themselves as a beacon of integration in a city where ethnic communities have become more segregated over the years. In a report written after the 2001 riots, Ted Cantle said: 'Separate educational arrangements, community and voluntary bodies, employment, places of worship, language, social and cultural networks, means that many communities operate on the basis of a series of parallel lives.' Pockets of Bradford, wrote the *Daily Telegraph*'s Anita Singh, were almost entirely Asian. 'Streets that once featured greengrocers, dry cleaners and hardware shops now sell nothing but halal takeaways and shalwar kameez stores. Women in full-face veils are a regular sight.'

As Dewhirst pointed out, despite the good intentions, there might even have been an increase in divisiveness when Rehman played at Valley Parade: 'They gave out tickets and a whole block was dominated by Pakistani blokes waving green-and-white flags. You had the idiots in the Kop shouting, "England, England." Then you'd hear: "Pakistan, Pakistan." What the hell is going on? Every time Rehman got the ball you got this big shout. If someone else touched it, there was nothing there. We breathe the same air, we've got the same experience of the physical structure. The disappointment is that in this city it's so segregated that even when there is a multiracial presence in the stands, there is some segregation.' The flag-waving was, agreed Ashraf, 'a culture shock for some fans. They were not used to a noise coming from the Asian community. A section, who were in a minority, were not appreciating it but a lot of people were supportive.'

According to a 2015 FA report on ethnic participation in English football, more than a decade on from Rehman's breakthrough at Fulham, only nine out of 3,000 professional footballers in the top four divisions hailed from countries such as Pakistan, India and Bangladesh. In Bradford, about a third of its 300,000 population belong to ethnic minorities, mainly Pakistanis, with a smaller group of Bangladeshis and Hindu Indians. Most live on Valley Parade's doorstep – in Manningham, Bradford Moor, Little Horton and Toller. The club knows it makes good commercial sense to tap into this unexplored market, but they have barely scratched the surface. 'Bradford has had a growing Asian population since the 1960s, working in what remained of the wool industry,' noted Mike Harrison, the editor of *City Gent*. 'Very few have become regulars at Valley Parade, even though the ground lies in the heart of their community.'

To Harrison, this was symptomatic of a much bigger problem. Even during their two cherished Premier League seasons, the club had struggled with a modest fan base. 'For a city with a metropolitan population of nearly half a million (more than Manchester and nearly twice the size of Newcastle),' he wrote, 'Bradford has rarely come close to fulfilling its potential as a football centre.' Realising this potential, argued Ashraf, would act as a big step towards integration. 'Bradford is fighting, all the time, against a bad image,' he said. 'But football has shown it can change that image.' Despite the repeated failures of both the city's and club's lofty plans for regeneration – and the endless headlines about monocultural neighbourhoods and militant Islam – he remains optimistic. 'In the eighties,' he pointed out,

I played football all the time. It was how I integrated. It defused ethnic tensions. We were beginning to turn the corner in this respect. The fire was terrible and the club and the city have never got over it. I was at Islamic classes that Saturday getting extra Arabic lessons. It was just a thick black cloud that we could see from the mosque. There were people coming out of the ground covered in soot and lots of smoke. Some were crying. It brought different communities together and that's what football can do. That's what the Rehmans tried to do. But, at the end of the day, the big problem for Bradford is still very basic and straightforward: the wool industry which brought us here, and brought all the communities together, is no longer here. And nothing has yet emerged to replace it.

7

The Fall of the Republic

'When the steel and coal industries died or left the city and when local and national politicians no longer wished to subsidise ailing or non-profit-making production, Sheffield had to fight for its very survival. Some might say it lost the fight in the 1980s.'

Gary Armstrong and John Garrett,
Sheffield United FC: The Biography

THE CAR PARK PROTEST

22 March 1986. Bramall Lane. Sheffield United vs Norwich City. Towards the end of the game, Keith Edwards comes off the bench to score twice for the Blades. But it's too late. The visitors, who are powering their way to the Second Division title, had banged in five goals to secure their fourteenth win in sixteen games. Despite United being ninth in the table, and only five points outside the promotion spots, there are calls from the home crowd for manager Ian Porterfield to be sacked. When the City goals start going in, one fan jumps out of the stands and bangs loudly and repetitively on the corrugated plastic roof of the dugout before being led away by stewards to cheers from his fellow supporters. After the match there is a car-park demonstration by hundreds of United fans. Five days later, despite having five years left on his ten-year contract, Porterfield leaves the club.

'People always say to me "You missed out on the big money,"' says Keith Edwards, as he prepares to board his lorry. 'That's true. But I didn't miss out on the great characters. I would have given anything to sign for Sheffield United when I was starting up. Or anybody really. All I wanted to be was a professional footballer.' Edwards had two spells at Bramall Lane: he was a fringe player in the great mid-seventies team that included such legends as Tony Currie and Alan Woodward and a key figure in the Porterfield side which rose, in the first half of the eighties, from the fourth to the second tier. He still can't work out why his gaffer was sacked by owner Reg Brealey after the Norwich defeat. True, fans were angry with Porterfield for leaving Edwards on the bench, they had just conceded five goals at home and the style of play was a little on the dull side. But the Scot was one of the game's brightest, up-and-coming young managers – he would go on to kick-start the Chelsea revival – and he clearly lacked the financial backing to get the team back into the top flight. Edwards retired from the game in 1991, the year before the Premiership was formed, and now earns his living driving long-distance, 40-tonne, articulated lorries, delivering insulation for a Sheffield company. According to the blurb on the back of his autobiography, his story 'reflects the humour, and sometimes bitterness, of the realities of the game behind the scenes in the 1970s and 1980s before the explosion of media coverage and influx of money changed the landscape and character of English football forever'. Before leaving to meet Howard Wilkinson, who lives a few miles away in a leafy, south Sheffield suburb, I chat to Edwards' co-driver, Paul Widdowson. A long-time Blade, Widdowson says he pinched himself when his hero suddenly turned up at the depot seven years ago. 'The first game I watched was in 1981, just before Keith re-signed,' he says. 'We went down to the Fourth Division. I watched Keith right up to him leaving in 1986. From age nine until I was fourteen. I had pictures of him on my bedroom wall. He was one of them players who, if he were one-on-one with a goalkeeper, he'd always score. For that Norwich match, Porterfield got stick because Keith was on the bench. Keith then went and signed for *them*. In the seventies and eighties, if we had a decent player they were always sold to Leeds.' Like Mick Jones, Tony Currie and Alex Sabella before him, and Brian Deane a few years after he retired, the free-scoring Edwards ended up at Elland Road. As, indeed, did Wilkinson, whose five years at Sheffield Wednesday brought the Owls a promotion to the First

Division and a top-six position. 'Leeds in the mid-to-late eighties had a lot more going for it as a city,' says Wilkinson, as he brings me a coffee from his cappuccino machine. 'It was becoming a big financial and banking centre. There was a lot more wealth than in Sheffield. I dropped down a division to manage them, but I felt that Leeds had more potential.'

BIG BANG

In times of extreme economic distress, Sheffield United have always had a tendency to offload their best players. Two years before losing to Arsenal in the 1936 FA Cup final, for example, they upset fans by cashing in on leading scorer Jimmy Dunne. In an apologia published in the match programme, an unnamed club spokesman explained that selling their goal machine – to the opulent Gunners, known in the thirties as the 'Bank of England club' – had been a response to the world economic depression. It was also a symptom of that decade's shift in power and wealth from the north to the south. Dunne had made his debut in a 4-0 home win against Arsenal in 1926, a year after the Blades were crowned English champions. During the following decade, as northern towns bore the brunt of the recession, parts of the south enjoyed a mini-boom, experiencing rising living standards and prosperity. As northern teams suffered the effects of high unemployment and reduced gate income, Arsenal emerged as English football's pre-eminent side – thanks to the genius of another Yorkshire export (and miner's son), Herbert Chapman – and London 'upstarts' like Brentford, Chelsea and Charlton began to break into the big time. Chapman's team, boasting an irresistible front line of

Jack Lambert, David Jack and Cliff Bastin, became the first club from the capital to win the title in 1931, finally breaking the stranglehold of the industrial north.

A similar, and even more decisive, power shift began to take place after 1986. 'Big Bang' gave London's globally connected, finance-driven economy a huge boost, accelerating the transition from a manufacturing to a service-based economy and accentuating the north–south divide. As obituaries were being penned to Old York-shire – this was the year its most famous sportsman (Boycott) retired and its most famous broadcaster (Waring) died – a rejuvenated City of London began to disburse capital and credit around the globe. As the stock market was opening up the capital's square mile to interna-tional banks, and the government was hatching a new, far-reaching programme of privatisations, ITV executive Greg Dyke held a secret meeting with the directors of Manchester United, Liverpool, Everton, Tottenham Hotspur and Arsenal. Just as the suspension of controls on mergers and acquisitions would eventually allow banking's big four – Lloyds, NatWest, Barclays and Midland – to subvert the City's old-boy networks, so football's big five aimed to sweep aside the stuffy FA and create a new, deregulated structure based on a super-league of top teams. 'Although what one economist dubbed "Mrs Thatcher's economic experiment" ran a little ahead of the one brewing in football,' noted Dave Russell, 'it set the tone for much of what was to follow in the game.' Six years before the formation of the Premier League – the main item on the agenda at Dyke's meeting – the big five had fired the first shots of their revolution, securing an upward redistribution of resources. Four of the nine places on the Football League's management committee were reallocated to the First Division, which was awarded half the league's income. Two years later, the top-flight clubs agreed to gobble up 75 per cent of the £44 million Dyke paid out as part of ITV's new, live-football deal. The game's monetisation was to about to evolve at a furious speed.

After Big Bang, the British economy became increasingly dependent on the London-based financial-services sector while Sheffield, like Hull, Rotherham, Featherstone, Barnsley, Bradford and many other northern towns and cities, struggled to establish a post-industrial identity. Nineteen eighty-six was a watershed year for the steel city and its two famous football teams. Wilkinson's Wednesday finished sixth in the First Division, the culmination of a meteoric rise under its locally born manager. His board, however, were unwilling to bring in reinforcements and, as his team slid down the table, Wilkinson became restless. In 1988, the year Brealey brought in Dave Bassett to revive his ailing club, Wilkinson left for the greener pastures of Elland Road. Porterfield had steered the Blades from the fourth to the second division, but when Bassett arrived the team were hovering precariously close to the bottom of Division Two. 'There was no money, large debts and the club had lost their connection to the fans,' said Bassett. 'I arrived from the south and Sheffield, by comparison, felt very depressed.'

THE SOCIALIST REPUBLIC

In the first half of the decade, the Socialist Republic of South Yorkshire – viewed by Thatcher, like militant miners and unruly football fans, as a symptom of everything that had gone wrong in post-war, social-democratic Britain – had led the charge against New Britain. Every May Day its left-wing council had hoisted the Red Flag over the town hall. The 'republic' had heavily subsidised public transport, declared its city to be a nuclear-free zone, introduced Peace Studies into schools and, in 1983, became the new headquarters of the NUM. When the prime minister visited the city, it had taken around 1,000 baton-wielding policemen to keep a 5,000-strong protest group at bay. 'The scene had a whiff of 1789 or 1917 about it,' wrote John Cornwell, deputy leader of South Yorkshire County Council and a sometime member of Sheffield City Council. '[There were] shrieking, chanting demonstrators on one side of the road and buses arriving with "toffs" in evening dress looking down on them from their seats in the coaches.'

The steel city had a long tradition of rebelliousness, frequently setting the tone for militant national movements. It supported the early ideals of the French Revolution, was a stronghold of Chartism and has spawned, over the years, many radical MPs. In the early eighties, run by a new generation of idealistic socialists, it stood alongside Liverpool and the Greater London Council in the vanguard of the anti-Tory resistance. There were a couple of memorable early triumphs. In 1980 it had superintended a national steel strike of almost 100,000 workers, which had lasted thirteen weeks and involved the mass picketing of the vast Hadfields East Hecla Works in the Don Valley; the steel union won a 16 per cent pay rise, ten per cent higher than the management offer, for its members. A year later, the threat of strike action by the NUM, whose headquarters had been relocated to the city, forced the coal board to withdraw its pit-closure plan and the government to increase its subsidy to the industry and improve miners' employment terms. The *Sun* ('Surrender!') was not amused.

Sheffield's truculent opposition to Thatcherism was, in part, a hangover from its seventies militancy but also a response to the government's double-pronged attack on its local economy and services. Arguably, the council's commitment to low rents, cheap transport and new jobs – it set up the first-ever local government employment department – helped immunise the city from the violent rioting that broke out in 1981. Its subsidising of bus fares – the city had the cheapest public transport in Europe – and resistance to compulsory competitive tendering – which required leisure facilities to be put out to tender – brought it into direct conflict with an ideologically driven Conservative Party intent on slashing local authority expenditure, forcing councils to sell off its housing stock and eliminating municipal socialism as a political force. It felt, at times, as if the government were fighting a civil war against the city.

The republic's flagship battle was against a rate-capping policy that undermined the principle of the local, collective provision of services. According to its leader, David Blunkett, 'it removed powers of local government which had existed since 1601.' Accused by his critics of a Scargill-esque attempt to bring down the Tories, the future home secretary pointed out that capping would close down old people's homes and special schools for maladjusted children. A big fall in business rates, caused by the collapse of the steel industry, was exacerbated by the government's reduction of the rate support grant, from 53 per cent of council income in 1981 to 26 per cent in 1987. Blunkett became the leader of a national campaign to preserve local services, something councils could only do by pushing up the rates. On 7 March 1985, two days after the miners returned to work, he and his fellow councillors defied the government by deferring the setting of a legal rate. 'There was a "this world's against us" mentality,' said Clive Betts, the council's deputy leader.

The rate-capping campaign was a community response to several years of massive government cuts. This was Sheffield and its people against Thatcher and her government. Well, that's what it felt like. It brought Sheffield against the Establishment down in London. Sheffield had a real sense of identity, a sense of purpose. It was a city which was making a significant contribution to the UK and the world. There was a tradition of very high-skilled jobs and high-quality products and steel and no feeling that was ever going to change. You had this incredible tradition of sons following fathers and grandfathers into the steel industry and going to the same company. You would literally follow on from your father's footsteps. People met their partners there, in offices and shop floors and canteens. Then there were the social clubs built around the steelworks. There were very strong cricket works' leagues and football leagues. Community, family, industrial purpose and sport combined – and then almost got ripped apart by the government in the 1980s.

The month after the deferral vote, in one of the most dramatic meetings in its history – and after the government had threatened councillors with disqualification and individual surcharge – the authority felt it had no choice but to back down. Its decision to set a legal rate, according to the *Sheffield Star*, 'left the [Labour] party's pride and unity in tatters' and followed 'a three-way split in the seemingly impregnable ranks that have controlled the City Council almost without interruption for the past 50 years.' A year later, in the same month as the Bramall Lane car park protest, the county council, shortly to be abolished by the Conservatives, voted to stop subsidising cheap bus fares. The republic was over.

THE STRAIGHT ROAD

The city, like its football teams, has traditionally derived its strength from its powerful steel industry. In the mid-nineteenth century, the three-mile stretch along the River Don, running north-east of the city centre towards Rotherham, had (along with Pittsburgh in the USA) been the most concentrated area of steel production in the world, as illustrated by the two legends imprinted on the nation's cutlery: 'Sheffield Steel' and 'Made in Sheffield'. 'The city made by fire out of water changed the world with its ingenuity in steel production,' wrote Sheffield United historian Gary Armstrong, 'and in doing so produced a proud populace who laboured hard to send the steel around the globe. The same people played hard. The soil and sinews, leather and limbs that combined to make football the only global idiom was a product of the same people.'

Sheffield's emergence as an international centre of steel-making enabled it to lead the way in modern sport. The first cricket matches in Yorkshire were played in 1771 by a Sheffield eleven and, by the 1820s, this city team had become the unofficial county one, producing a series of prodigiously talented bowlers as if on a fast-moving assembly line. According to the great cricket correspondent J. M. Kilburn, Bramall Lane, which had been built in 1862, was a place of 'sharp wit and comment' and universally regarded as the spiritual home of the hardest players in cricket. Asked about his impressions of Niagara Falls during an 1879 tour of North America, batsman Ephraim Lockwood replied: 'Nowt. If this is Niagara, give me Sheffield any day.'

'Foot-ball' was played in the industrialised footholds of the Peak District long before the London-based Football Association was formed in 1863; the first recorded match, a six-a-side game between Sheffield and Norton, had taken place some seventy years earlier. In the late nineteenth century the city remained football's most fertile territory. It was the home of the oldest club in the world, Sheffield FC, who were founded in 1857 and three years later took part in the first-ever local derby, against Hallam FC. Bramall Lane is the world's oldest football ground. 'Sheffield rules', an alternative code to the one used in public schools, was a huge influence on the laws of the modern game. It restricted hacking and handling, allowed forward passes and introduced corner flags, umpires, corners, goal-kicks, throw-ins, crossbars, the half-time change of ends and the drawing of cup ties from a hat. The city was responsible for a number of football firsts: paid player, floodlit match, cup competition, printed fixture list, football columnist, shin pads and Saturday night sports newspaper. 'Playing such a role in [football's] invention and early growth,' wrote Daniel Gray, 'created an ethos among Sheffielders – conscious or otherwise – that what they said mattered, and that their actions could change England . . . More than any other place, Sheffield explains how English football began.' Indeed, association football owes as much to the blasting furnaces of its steelworks as it does to the playing fields of Eton. To begin with, the likes of Rotherham Town, Stoke City and Nottingham Forest preferred to play under Sheffield rather than FA rules. As one club official explained: 'We firmly believe there is a much greater vitality in the cutlery town's society than there is in the so-called national one.' The Sheffield FA held out until 1877, when they finally accepted administrator Charles Alcock's invitation to merge with the London association – in the process, according to Cameron Fleming, 'exchanging their status as northern moguls for that of FA provincial satellite'.

The sense of being part of a pioneering, autonomous and alternative sporting culture clung to both United and Wednesday in the late-Victorian, early-Edwardian era. Between 1896 and 1907 they won four FA Cups and three First Division championships between them. Bramall Lane was home to many legends, from Arthur Wharton, the first black professional player in Britain, to goalkeeper William 'Fatty' Foulke, who led United to a title win in 1899. In the following four years the Blades appeared in three cup finals and were runners-up in the league. Fred Tunstall's winner against Cardiff City in the 1925 FA Cup final brought them their fourth trophy. Their failure to win a major prize since then – Wednesday are perceived to be the more successful of the two clubs but have captured only one trophy in the eighty years since they last won the FA Cup – can be attributed, in part, to the gradual shrivelling of the steel industry. In 1920, it employed 70,000 people – by the early nineties that figure had fallen to under 10,000, with the council becoming the largest employer in the city. Sheffield's de-industrialisation drove the great cutlery factories and the old trades from the city centre, its traditional manufacturing districts sliced wide open by a new motorway and super-tram system. 'The big factories, like Hadfield's, used to employ several thousand people on the same site,' remembered Blunkett. 'People had their social interaction at work. It was part of their life. The community shared both their joys and their sorrows about football. And the boardrooms of their football clubs had their interests at heart.'

Those boardrooms were, on the whole, run by benign industrialists who had devoted their lives to good works. The tone was set by Charles Clegg, a legendary administrator known for the maxim: 'Nobody gets lost on a straight road.' Clegg began his football career as a Wednesday player, helped form United in 1889 and then rose to the position of FA chairman. The first man to be knighted for services to football, he was a strict teetotaller and non-smoker and, as David Conn noted, 'believed it was anathema ever to take a penny from the game. [He] always claimed high moral values for Sheffield Wednesday, the FA and the game of football itself.' Clegg's advocacy of a social bargain between employer and employees was praised in a whimsical, 99-page, 1901 essay by United captain Ernest Needham. After praising the 'great old man of football', Needham pointed out two universal truths: first, that soccer had always provided Shef-fielders with a safety valve for their subversive feelings – and second, that local businesses would always benefit from a healthy, distractedly contented workforce. The city's largest employer, steel magnate Sir Robert Hadfield, wrote a letter in agreement, praising the game for improving his employees' fitness and productivity.

United were, by this time, a limited liability company. Their shares had been bought by modestly wealthy supporters, many of them egalitarian-minded Methodists renowned for possessing a social conscience and opposed to the idea of one person owning a block of shares. Until the Brealey era, in fact, the club had been run by around 400 people, mostly local businessmen and city dignitaries, all committed to the principles of good works and charity. In the 1940s, for example, a silversmith, fruit market wholesaler and builders' merchant sat on the board alongside the Lord Mayor of Sheffield. The personification of this Sunday School Chapel philanthropy was the director George Lawrence who, during the 1930s, funded an annual pre-season day out and dinner for the entire United squad and, with his own money, built a roof over the Kop embankment. During the Great Depression, the club reduced admission prices for the jobless – until the Football League banned the policy. Before the final home game of the 1938–9 season, they hosted a physical training display by the unemployed. 'Those who controlled football [at United],' wrote Armstrong, 'were upright men, moderate in their social life and keen to be seen living on the straight and narrow. They led by example and epitomised the belief that hard work and sobriety brought rewards ... Their financial commitment to the club was primarily one of guaranteeing loans, usually with low interest. Their return was the glory by association of any footballing triumph and the hope that on leaving the board their money would be returned.'

THE REG REVOLUTION

Throughout his decade in charge at Bramall Lane, from becoming finance director in 1980 to selling his shares in 1990, Brealey was an exemplar of the new breed of Thatcherite entrepreneur. A financial contributor to the Conservative Party, he perfectly encapsulated the values of New Britain. The Iron Lady's revolution, he insisted, had created a freer, more informal economy, allowing him to turn the Blades into a profitable business. He was the first outsider to take control at Bramall Lane, being born and bred in Lincolnshire and a past member of the Lincoln City board. This was not the only way in which he was a departure from a local and paternalistic tradition that had shaped the club for almost a century. A driven, ambitious, internationally connected wheeler-dealer, as well as being a member of the General Synod of the Church of England, he owned a heli-copter and a Rolls-Royce and had made his vast fortune – he initially put £2.5 million, then a huge investment, into United – from a chain of hotels in London and the Mediterranean and his construction company. 'He had his finger on the pulse of Thatcherite Britain,' wrote Armstrong. 'His wealth impressed the generally working-class supporters of Sheffield United. He wasn't one of us. Perhaps God had sent him to sprinkle moon-dust on the then grimy, low-income, ugly industrial city that was Sheffield.'

Brealey's first commercial venture, inspired by Scholar's flotation of Tottenham Hotspur, was an attempt to recapitalise the club by launching a share issue. 'He was a proponent of the New Right philosophy of wider public share ownership,' explained Armstrong. 'To this end he wanted supporters to purchase most of the shares. But £500 per five new shares was a lot of money in 1981 in a city still trying to recover from the steelworkers' strike the year before and which had no great history of shareholding or, indeed, Thatcherite monetary policies. The take-up was far short of what he anticipated.' Undeterred by this failure, he then came up with his Big Idea: redeveloping Bramall Lane into the Bramall Centre, which he claimed would transform Sheffield into the sporting capital of the north. The futuristic complex, incorporating a shopping mall, wine bar, sports club, eight-lane running track, conference centre, hotel and car park, would fund a new, all-seater Kop and provide a secure financial base for the future. A multi-purpose sports stadium, capable of hosting international events, it would promote the name of the city around the world, just as Sheffield's cutlery had once done. The council, however, spurned the plan – despite Brealey upping his offer for the site from £5 million to £20 million – citing the adverse impact it would have on town-centre trade. 'He mistook a football club for a redevelopment site,' argued Blunkett. 'That is not unknown in the commercial world, but it was not something we had to take account of.'

United fans saw this rejection, according to Armstrong, 'as The Tory capitalist not being allowed to develop facilities for which the renowned socialist council had their own plans'. Brealey attacked the authority for leading him 'along the path into their political arena for slaughter. In the light of this, the government should remove all authority from this council in the interests of the community. Their misadministration is unbelievable . . . they are nothing but a bunch of cheaps'. Blunkett responded by pointing out that the local community had hated the idea of an intrusive hotel, with its noise and traffic, on its doorstep and denounced Brealey's cavalier approach to business dealings. 'Many United-ites didn't trust Brealey and what he was up to,' said Betts. 'I think they thought he was using the club for particular ends. This plan to redevelop the ground was, quite frankly, a nonsense. He hadn't consulted the local community. He was going to put an athletics track in without consulting local athletics organisations. It just didn't stack up. It was a pie in the sky adventure.'

According to Blunkett, Brealey's approach was indicative of a new economic philosophy. 'It's inevitable that if people's lives are so heavily bound up with something that matters to them,' he said, 'and the game itself is coming into being as a business – as we see now an international business – in the very early stages, in the foothills if you like, it was inevitable that football itself would be infiltrated, and affected, by that philosophy. And Reg Brealey was merely an early expression of it. He was probably one of the early pioneers. Since then, globalisation has accelerated and just about everything moving is owned by somebody from outside Britain, whether it's water, electricity, high-speed trains or whatever, even nuclear power stations owned by China. It was almost an inevitability that football would go the same way.' The council's anti-Brealey stance was not based on ideology alone. Blunkett, Betts and many of their colleagues were passionate Wednesday fans. 'Despite the different football allegiances we had good working relations with people at United,' insisted Betts. 'But not Brealey. He never even spoke to us. We had several discussions about United moving to a new stadium. In principle they were up for looking at that. But Brealey vetoed it. For all this entrepreneurial vision he had, when he was offered a new stadium, at Don Valley, which was a reasonable area to develop and commercially viable, he – and Wednesday – turned it down.'

Undeterred, Brealey pressed ahead with yet more marketing innovations. Commercial insignia appeared on the players' shorts a few months after the first £1,000-a-week footballer had appeared on the club's books. Innovatory fund-raising schemes were introduced and he attempted to rebrand United as 'The Friendly Club'. In a 1982 interview with the *Sheffield Star* he explained: 'There is the recession, unemployment and the associated social problems. We see football as a great safety valve, and making our club the friendly club is I feel a contribution we can make.' He pursued new markets in the Middle East – unheard of at the time – launching one of the first attempts to gain a commercial foothold in Asia. After he struck a deal with Simonds Cutting Tools, who had an office in China, United were invited to tour the world's most populous country. In one of the matches, broadcast live on television, the team displayed the company's name on their shirts in both English and Mandarin. 'In truth,' Armstrong pointed out, 'such football-related diplomacy was probably more important for Brealey's business world than for United.'

In 1986, however, the Reg revolution hit the buffers. Porterfield's team had stalled and the crowds had plummeted; in the 1986–7 season United recorded their lowest-ever attendance of 9,992. Following the repeated failure to win approval for his stadium plans there had been further conflict with the council over the financing of the police's match-day services. The plateauing of Porterfield's ageing side, rammed home by the humiliating 5-2 home defeat to Norwich, was the final straw. It provoked not only the departure of a promising young manager but also Brealey's last, do-or-die attempt to remake his club in the image of New Britain. Like his heroine, who was about to win a third term and pursue an even more radical programme of deregulation, Brealey decided to reboot his revolution. The 'Blades' revival lottery scheme', which offered cash and other prizes and would raise money to buy players, was given an expensive, glitzy launch at the Roxy. A crowd of 3,500 packed inside the town-centre nightclub to hear him describe, in quasi-religious terms, 'a revival of faith, hope and courage' and a 'new spirit' at the club.

Four years later the scheme, like Thatcher's reign itself, was dead in the water and Brealey was under investigation by the stock exchange and Crown Prosecution Service for insider dealing in the Ganges Delta (although the case against him subsequently collapsed and he was acquitted). Exhausted, battered and beleaguered, he sold up. 'I guess you could draw parallels with the dominant political ideology of the time', noted Paul Blomfield, who led a fans' campaign to remove United's one-time messiah and is now a Labour MP.

Some people might see him as a bit of an asset stripper. He was certainly seeking to make money out of football. He had one big development plan which he tried to bulldoze through against community opposition. The council backed the community.

When the council resisted and supported the community, Reg took the view that it's just bloody politicians and Wednesday fans. We had a whole season where we had this scar in the ground. It seemed to typify his failure to deliver.

For Steve Hodkinson, another anti-Brealey campaigner, the Reg Revolution signalled a shift in the football club 'from a paternalistic environment to a business environment. He was like many brash businesspeople in the age of Thatcher. He knew what he wanted to achieve and the market allowed him to do that. It was an "I can more or less do anything and never mind the rules" attitude. The disconnect is that the fans wanted money put into the players and the stadium, not into the club as a corporate body.'

THE LAST OF THE OLD BREED

As Brealey was trying to swat away those pesky Wednesdayite lefties, another battle had been raging across the city. During the miners' strike, Wilkinson had frequently spoken up in support of the coal industry's embattled communities. He had built his Wednesday side on a tidal wave of Old Yorkshire defiance, harnessing a powerful, and at times, negative energy for the collective good. 'The chairman gave me a very serious talking to for some of the things I was saying in public,' he recalled. 'It was all pro-miner stuff. I got in trouble over Orgreave. I got a phone call from the chairman, Bert McGee. It took him a long time to get round to it but he didn't think I should be making political references in some of the things I was saying and writing. But I'm a Sheffield lad. I'd come back to Sheffield to manage a Sheffield club. We'd got a lot of fans from around the area and a lot of them were miners. So I didn't stop what I was saying.'

Wilkinson, a miner's son and former Wednesday player, saw how the strike had left deep wounds on the city's psyche. His team's style of play – fast, furious and fearless – spoke to Sheffielders' sense of themselves as the forgotten, the wronged. 'My dad worked at Nunnery Colliery,' he said, 'two tram rides away from our house. They closed that and then he moved out to Treaton and then Orgreave, the scene of Mrs Thatcher's greatest hour, bless her. One of the good things about the time was the sense of community, particularly in South Yorkshire and the mining areas and villages and the mining people. It seems to me that politics is more than just about making good, sound business decisions. It's also about the values that you want to see represented and, to me, to take away what the miners had and not replace it with anything – that was the crime. Not whether they should close them or not. If they do decide to close them at least have a plan B that allows what's happening to continue to happen. In so many ways you paid for that. You paid for putting an axe through what is a very strong culture of community and joint responsibility. And no more so than in mining. My dad had worked before they were privatised and that culture was even stronger then. There was a great sense of community, of neighbourliness.'

Wilkinson wanted his players to appreciate the hardships and perils, and display the courage, honesty and togetherness, of working underground. 'If you worked in a team and you were a shirker who kept having days off, no chance,' he said,

because you were letting the team down. Down there it was death. So if you had someone who didn't act with a sense of responsibility, who didn't care about what he was doing, who wasn't aware of his responsibilities to the rest of them, it could be fatal. That was where it really mattered. Because I'd been brought up with that and I'd listened to my dad talk, there was a strong sense in the pit of responsibility and letting people down. Team implies teamwork, working together, common goals, common objectives, agreed ways of doing things. You can have all of those things, a sense of direction, but at the heart of that there's got to be trust. And trust is about values. You can be the best coach and tactician, but if you do not have those strong beliefs and values, it's difficult to get that trust. Look to your right, look to your left, look across the dressing room: if you ask yourself, 'Can I trust him?' and the answer's yes, we're on our way. It's possibly more difficult to get that trust nowadays.

Stamped from the presses of Sheffield's fast-fading industrial past, the Wednesday team Wilkinson led to a top-flight promotion, five FA Cup quarter-finals and a semi-final side combined the gritty, egalitarian tradition of their steel heritage with the meticulous planning of a fiercely ambitious disciplinarian. When he arrived in 1983, the team having just been promoted to Division Two after five seasons in the third tier, the former PE teacher introduced long cross-country runs in the north Sheffield hills and arduous, military-style drills to improve fitness and discipline. On his first day in charge he lived up to his nickname of Sergeant Wilko – a play on the name of the TV character Sergeant Bilko – by locking the gates of the training ground, only letting his charges out, on their hands and knees, at dusk. 'Not true,' he protested, 'it was a week later.' He pinned up posters in the dressing room urging players to 'Think Positive' and fined those who forgot his designated phrase of the week. Another of his notices declared: 'It's Amazing What Can Be Achieved If No-One Minds Who Takes The Credit'. He took the whole squad to a factory – 'I told them that these are the people who turn up Saturdays' – and insisted on an innovative pre-match ritual where 'we held hands in a circle that was meant to mark our coming together as a clan. It was a symbolic act to show that we were going out as a team'. The team spirit, midfielder Gary Shelton would later point out, 'wasn't just for each other but for the supporters as well. We all knew how they felt and we wanted to celebrate not just among ourselves but with them. When times were hard and we needed their support, they were there – they kept us going.'

The Sergeant's long-ball, percentage-football approach was not always pleasing on the eye but, in his five years at the club, Wilkinson built a winning team on low resources. Before the new football order began to be shaped by mega-wealth, they were Old Yorkshire's beacon team, viewing success as a function of will and spirit, an anti-money tale of shrewd scouting, discarded players out to prove themselves and close-knit togetherness. 'I've been wrong about Howard Wilkinson,' admitted the *Sun*'s John Sadler in a mid-eighties column about Wednesday's unfashionable, generally unloved, upstarts. 'He's produced a team of highly-disciplined players adopting a direct style of football ideally suited to capturing the identity of a hard-working area in which 15 per cent can't find work at all.' In the 1984 documentary *Steel City Blues*, commemorating the Owls' promotion back to the First Division after a fourteen-year absence – in Wilkinson's first year in charge – the manager argued that 'football has to be responsible to the spectators because it exists for the spectators. It can't exist without them.' Referring to a rare defeat at Southampton he said the home crowd had understood 'that we got beat but we didn't surrender.' When Wilkinson played for Wednesday in the sixties, explained the documentary's narrator, 'both club and city were riding high. There was First Division football and full skilled employment. But both were on the threshold of a decline. [Today] there must be one out of five out of work.'

Wilkinson brought confidence back to a club which, since winning the 1935 FA Cup, and enjoying a few years of success in the early-to-mid sixties, had faded to the point of obscurity. In just a few years, he transformed the team. Wednesday's meteoric rise had made them profitable, frequently posting surpluses. According to a board minute from March 1985, they showed a credit balance of £689,000. And yet their chairman Bert McGee repeatedly rejected the manager's request to bring in new players. In *Steel City Blues*, Wilkinson had said: 'I came here to win the European Cup.' McGee had appeared to back his manager's ambition, at least verbally. '[The crowd] yearn for a winner,' the chairman declared in the documentary. 'I've sat here on a Saturday afternoon and tried to suck a goal between the goalposts . . . wanting this club to be restored to its former glory. It's been a long time, too long in my opinion, but we're going now. We're going now.' Behind the scenes, however, Wilkinson's argument that a team of triers would ultimately fail to trouble an increasingly affluent elite, had fallen on deaf ears. After steering Wednesday to fifth, their highest league position for twenty-five years – and which, but for the Heysel disaster, would have seen them qualify for Europe – they drifted into mid-table mediocrity. Forced to sell good players, and with the board's low-wage policy prohibiting the recruitment of top-class replacements, they finished thirteenth and, the following season, eleventh. Good organisation and high levels of fitness and commitment, argued Wilkinson, would only get you so far. 'To stay ahead of other teams,' he said, 'you have either got to invent new tactics or produce or bring in better players.' After failing in his final attempt to persuade McGee to bring in reinforcements, he reluctantly jumped ship.

At Elland Road, he immediately enjoyed the benefits of a more expansive financial approach. The city of Leeds had taken a big hit during the early-eighties recession and its cash-strapped football team had been forced to sell their stadium to the council for £2.5 million. However, as well as aggrandising the City of London, Big Bang had triggered Leeds' growth as a financial services centre. It had quickly become a mecca of shopping, confirmed by the opening of Harvey Nichols' first store outside the capital in a city centre now offering consumerist affluence to rival London's. Within four years of his arrival, Wilkinson's new club were crowned First Division champions. In his autobiography he pointed out the contrast in economic fortunes between the two rival cities and argued that

if things had gone differently . . . what was happening at Leeds might have happened with Sheffield Wednesday. Even given my genuine grievances, the day I finally departed Hillsborough was heart-breaking for me. I spent five minutes talking to the office staff and secretary before I was close to breaking down and realised I must head for the dressing room. I then met the players and conveyed to them that life must go on and they would succeed without me. Towards the end of that meeting the emotions welling up inside me forced me to walk out and

I rushed to the bootroom as a bolthole. I grabbed a large blue towel and sobbed into it for ten minutes. I remember bitterly saying: 'If it wasn't for those bastards in the boardroom I'd still be here.'

As every pub quizmaster knows, Wilkinson was the last English manager to win the top-flight title. Leeds had spent most of the eighties mired in mind-numbing mediocrity but the Sergeant, once again, managed to drill discipline into a lacklustre squad, steering them to promotion as Second Division champions. This time, however, he was given the money to 'move to the next level', as he put it, signing top-class players like Gordon Strachan, Gary McAllister, Rod Wallace, Tony Dorigo and, of course, the mercurial Éric Cantona. His failure to court publicity and play the media game eventually, in a new age of spin, did for him. And yet, at both Hillsborough and Elland Road, he had been ahead of his time. His bluff Yorkshireman persona concealed a deep thinker opposed to the myopia of English football's pell-mell culture. At Leeds, he introduced foreign-style dietary habits, a visionary ten-year plan and a new emphasis on nurturing young, homegrown players; his state-of-the-art academy ended up producing three generations of talented youngsters. But, four years after winning the title, and despite having just guided the Whites to a League Cup final, he was sacked.

As the Premier League morphed into a global monster, Wilkinson was written off as yesterday's man, out of step with the post-Hillsborough era. Foreign-owned clubs began to bring in foreign managers and English bosses in the Sergeant Wilko mould went out of fashion.

Wilkinson's legacy at Leeds was squandered by a notoriously

spendthrift board who borrowed £82 million against future gate receipts in a wild gamble to restore the club's past glories. Although they reached the Champions League semi-final in 2001, the Whites' failure to re-qualify for the competition set in motion a series of fire sales, financial meltdowns, administrations and points deductions which condemned them to an ignominious free fall down the divisions. 'If Leeds had stuck with Howard I am convinced they wouldn't have become so reckless and debt-ridden,' said Leslie Silver, who resigned as chairman a few months after Wilkinson's departure. 'They had so many young players coming through. There was no need to buy so many expensive players on such high wages. Howard was building things up steadily, but his long-term work was undermined, after he left, by an irresponsible approach. Howard was an innovator but he was also down-to-earth and didn't tolerate fools – and his Leeds side reflected that ethos. He was, sadly, the last of a kind.'

8

The Jewel in the Crown

'Hillsborough, a stain on British history like no other, can only be fully understood as part of the Thatcher era that gave rise to it . . . Hillsborough was never simply a football disaster; it is the tragedy of this country in the 1980s. An entire class of people abandoned by those in power.'

Adrian Tempany, a Hillsborough survivor
and author of *And the Sun Shines Now*, 2016

THE SEMI-FINALS

12 April, 1987. Hillsborough. FA Cup semi-final. Coventry City beat Leeds United 3-2. Despite Leeds having the larger support of the two teams, the South Yorkshire Police insist their fans are housed in the smaller Leppings Lane end, behind the goal where away fans are traditionally located for Wednesday games. Serious overcrowding leads to a crush with many Leeds fans only able to escape by being pulled up from the terrace to the upper stand. The kick-off is delayed by fifteen minutes.

9 April, 1988. Hillsborough. FA Cup semi-final. Liverpool beat Nottingham Forest 2-1. Again, it is Liverpool fans, despite having the bigger support, who are allocated the Leppings Lane end, with Nottingham Forest fans given the larger-capacity end. Hundreds of Liverpool fans miss John Aldridge's winning goal following a crush in pens three and four behind the goal.

15 April, 1989. Hillsborough. FA Cup semi-final. Liverpool vs Nottingham Forest. More than 24,000 Liverpool fans travel to Sheffield for the tie. In the period before kick-off, as a large crowd builds outside the turnstiles at the Leppings Lane end, an order is given to open an exit gate to relieve turnstile pressure. In the five minutes gate C was open, around 2,000 Liverpool fans enter the stadium. A 'significant proportion' head via a tunnel to the terraces behind the goal, entering 'relatively full' central pens that are fenced on all sides. There is a severe crush. After the police signal to referee Ray Lewis that fans are spilling onto the pitch, he calls a halt to the match. Ninety-six men, women and children die as a result of the crush.

Anthony Garratty was a steward at all three semi-finals. A lifelong Sheffield Wednesday fan, he only started going to their stadium again in 2015 after giving evidence at the Hillsborough inquests. While describing the aftermath of the crush in court he broke down. 'I hadn't been back to the ground for years,' he explains, speaking a few months later in his village local. After 'doing my little bit' at the inquests he was visited in his hotel room by Trevor Hicks, whose two teenage daughters, Sarah and Vicki, had died in the disaster. Hicks thanked Garratty for trying to revive Vicki and introduced him to other bereaved family members, who told him how much they appreciated his efforts. 'They suggested I get on with my life,' he recalls. 'For years and years I worried that people would hate me for letting their sons and daughters die. Then when I met the Hillsborough families they were absolutely amazing. They said they were still Liverpool fans and that I should still be a Wednesday fan. I helped about seventeen or eighteen people that day.' Liverpool supporters had begun arriving from midday, entering the Leppings Lane end through a small number of turnstiles. After the police ordered a large exit gate to be opened to alleviate the congestion outside, more than 2,000 of them made their way to the central pens, almost double the number regarded as a safe capacity. This caused severe crushing and, six minutes in, the game was abandoned. Garratty 'ran around like an ant', using advertising hoardings as makeshift stretchers to carry bodies to the gymnasium, which was being used as a mortuary. 'The last one I helped was this young lad,' he says.

I was fit as a fiddle because I worked on the bins. I picked him up in my arms and carried him over. It's a long way from the Leppings Lane end to the gymnasium. All the time I was talking to him. I remember he had fairly biggish ears. I kept nipping his ear and touching his face to see if I could get some response. But he never responded. I took him into the gymnasium and passed him on to the St John's Ambulance people. A doctor said he thought he was dead. He reminded me of my brother. He was right skinny, light as a feather. I couldn't leave him on his own.

Garratty can't remember anything that happened during the following two weeks. 'My mind is blank when it comes to that fortnight. Apparently I had been walking around like a zombie. I had always thought the police spoke to me the day after the disaster, but I'm told they actually came for my statement two weeks after.' The next time he saw that statement – twenty-six years later, just before he appeared at the inquests – he noticed that large parts of it were missing.

THE SHOW MUST GO ON

'It is so sad,' reflected *Sheffield Star* sportswriter Paul Thompson two days after Britain's worst-ever sporting disaster, 'that one of football's old clubs, run by decent men, is now synonymous not with sport, but with death on a grand scale. That is why the club and its followers can barely comprehend what has happened to them.' The Wednesday manager at the time, Ron Atkinson, put it more bluntly (and offensively): the club, he declared, had 'suffered enough'. Eighteen months later, writing in a match programme ahead of the re-opening of Leppings Lane as an £800,000 all-seater stand,

Wednesday safety officer Graham Mackrell insisted that it was now time to move on. 'The empty terrace has been a constant reminder of the tragedy,' he said, 'and although it will never be forgotten we do need to press on. That is not a callous remark.' To the bereaved families it certainly appeared so.

It took the club twenty-one years to put up a memorial to the ninety-six supporters who perished at their ground. 'There was a denial when it came to accepting their responsibility,' said *Just Another Wednesday* fanzine editor Dan Gordon. 'What surprises me about being in Sheffield and being a Wednesday fan, knowing what type of city Sheffield is and how brutalised by the police and the Thatcher government Sheffield was in the eighties, with the steel strike and the miners' strike, is that many football fans in the city still thought: "Actually the police were right and it was the Liverpool fans."' After 267 days of evidence, the jury at the inquests concluded that none of the Liverpool supporters had been responsible for the tragedy.

Wednesday's negligent approach to safety, however, was singled out for criticism: Hillsborough's safety certificate had been unchanged since 1979. Despite the introduction of radial fences to create pens in the Leppings Lane standing area, the club had overestimated the capacity of that area; the fences had made them unsafe and the club's plans to build more turnstiles, which would have allowed the number of fans entering the area to be monitored, had been dropped due to cost.

Much of this was not new. The interim Taylor Report, published in the aftermath of the disaster, had described Leppings Lane as 'unsatisfactory and ill-suited to admit the numbers invited'. Richard Chester, their secretary between January 1984 and October 1986, told the inquests he had been aware that breaching the safety certificate's conditions was a matter of potential criminal liability. And yet Wednesday had refused to accept any responsibility for the tragedy. Atkinson's attempt to portray the club as victims reinforced a shameful narrative, encouraged by policemen, politicians and newspaper editors, which blamed 'drunk' and 'misbehaving' Liverpool fans for the crush. 'I didn't see any who were drunk,' said Garratty. There had been, he recalled, several previous close shaves at the stadium. 'My father-in-law once had to stand in three foot of pee during a crush. The club were complacent. They'd had crushes and nowt had ever happened. I think they thought they were infallible, that it was never going to happen. There was a lack of safety.'

A TRAGEDY WAITING TO HAPPEN

As in Bradford, the demise of Sheffield's staple industry had created a vacuum that the city tried to fill with mass entertainment. Or, to quote one of the steelworkers-turned-strippers in *The Full Monty*, by 'putting on a show'. Hosting one of football's biggest 'shows', the FA Cup semi-final, guaranteed a high profile, not to mention huge gate receipts, for its historic stadium. 'To me, and lots of football fans, the semi at Hillsborough was the biggest match in England,' said Garratty. The Cup meant a great deal more in the seventies and eighties than it does today. This was due to a series of thrilling upsets – this being an era when Second Division sides like Sunderland, Southampton and West Ham, and unfancied teams like Coventry City and Wimbledon, defeated more illustrious opponents to win the trophy – and the fact that, until 1983, apart from the England vs Scotland internationals, a few European club matches and the World

Cup, the FA Cup final and the competition's last-four showpieces were the only live football games shown on television.

Thanks to Wednesday's general secretary Eric Taylor, Hillsborough had established itself almost as an annual venue in the sixties. But in 1981 it was dropped by the FA. During the Tottenham Hotspur vs Wolves semi-final, disaster was only narrowly averted as a Leppings Lane crush forced a large number of Spurs fans onto the pitch. Before the match started there had been chaos outside the ground as they tried to get through a limited number of turnstiles. Luckily, once inside, there had been no perimeter fences to hem the supporters in; a gate at the front of the open terrace had been quickly opened to relieve the pressure and over 200 people managed to escape on to the perimeter track. Thirty-eight of them, however, were injured, with some requiring medical treatment for broken arms and legs. After the game, a policeman told Wednesday chairman Bert McGee it was just a matter of luck that no fans had died and suggested safety precautions should have been taken. 'Bollocks,' replied McGee. 'No-one would have been killed.' McGee even managed to turn the criticism around, attacking police officers for allowing Spurs supporters to spend the remainder of the match sitting on the track against the perimeter fence wall. According to the minutes of a post-match meeting, he claimed this action had been 'completely unnecessary and made the ground look "untidy".'

It would be another six years before the club was allowed to put on another semi-final show.

McGee's claim that the indecorous sight of Spurs' goal-line fans had put off the TV companies was simply wrong: it was the crush itself that had kept the cameras away. Despite this, when Coventry and

Leeds contested the 1987 semi-final at the ground, the chairman appeared not to have learned any lessons. The police's warnings that capacity had become too high were not heeded. The board, once again, prioritised crowd control over crowd safety. They had already rejected, as too costly, a £130,000 scheme to monitor the safe influx of supporters into Leppings Lane – despite receiving grants of over £1 million for ground improvements. And, despite Popper's report on the Bradford fire underlining the dangers of draconian perimeter fencing, blue-painted metal fences had been installed, along with crush barriers, segregating the terrace into separate pens. Incredibly, despite the fifteen-minute delay to the game, the post-match police debrief failed to mention any overcrowding or crushing. Ted Heaton, a Leeds fan who sat in the Leppings Lane upper stand, described how 'about fifteen minutes before kick-off we could see that the centre section of the standing area below us was extremely full. It's easy with hindsight but we didn't realise just how bad it could become. Lads were turning and looking up to us. A lot were being squashed and unable to enter the rest of the stand below. We started pulling fans up into the seats and out of the crush for a good while. My memory isn't exact but we were still helping people out of the standing area after kick-off.' Another Leeds supporter, John Murtagh, remembered a man next to him fainting and being lifted to safety. 'I believed then and I still hold this opinion,' he said, 'that the police wanted us like that: fenced in and too packed to cause any trouble. To me it seemed like their idea of effective crowd control.'

In 1988, some Liverpool fans suffered broken ribs and fractured limbs in a crush. After watching his team beat Nottingham Forest 2-1 in the following year's semi-final, a Liverpool fan wrote a letter of complaint to Peter Robinson, the Reds' chief executive, protesting 'in the strongest possible terms at the disgraceful overcrowding that was allowed to occur in the Leppings Lane terrace area . . . the whole area was packed solid to the point where it was impossible to move and where I, and others around me, felt considerable concern for my personal safety.' Robinson then wrote to FA general secretary Graham Kelly suggesting that the tie be moved to Old Trafford, a stadium more appropriate for a following of Liverpool's size. Another Liverpool fan outlined to the FA his experience of congestion, which had begun in the tunnel feeding the central pens. Once out of the tunnel, he explained, 'if anything the situation became worse and the pressure behind became worse, causing many fans to stumble and fall down the steps only to disappear under the crowd.' A third fan wrote to the governing body, warning them that Leppings Lane 'will always be a death trap'. The FA's safety consultant Ken Evans, however, bizarrely decided that 'the tie [had gone] well' and made no mention of the crushing in his report. This led the governing body's chief executive, Graham Kelly, to conclude that 'the identical 1989 tie was not regarded as a problem match.'

THE WEMBLEY OF THE NORTH

During the late eighties, Hillsborough was still being marketed as the 'Wembley of the north'. Never mind that it had become an antique and ill-designed public facility, its chequered safety history rendered it unfit to stage a mass event. It was, after all, the only football ground, apart from the London stadium itself, to be mentioned in Nikolaus Pevsner's magisterial, post-war inventory *The Buildings of England* and was deemed by Simon Inglis, in his seminal *Football*

Grounds of Britain, to be the perfect sports venue. In the sixties, however, thanks to Eric Taylor, it was elevated to an even higher plane. The club's general secretary, known locally as 'Mr Sheffield Wednesday', had designed a new, 10,000-seater, cantilevered stand that was entirely in keeping with the city's other visionary super-structures. Like Sheffield's post-war modernist housing estates, it was designed by local engineers and constructed with local materials. Park Hill, an expanse of blocks built into the city's up-and-down topography, was praised by international architects for its pioneering 'streets in the sky', taking its place in a radically transformed skyline alongside other futuristic icons: Hyde Park, Broomhall, Kelvin Flats, Gleadless Valley and the Miesian university. This brutalist beacon was a rejoinder to all those cultural tourists who, ever since Sheffield's industrialisation, had recoiled from the city's muck, mess and squalor. In *The Road to Wigan Pier* Orwell had called Sheffield 'the ugliest town in the Old World'.

In the sixties, the city was still dependent on mining, iron and steel. But, as its marketing department put it, it was 'on the move'. Its town centre might have been pounded by German bombers but its civic leaders were determined to build a New Jerusalem from the rubble. 'The task in hand was to build a better Britain,' noted the writer Hugh Pearman, 'and state funds, from Labour and Tory governments alike, were made available to do so.' 'Of all the northern cities,' wrote the architectural critic Owen Hatherley, 'Sheffield went furthest towards becoming some sort of viable modern city . . . using its topography – this is a city practically built into the Peak district – as an advantage.'

Like many of Sheffield's planners and architects, Taylor was the product of post-war upward mobility; in his forty-five years at Wednesday, he had risen from office boy to secretary, then to manager and finally to general manager. His ascent had taken place during an era when Britain had risked bold architectural and civic experiments to remake towns and cities fractured by bombing and shortages. He saw himself as football's answer to the Sheffield-born modernist Alison Smithson and all the unsung idealistic architects who, from the forties to the seventies, had worked in the public sector. With her husband Peter, Smithson had been in the vanguard of a social architecture movement often convoked with the era's angry, young, northern realist writers.

The modernists' soaring monuments to civic optimism were venerated in books such as *Sheffield: Emerging City*, *Ten Years Of Housing in Sheffield* and even the Shell Guide. Such self-mythologising peaked with the council's 1970 marketing film, predictably entitled *Sheffield: City on the Move*. Famously mocked, two-and-a-half decades later, during the opening titles of *The Full Monty*, the promotional short showcased Sheffield's dynamic football scene and myriad landscapes of outstanding natural beauty. As the council officer who commissioned it explained, 'we have the cleanest atmosphere of any industrial city in Europe. [Visitors] might be surprised at the extent and variety of the city's parks, at the housing developments, and progress in slum clearance.' Writing about Taylor's conspicuously grand North Stand, opened in 1962 by FIFA president Sir Stanley Rous, Inglis rhapsodised: 'There is not a misplaced line in this remarkable stand. From any angle [it] is quite breathtaking. It is like an architect's model of the dream stand of the future, a space age stand.' 'People were sure it would be a white elephant,' recalled Derek Dooley, a legend at both Sheffield clubs. 'But the World Cup came to Hillsborough in 1966 and after that we got the cup semi-final every other year. Eric knew how to sell Wednesday to the public.'

He also knew how to sell the 'Wembley of the north', as he called it, to the FA. A shrewd administrator, and a mover and shaker in national football circles, Taylor believed that hosting regular semi-finals would boost Sheffield's reputation as a vibrant, progressive city. Hillsborough, which had first opened in 1899, had always been an architectural treasure and used for big games, but in the sixties he did more than anyone to transform it into a national institution. Out of all his achievements, on and off the pitch, this became his greatest legacy. He travelled widely abroad, visiting stadiums that prioritised spectator comfort, and came back from a trip to the 1962 Chile World Cup determined to secure Hillsborough as a venue for the upcoming, home-based global extravaganza. The increased seating from the North Stand brought in greater revenue and, after hosting three group games at the 1966 World Cup, the club received funding from the FA for further ground improvements, which led to Leppings Lane being redeveloped. Taylor was a great innovator. He used a mascot, Ozzie Owl, to market merchandise to the fans, lured Pelé's Santos and other foreign teams from central Europe and Russia to the ground, built a revenue-generating gym and South Stand restaurant and initiated countless other money-making schemes. Under his management, Hillsborough increased its capacity to 55,000 and became one of the first stadiums to install floodlights. There was a big difference, however, between his civic-minded approach to modernisation and the monetised version that emerged in the eighties. In describing the stadium's metamorphosis into a national icon, he preferred the language of identity, pride and prestige to that of revenue streams, brand loyalty and stakeholders. According to local legend, he even turned down a lucrative offer to develop the new, North American Soccer League so that he could finish painting his house in the club's traditional colours of blue and white.

Taylor saw Hillsborough as a symbol of civic grandeur rather than a booming sector of the corporatised entertainment industry or a remorseless, money-making machine. While unambiguously embracing the future, his revamped stadium was a continuation of the paternalistic tradition – common to both Sheffield clubs – that had shaped Wednesday since Clegg willed the club into existence back in 1867. He was appointed office boy in 1929 when Clegg was still chairman and immediately took his mentor's 'straight road' maxim to heart. Taylor regarded all his staff, playing and non-playing, as part of a giant family. 'He was part of my boyhood,' wrote Hattersley. 'In the early 1940s, I would see him most days as he cycled off from home in the morning, doubling up his job at Hillsborough with essential war work in the steel industry . . . In 1966, my father was too far back in the queue to get us Cup Final tickets. Then, at Eric Taylor's suggestion, the box-office "found" two, still waiting to be sold.' More importantly, wrote Hattersley, Mr Sheffield Wednesday ensured 'that Hillsborough hosted a semi-final almost every year.'

This reverence was not shared by Harry Catterick, the club's manager. In his autobiography, Catterick complained that his early-sixties Wednesday team had been held back by Taylor's obsession with ground improvements. '[He] had very strict rules that no-one should train on his beloved Hillsborough pitch,' wrote Catterick, who in successive seasons led the Owls to a Division Two title and runners-up in Division One.

So the arrangements were as follows: the local greyhound stadium had a good playing area inside the dog track which was ideal for training purposes. The players changed at Hillsborough and proceeded to the greyhound stadium . . . I stormed back to Hillsborough and confronted Eric Taylor. Eric's cool, calm exterior was certainly ruffled but his only comment was 'That's your problem' . . . The ambitions of Mr Taylor and I just did not mix. Mr Taylor's number one aim was the improvement of Hillsborough as a soccer stadium. My number one aim was the improvement of the team. It was as simple as that.

Taylor prevailed and, after a dispute about a new contract, Catterick left for Everton, getting his revenge in the 1966 FA Cup final when the Merseysiders came back from two goals down to beat his former club. Catterick's huge budget at Everton, a club known at the time as the 'millionaire set', enabled him to not only win the cup but also two First Division championships.

PUTTING ON A SHOW

According to some estimates, a sixth of Sheffield's workforce lost their jobs when the steel industry collapsed. At the end of the eighties, unemployment in the Sheffield Central constituency, which contains Bramall Lane, reached 18.4 per cent, the highest level of joblessness in Yorkshire. The seemingly unending social misery had taken its toll long before the bus fare and rate-capping defeats had forced a retreat from the battle-weary republic and the adoption of a more pragmatic strategy of public–private partnerships. In the first half of the decade, there had been hardly any retail, commercial or industrial development in the city. To lure new investors, the council was advised to emphasise Sheffield's potential for cultural regeneration and its unique location on the doorstep of the Peak District. According to Cornwell, a chief officer warned them 'that the name Socialist Republic was not the best slogan with which to attract new investment'. If they failed to shed their uncompromisingly militant image, the adviser continued, they would remain stuck in a time warp, increasingly isolated from New Britain's booming enterprise economy.

After their 'surrender' to the government, and a few self-indulgent months licking their wounds, the council underwent something of a sea change in their thinking. In seeking to adapt to the changing economic climate, and stop the city being cut adrift from the rest of the country, they ditched their 'us against Thatcher' rhetoric, replaced their old-style officers with professional planners and cast around for a new vision to revive the local economy. They didn't have to look very far. For a creative revolution had already been taking place on their doorstep. Despite severe social problems, including mass joblessness, sink estates, heavy drinking and heroin addiction – or, quite possibly, as a reaction to them – a fresh-faced batch of penniless indie bands had sprung up on the local music scene. Their austere, gritty sound, a response to both the clanking and shrieking of the steel industry and the electronic technology that had contributed to its demise, had initially consigned them to the avant-garde underground. They had seen themselves, in the beginning, as musical outcasts, transforming their poverty into a costume of defiance. Their distinctive 'Sheffield Sound', merging the anarchic fury of punk with the lushly romantic lyrics of experimental dance music had been, according to Heaven

17's Martyn Ware, 'like a heartbeat for the whole city. [At night we'd] hear the drop forges hammering away like a metronome.'

To Pulp singer Jarvis Cocker, such outlaw dissidence was Old Yorkshire's up yours to the new culture of money, glamour and power. The movement, he declared, was a musical updating of sixties social realism. He pointed out that one local band had a song called 'Don't Let the Bastards Grind You Down', an allusion to the famous line spoken by Arthur Seaton in Alan Sillitoe's *Saturday Night, Sunday Morning*. 'I was impressed,' he wrote. 'Here was a belligerent protest against the very system that had both spawned and destroyed [the steel] industry. Plus it had a catchy chorus. A sensibility was born. *This Sporting Life* (1963), *A Taste of Honey* (1961), *The Loneliness of the Long Distance Runner* (1962) – there are a host of other 1960s "kitchen-sink dramas" that were inspirational touchstones for people like me in indie bands in the 1980s. But of course, the daddy of them all is *Kes* . . . the most enduring image of that entire film, the one that's now on the cover of its DVD edition, is the one in which Billy Casper "flicks the V's" at the movie camera. It's the ultimate act of defiance.'

As indie music went 'overground' (ideological purists preferred the phrase 'sold out') many of the city's cutting-edge bands went over to the 'dark side', throwing in their lot with the Thatcherite New Romantics. Like the books and films that had inspired Pulp, the Sheffield Sound had been the final flourishing of a lineage that was rapidly disappearing. The lyrics of Cocker's 'The Last Day of the Miners' Strike' were a paean to a vanishing culture, expressing, as an admiring Hatherley noted, 'the feeling of power and solidarity' but also conjuring up the sounds of hoofbeats and a life-or-death-struggle, '(in nearby Orgreave no doubt) and a defeat so drastic and conclusive'. But with the melting away of the great ghost armies of labour, at whose head Sheffielders were to have marched triumphantly into an egalitarian future, a different landscape had emerged – of 'mass unemployment, a seemingly unending slump [and] an ever-widening north–south divide'.

This landscape of desolation was being reimagined, in endless pop videos and a tedious procession of men's style magazines, as the sunlit uplands of unfettered capitalism. As well as redefining youth culture and conquering the fashion world, fiercely ambitious London bands like Culture Club, Spandau Ballet and Wham! promoted an acquisitive individualism entirely in tune with Thatcher's deregulated anti-society. Their international success prompted Sheffield bands like Heaven 17, Human League and Vice-Versa, who quickly changed their name to ABC, to undergo what Andy Beckett described as a 'psychological rewiring, [rethinking] their sounds and looks, and their reasons for being. [They now] spurned the dour mass youth fashions of the 1970s for a new peacock individualism.' Inspired by ABC's commercial breakthrough – their glossy, escapist masterwork *The Lexicon of Love* – the local council set up a Cultural Industries Quarter next to the railway station.

At the beginning of the decade, Sheffield had been the go-to place for Yorkshire noir, its abandoned buildings, run-down housing estates and crumbling industrial complexes forming the ideal backdrop to gritty, black-and-white films like *Looks and Smiles*. In Loach's early eighties movie, set against the first wave of steel redundancies and closures, and in the post-apocalyptic 1982 movie *Threads*, Sheffield was a place devoid of hope, doomed to a terminal, post-industrial decline, broken seemingly beyond repair. Instead of basking in the romantic glow of its spectacular ruins – the deserted Sheffield

Victoria station, one writer noted, was 'where you went when you wanted to feel like the world had just ended' – the civic boosterists now insisted it was time to make their peace with New Britain. In a new globalised world of consumption and lifestyle choice, the creative industries would be the route to economic salvation. The council provided facilities for music and film production – including, in 1986, Red Tape Studios, the first municipal recording studio in the country – and set up a number of arts and music festivals. This policy peaked in 1999, with the opening of the giant, steel-domed, £15 million National Centre for Popular Music, filled with memorabilia such as ABC's gold lamé jackets.

A year later, however, Britain's first-ever museum of pop music was closed down due to lack of interest. Some 400,000 people had been expected to pass through its doors each year, but only 104,000 visited in the first six months. Still, as in Bradford, there was more than one way to fill the void. The £450 million Meadowhall shopping centre, built on derelict land once occupied by the sprawling Dunford Hadfield's steelworks, had already spearheaded the expansion of a service sector that employed 150,000 people. A decade after hitting the headlines as the battleground of mass picketing, the out-of-town mall had transformed a one-time bastion of industrial militancy into a temple of mass consumerism. Built by the Barnsley tycoon Paul Sykes, and coming in the middle of a wave of out-of-town developments – it was preceded by Brent Cross, Merry Hill and the Metro Centre and followed by Lakeside, White Rose, the Trafford Centre, the Mall at Cribbs Causeway, Bristol and Bluewater – the giant mall immediately replaced the Tinsley cooling towers as the M1's South Yorkshire landmark.

Name-checked by Cocker on Pulp's *His 'n' Hers* album it had, by the end of the nineties, become a metaphor for consumer hell, a place to be endured rather than embraced, accused of sucking business out of both Sheffield and Rotherham town centres. In 1989, interviewed while it was being constructed, Sykes had explained that his aim was simply to make a profit. When he sold up a decade later, a lot wiser – and £280 million richer – he denounced the way its consumerist values had got out of hand. 'Meadowhell', as a minority of dissenters had renamed it, was close to becoming a secular religion. 'It has gone way beyond whatever I imagined,' he admitted. 'I did not think people would become obsessed with it.'

If the city's creative industries and shopping malls weren't the answer, then why not return to its earliest, and most enduring, attempt at mass entertainment? The council's inner circle were all huge football fans – according to Betts they were not above scheduling meetings around Wednesday games – and keen on the idea of using sport, as one of them put it, 'to once again fly the flag'. Taylor's modernised Hillsborough had shown, in the 1966 World Cup, how hosting an elite sporting event could put the city on the map. A local newspaper greeted news of the successful bid to host the 1991 World Student Games with the headline: 'The greatest day in the history of Sheffield'. Three new sporting facilities were built for the occasion: the Don Valley Stadium, Sheffield Arena and the Ponds Forge complex.

However, in its attempt to remodel the city as a 'twenty-first-century global venue', the authority ended up making a £10 million loss. The ski village's pristine slopes, after a series of arson attacks, had to be abandoned. The cost of hosting three weeks of games has left Sheffield taxpayers covering debts of around £25 million to £30 million a year, repayments that they are due to make until 2024. The £29 million, 25,000-capacity Don Valley Stadium, the second-largest athletics venue in the country, became famous for being the home track of Jessica Ennis. It cost £700,000 a year to run and, when the council faced a £1.6 million repair bill, was targeted for closure by the government. Ennis, who had been talent-spotted at the stadium's summer camp as a ten-year-old, was the 2012 Olympic Games' poster girl and hailed as a global ambassador for her home town. A year after she won her Olympics gold medal in the heptathlon, Don Valley was bulldozed to make way for medical research facilities.

For Cocker, the rot had set in the moment the republic had laid down its tools by abandoning its cheap bus-fares policy. 'That's why buses are mentioned quite a lot in our songs,' he said. 'People came from Japan to see our bus service.' The city's modernist superstructures had been emblems of social change, an antidote to both the deleterious back-to-backs and inhospitable high-rise towers that destroyed working-class communities. 'I'd grown up reading the local paper and seeing "Sheffield, city of the future" with a map of how it's going to be and pictures of everyone walking around in spacesuits,' explained his band-mate Russell Senior. 'But we're the only ones who took it seriously. We were brought up on the space race – now they expect you to clean toilets.'

Sheffield's final bid for a sporting event – the 2005 World Athletics Championships – fell at the first hurdle, prompting a Ruskin-esque backlash against the very idea of such a gloomy, post-industrial wasteland becoming a twenty-first-century global venue. Told-you-so critics like Michael Fabricant implied that the city would always be weighed down by its industrial past. Burdened by its dour, downbeat Old Yorkshireness, it lacked the glitz, glamour and razzmatazz needed to host international events. 'It is not sexy,' declared the straight-talking Conservative MP. 'It is old and dirty.'

POLICING THE SHOW

Coming only a few years after Orgreave, one of the most violent confrontations in modern British history, the Hillsborough disaster brought to a close a decade in which mistrust between police and working-class football fans had been high. Throughout the eighties, a more aggressive and politicised approach to policing had been pursued. Football hooliganism, quite clearly, was a problem – although, despite the relentless moral panics stoked by sensationalist tabloid headlines such as 'Smash These Thugs!', 'Savages!' and 'Murder on a Soccer Train!', it actually declined during the eighties – and there was an obvious need to prevent pitch invasions and eradicate disorder. But while the public accepted that such tactics might be necessary to combat political extremists, especially enemies of the state, it came as a shock to see them being used against ordinary fans.

'We sent our children and loved ones to a football match,' said Margaret Aspinall, whose eighteen-year-old son James died in the Hillsborough tragedy. 'We entrusted their lives to the care of those policemen.' The jury at the Hillsborough inquests ruled that there had been an absence of care: officers had flouted their duty to protect the safety of the 54,000-strong crowd. The ninety-six victims, they concluded, had been killed unlawfully. The actions of David Duckenfield, the inexperienced South Yorkshire Police chief superintendent in charge of the semi-final, amounted to gross negligence; his decision to open an exit gate and allow a large number of supporters into Leppings Lane, while not taking steps to close off a tunnel leading to the overcrowded central pens, was deemed to be the main cause of the crush. He admitted to failing to prepare for the match, that his focus beforehand had been on dealing with misbehaviour rather than the need to protect people from overcrowding or crushing and that after the disaster he had lied about key decisions taken on the day.

The jury also heard evidence that the police had actively amended statements to point the finger of blame at Liverpool supporters; that immediately after the disaster, a police cover-up had taken place, with inaccurate and untrue information being planted in the media.

There were clear similarities with the black propaganda put out by the South Yorkshire force after Orgreave, particularly the frame-ups, the fabrications and the narratives about mindless thugs. The response to the mass picket outside Sheffield represented a fundamental shift in policing techniques.

The image of the blue-helmeted, unarmed Bobby, patrolling on foot in all weathers, protecting the people who paid their wages from criminal and disorderly elements was supplanted by the *Spitting Image* caricature of sinister coppers kitted out in riot overalls, helmets, visors, shields and batons. Following on from several infamous miscarriages of justice and clashes with trade unionists, inner-city youth and ethnic minorities, the tragedy further eroded public confidence in the integrity of policing; a BBC poll in the early nineties revealed that two-thirds of the population were convinced officers bent the rules to gain convictions. Twenty-five years later, the reputation of the South Yorkshire police sunk to an all-time low: in a makeshift courtroom in Warrington, a jury heard how the force had become disconnected from the citizens it served. They were told about an appalling catalogue of incompetence, lies and cover-ups and reminded that this was neither the first nor the last scandal to have hit the police in the area. In 1963, Sheffield detectives admitted that suspects were routinely beaten with stolen weapons to elicit a confession and that evidence was regularly tampered with. In the year the inquests began, the Jay Report disclosed that, between 1997 and 2013, at least 1,400 children had been raped, trafficked and abused in Rotherham under the noses of the police. A picture emerged in court, wrote David Conn, 'of a drinking culture in the South Yorkshire police, with most stations at the time having a bar. In the midst of a hard-faced culture in which officers rarely talked about their feelings, some drank heavily after the disaster. Police Federation minutes noted that officers "got considerably drunk" that night while bereaved relatives were queuing outside to enter the hell of the gymnasium – where police would interrogate them about drinking.'

The confrontational policing of the miners' strike – symbolised by officers waving their overtime payslips in the face of striking miners – had broken longstanding bonds between local communities and local officers. The strike might have made the latter lots of money, but it also made them lots of enemies and their politicisation, and apparent freedom to operate beyond both the law and local account-ability, created a dangerous rift. 'The Thatcher government,' noted former Labour home secretary Jack Straw, 'because they needed the police to be a partisan force, particularly for the miners' strike and other industrial troubles, created a culture of impunity in the police service.' Police pay had been at the top of the agenda when the first Conservative Cabinet meeting took place after the 1979 election. Between 1979 and 1989 it increased in real terms by 41 per cent, while other public-sector employees saw their salaries, numbers and resources all squeezed. The public begin to see them, as one senior officer admitted, as 'Maggie Thatcher's private army'. This perception was reinforced by the South Yorkshire force's smearing of Liverpool supporters, which confirmed a culture of malpractice that had first come to light four years earlier in the aftermath of the quasi-military operation against pickets at Orgreave. Then, controlled by the same chief constable, Peter Wright, they had prosecuted ninety-five miners for rioting – all of whom were subsequently acquitted.

After Hillsborough, senior officers, overseen by Wright, ordered junior officers to rewrite their statements, remove their criticism of the operation and highlight the Liverpool fans' 'misconduct'. It took twenty-six years for Duckenfield to admit, under pressure of an inquest, that his failings had been the prime cause of the tragedy. A videotape of CCTV footage went missing on the night of the disaster – a theft for which no culprit has ever been caught – as the forced-open-by-fans version, faithfully broadcast on TV, seeped into the national consciousness.

Even though the vast majority of football fans were peaceful and law-abiding – and hooliganism was on the wane – they were consist-ently portrayed as a uniformly frightening group, a lumpen problem mass. Like the miners, they were the enemy within. Working-class crowds, once feted for their loyalty, pride and collectivity, became an object of fear, loathing and social control; herded in and out of pens, they were demonised as an undifferentiated mob, unworthy of the effort and expense of adequate protection. 'Lurid press reports of fan violence,' wrote *When Saturday Comes* editor Andy Lyons, 'would have led anyone who didn't attend matches to think that football stadia were life-threatening environments, teeming with drunken, dart-throwing maniacs.' Shortly before the 1989 semi-final, the Foot-ball Spectators Act made ID cards compulsory for all fans. Dropped after the introduction of all-seater stadia – the Taylor Report had called it counter-productive – the legislation provided a revealing insight into the government's authoritarian mindset. A Football

Licensing Authority was to be run by a civil servant renowned for putting down prison riots. Supporters failing to possess the cards would have faced draconian penalties. According to sportswriter Mihir Bose, the cards 'would have meant English football supporters would have become the first people since the war to be obliged to identify themselves on demand to the police. On match days they would have been subjected to stop-and-search powers if a police officer thought that they might be journeying to a football match. They could have been banned from public places and public transport and denied the right to buy alcohol. They would have had to undergo this regime for the dubious pleasure of watching a football match in dismal, disgusting and dangerous conditions, crammed into pens and ordered about by police and stewards.'

THE NEW SHOW IN TOWN

In the post-Hillsborough era, as New Britain established its grip on sport, Old Yorkshire tried desperately hard to reinvent itself for the 'new show in town': the modernised, monetised, globalised, Sky-driven TV age. Its football clubs displayed sporadic bursts of ambition, fired by a combination of financial hubris and Casper-like defiance. These tended to be, in the main, short-lived, unsustainable adventures and were often followed by ignominious, debt-ridden implosions. Occasionally, when a plucky, lower-league, White Rose David, sprinkled with transfer-market bargains and discarded journeymen with points to prove, knocked a mighty, billionaire-owned Goliath out of one of the cups, there was a nostalgic yearning for the *Kes*-like grittiness of yesteryear. But these hugely hyped one-off dramas have always turned to be exceptions confirming the rule of a new, ruthless, cash-driven, overclass.

At the turn of the millennium, after Paul Jewell left Bradford City – despite keeping them in the top flight – he spent a miserable eight months failing to restore Sheffield Wednesday to their post-Wilkinson heights. During an after-match drink with Graham Taylor, whose Watford side had just turned the Owls over, the former England manager told Jewell he'd smelt defeat in the air. 'There is no question that rot can set in,' said Jewell. 'You can develop a losing mentality. It is little things. Look at the grounds. Hillsborough, Elland Road, Valley Parade; they look tired. The fans turn up because they have to, not because they want to. It is a vicious circle. It can be hard to break out.'

The teams that play at these famous old stadiums now belong to football's new underclass. Along with Barnsley and Sheffield United, they enjoyed some success (mostly fleeting) during the post-Hillsborough boom years but have become, like many other Old Yorkshire institutions, resigned to life on the margins, cut off from the sporting elite. They first began to get left behind in the eighties, when Thatcher's great 'liberating' wave of deregulation transformed the sporting landscape. As a new, commercialised order was taking shape, fans returned to the game – and so did the money. In 1989, three years after Big Bang, Murdoch launched Sky, which has changed the way football is financed, presented and even played.

Through his new channel's exclusive acquisition of live Premier League coverage, consumers were persuaded to invest in both satellite equipment and the monthly subscription charges the service commanded. The top flight was renamed the Premiership and immediately repackaged as England's showcase top division. As TV viewers were urged to 'eat, drink and sleep football', the elite clubs started to make unprecedented returns on their investments. In exchange for providing Sky's 'content', they were able to pursue commercial activities unencumbered by regulation. 'The clubs cried poverty on the edge of the pay TV bonanza they all knew was coming,' wrote Conn, writing about the government subsidies for their new stands. '[They] got rich and cashed in.'

The 'cashing in' was, supposedly, the defining moment in English football history. After the Taylor report, according to this narrative, came the lucrative rebirth of football: the top clubs' breakaway from the old Football League, the TV rights-led enrichment of the new Premier League. A new sporting order – reckless, risk-taking and individualistic – came into being. Hillsborough, as Goldblatt has argued, 'was a summation of many of the changes that football and the nation had undergone'. In their desperation to cash in on their biggest brand, Sheffield Wednesday, like so many other clubs, had lost sight of what football is, and always should be, about.

Conclusion: The Invisible Fingerprint

'And, you know, there's no such thing as society. There are individual men and women and there are families.'

Margaret Thatcher, 1987

Jackie Elliot, a miner out on strike, takes his son Billy to the local sports centre to learn boxing. Unbeknown to his father, Billy joins the ballet class instead. He misses an audition at the Royal Ballet School because his brother Tony is arrested during a skirmish between police and striking miners. Jackie is furious about the ballet lessons but, after seeing his son dancing in the gym, decides to do whatever it takes to help him realise his dream. Fourteen years later, now settled in London, Billy performs the lead in Swan Lake at Covent Garden, watched by Jackie and Tony.

In a celebrated cartoon of the mid-1980s, drawn by the *Observer*'s Trog, the sun shines on a champagne-swilling pair of yuppies in the south, whilst in the north the rain falls out of a dark sky on to a stooping middle-aged couple, who plaintively ask: 'They've got their prime minister, why can't we have ours?' By the end of the decade a similar borderline, between New Britain and Old Yorkshire, divided the sporting landscape. The decade had seen the emergence of an ideology which, as Andrew Gamble argued, was good 'for financial Britain, for multinational Britain, for rural Britain, for share-owning and upper-income Britain, but not so good for working-class Britain, for manufacturing Britain, for trade-union Britain'. Neoliberalism, it must not be forgotten, was also a disaster for sporting Britain. While it has undoubtedly enriched the governing bodies of football, rugby league and cricket, it has shifted the locus of power from the grassroots to the wealthy elites. Although the Sky revolution brought about a long-overdue modernisation of these sports, and clearly improved safety and comfort at matches, there is no doubt that a damaging, and ever-deepening rift, has become a dominant feature of twenty-first-century English sport.

The Thatcher decade was bookended by the Headingley miracle and the Hillsborough tragedy. In the public consciousness, these two internationally renowned stadiums remain relics of an old, decaying, divisive Yorkshire. Hillsborough is a byword for a powerful elite's mistreatment of what it deemed a lumpen herd. Headingley – still, despite Leeds city centre's metamorphosis into a beacon of shiny, post-modern, consumerism, in a dilapidated state – is haunted by its civil war. Thirty years after his retirement, Boycott's attempt to rejoin the Yorkshire hierarchy was narrowly rejected by the board, the club chairman attacking his candidacy as 'disruptive'. A great deal was made of the seven gold medals (and two silver and three bronze) won by White Rose athletes at the 2012 London Games. But the success of Jessica Ennis, the Brownlee brothers and Nicola Adams, as well as other supremely talented, and heavily funded, athletes (investment in Olympic sports rocketed in preparation for the country's first tournament since 1948) only served to disguise the long-term failure of their communities' sporting teams, especially those based on a nucleus of local talent. These teams, today, are consigned to the margins, cut off from the centre of power; Yorkshire's disappearance from the Premier League, like Headingley's usual absence from the Ashes series and the continuing low profile of the county's 'national sport' (rugby league), is part of the wider drift towards sporting and cultural irrelevance.

God's own county no longer produces sportsmen and women in large numbers. There is no more whistling down pit shafts for defenders, fast bowlers and prop forwards; Kellingley Colliery, in North Yorkshire – the country's last deep coal mine – was closed in 2016. The occasional Billy Elliot keeps slipping through the net, dancing his or her way to the top of the pile, but thousands of Billy Caspers remain at the bottom, stuck in low-skilled service jobs, welfare dependency (or worse), and alienated from their local clubs, often lacking an emotional connection to the region. 'It is simply that a specific part of culture has been destroyed,' wrote Paul Mason. 'A culture based on work, rising wages, strict unspoken rules against disorder, obligatory collaboration and mutual aid. It all had to go.' The disappearance of the old, industrial, northern, working-class landscape was movingly commemorated by film director Danny Boyle in his 2012 Olympic opening ceremony. Explaining his decision to show the, no doubt bemused, watching TV millions a clip from *Kes*, Boyle pointed out that the movie had become a forgotten icon of British culture. 'Whether you've seen a film like *Kes* or not,' he said, 'it's part of [your] heritage. It's running in your veins. It's an invisible fingerprint that everybody carries, whether you ever sit down and watch it or not.' A similar sense of loss informed the tributes to Barry Hines, who died as I was finishing this book. Like Casper, he was hailed as the last of a dying breed, part of an extraordinary generation of novelists who wrote almost exclusively about the lives of the northern working class.

History belongs to the victors. By the time the Games were staged, in a capital city now monopolising the country's wealth, New Britain commanded not only the economy but the narrative as well. The ideology behind mass privatisation, the sale of council houses and financial deregulation had become 'common sense'. The idea of Billy Casper had been supplanted by the idea of Billy Elliot: self-determination, self-reliance, self-help. 'Jess has become a metaphor for modern Sheffield,' declared Creative Sheffield's Brendan Moffett, after Ennis won the heptathlon gold. 'High performance, high achievement and a can-do attitude.' Like Billy Elliot, she was also a metaphor for the new individualism. In the eponymous film, set in a mining community during the 1984–5 strike, Elliot follows his dream of becoming a ballet dancer. But his triumph comes at the expense of collective struggle; to raise money to travel to London for an audition at the Royal Ballet School, his father attempts to cross the picket line. 'It's for wee Billy,' Jackie explains to his other son, a union leader. 'I'm sorry, son. We're finished, son.' By 'we' he meant, according to the film's writer Lee Hall, 'community, identity and a collective politics which inspired generations of people'. Billy receives his letter of acceptance to the ballet school on the day the miners vote to go back to work. 'Jackie, have you not heard, man?' a devastated striker tells Elliot's dad when he excitedly reveals the news. 'We're going back.'

The Elliot story, like *The Full Monty*, encapsulates the American/Thatcherite dream of the individual who, against all the odds, makes good. Both films were made during a New Labour era that owed a great deal to the Iron Lady's legacy. In aspiring to run the market economy better than the Conservatives, the Blair–Brown governments rendered Thatcherism irreversible. *The Full Monty*, released three years earlier than *Billy Elliott*, might be renowned for its stripping sequence, but it was really about Old Yorkshire's attempt to come to terms with the new political economy. Its opening sequence cut away from a chirpy, early seventies marketing film, in which shiny, happy people were shown working in steel factories, playing football and drinking in pubs. Twenty-five years later, the steel had gone, the football was in decline and the men were standing around in unemployment lines swinging their hips in time to Chippendale routines. Toughness and togetherness are all very well, the film implied, but in a colourful, instantly gratifying world of fun, entertainment and big money – and mass unemployment – a new type of hero was required.

That type had first appeared in the eighties: from Botham to Eddie the Eagle – the sublime to the ridiculous – a new national story, based on a narrative of individualistic self-realisation, had emerged. 'When I first watched Billy Elliot,' said Chris Dean, the son of a Nottinghamshire miner, 'I thought, "Somebody's written my life story here." It was very much like that.' Dean was one half of an ice-skating duo that, during the miners' strike, cheered up a depressed nation. Writing in praise of the dancers, the *Daily Telegraph*'s Olga Craig declared that 'after years of economic gloom, a new Britain with a new attitude was finding its voice'. In the spring of 1984, 24 million people watched the pair win what commentator Alan Weeks called, a tad exaggeratedly, 'the most cherished prize in sport' – the world figure-skating championships gold medal – scoring an unprecedented nine perfect sixes for artistic impression.

'There is nothing more powerful than an idea whose time has come.' One of the entrepreneurs who had emerged during the Thatcher decades, the Hull City owner Assem Allam, was so taken with this quote that he emblazoned it on his office wall. The first half of the eighties saw a final flourishing of the Casper-ite idea; the scrawny teenager's defiance inspired several of the key sporting figures, and teams, of that period. Howard Wilkinson even revealed to a bemused journalist that he'd written an unfinished novel, explaining it was 'a bit like *Kes*'. His city's, and team's, rise-and-fall narrative certainly lent itself to the *Kes* treatment. By the time he had defected to Leeds, a team whose rise-and-fall narrative lent itself to the Icarus treatment, there had been, as the cultural critic Ian Macdonald noted, 'a shift from a society weakly held together by a decaying faith to a rapidly desocialising mass of groups and individuals united by little more than a wish for quick satisfaction'.

Like *This Sporting Life*, *A Kind of Loving* and *The Loneliness of the Long Distance Runner*, *Kes* captured the angry proletarian mood of the post-war era. Since that brief dawning, working-class collectivist narratives have disappeared from British culture. Where is the contemporary Billy Casper? Or, indeed, the contemporary David Bradley? Around half of Britain's best actors, according to a Sutton Trust study, are privately educated. As the image of the vulgar, boorish northerner has taken hold – from nineteenth-century *Little Britain* caricatures through poverty-porn reality TV shows to Sacha Baron Cohen's 'chav' protagonist in the film *Nobby* – literature, film and the arts have been taken over by the better off. Old Yorkshire appears to be an idea whose time has gone. Since the miners' strike, the former pit villages, steel towns and industrial cities have been faced with a choice: either dance to New Britain's tune or stagnate. In her eulogising of Torvill and Dean, Craig sensed the evolution of a 'new kind of sport', arguing that 'something new was happening, something old was dying. It was a defining moment in the battle between old and new Britain . . . The coal industry, loss-making and dominated by the NUM, a union that had the power to bring down the government, represented everything about the old Britain that dogged the new, blossoming ethos of free enterprise.' In the New Britain, noted Andrew O'Hagan, the working class have become attracted to 'new forms of transcendence offered by celebrity culture and credit cards and the bogus life of the fantasy rich . . . As a class in and of itself, it appears to be dead. The aims of society are not part of its ethos any more. The idea is as knackered as the Working Men's Institutes.' For millions of institute members, watching their local sporting clubs had once been the cornerstone of their lives. But as the industrial work of old has given way to welfare – and in some, extremely run-down areas – drug dependency, and the old bonds of class and community have faded almost to nothingness, that link has been broken.

It is one of the oldest clichés to say that sport mirrors life. Yet the decline of Yorkshire's sporting hinterland is clearly connected to the manufacturing collapse which wiped out almost a fifth of Britain's industrial base and left large swathes of the three ridings trapped in hopelessness and underachievement. Of the original twelve members of the Football League, formed in 1888, none hailed from London or the south. Yorkshire was late to the party, but Bradford City, Leeds, Huddersfield Town and the two Sheffields eventually joined football's aristocracy. With the exception of the yo-yoing

Hull City, the top flight has, in recent years, become a Yorkshire-free zone.

The romantic ascent of Leicester City (clearly a non-London success story but also owned by a billionaire Thai businessman and one of the top thirty richest clubs in the world) does not alter the game's long-term transformation from a paternalistic, relatively egalitarian sport to a global entertainment industry dominated by rapacious mega-brands. According to the co-authors of *Soccernomics*, Simon Kuper and Stefan Szymanski, there is now an 89 per cent correlation between wage spending and league position. 'It's very important for Premier League propaganda,' wrote Kuper, 'and for everyone who invests so much of their emotional life in the Premier League, to believe that the game is not all about money . . . But the true story of the Premier League is that it is almost all about money. In the short term you can get anomalies . . . but if you average it out over ten seasons the correlation between the wage bill and league position goes up to 90 per cent. Over ten seasons, luck evens out. [A Leicester] will only happen once every 20-plus years.'

The chances of a Sheffield United, a Bradford City or a Barnsley breaking into the cartel-like top tier are even more remote. These clubs are part of English football's invisible fingerprint. Their fans were once its heart and soul. Since Hillsborough, however, there has been a shift in the demographics of the game's support. Ticket prices now cost at least three times what they did in 1989; regular attendance is something that only a certain strata of society can afford. The working class have, by and large, been priced out of the market. A gentrification of sorts has even infected rugby league. Since Murdoch pumped £87 million into the game, in return for TV rights, it has been re-branded. Its post-1996 commercial modernisation injected a bit of transatlantic razzmatazz but ended, for ever, the possibility of a team like Featherstone Rovers ever winning the Challenge Cup again.

Boyle's homage to *Kes* reminded the nation, and the watching world, that a once-powerful, vibrant, collectivist culture had vanished from public view. Old Yorkshire, as an idea, can be sentimentalised, romanticised even, its insular and bigoted tendencies ignored by nostalgia-addled advocates. But the loss of a belligerent, solidaristic, communal culture is more than just a Yorkshire tragedy. It is a national one. Many of the county's clubs are no longer the heartbeat of their communities; their players, an ever-decreasing number of whom are recruited locally, exist in a completely different financial orbit. The communal to and fro of the old, standing terraces belongs to a disappearing world of well-paid skilled jobs, crowded pubs and terraced streets. The evisceration in the eighties of that world sounded the death knell for a simpler, purer, harder, edgier – and at times uglier – version of sport. It was not only trade unions, heavy industry and working-class communities that were crushed. It was also hope.

Acknowledgements

This book began life as a late-night conversation with Jon Riley. So, once again, many thanks to him for helping to hatch the idea – and for his inspirational editing. Also, like my friend and agent David Luxton, he gave me great support during a difficult time. Thanks, also, to Josh Ireland for his meticulous editing and to the four Davids – Conn, Goldblatt, Winner and Peace – for their books, company and always stimulating contributions. All are writers I greatly admire. The books and journalism of David Conn, in particular, have been a big influence. I'd also like to single out the two Ians – McMillan and Clayton – for producing so many pioneering works on Yorkshireness over the years.

Thanks, of course, to Alison Shelley, Rosa Clavane, Miriam Clavane, Matthew Clavane, Emile Clavane and Peter Clavane. Phil Caplan, who runs an excellent bookshop, showed me a bit of Rotherham and Mick Cusworth, over the course of two days, drove me around South Yorkshire. Tony Collins helped me understand rugby league's place in Yorkshire culture and Mark Perryman and Rob Steen provided thoughtful insights. Thanks also to Alan Dein, Duncan Hamilton, Gary Hetherington, Richard de la Rivière, Doug Sandle, Katy Shaw, the magnificent *When Saturday Comes* – and Krys Kotolo, for keeping alive the spirit of *Kes*. And here's to the next generation: Tom Whitworth and (so helpful on Sheffield), Aaron Paul.

And finally, thanks to all the interviewees who helped me during my research: At Hull: Pete Allen, Steve Bruce, James Clark, Alec Gill, Mark Gretton, Steve Hubbard, Geoffrey 'Sammy' Lloyd, Roy North, Katie Ogram, Adam Pearson, Nick Quantrill, Steve Saddington, Rick Skelton, Keith Tindall, Johnny Whiteley and Dave Windass. At Headingley/Yorkshire: Mark Arthur, Dickie Bird, Geoff Cope, Jason Gillespie, David Hopps, Chris Old and Stuart Rayner. At Rotherham: John Breckin, Jamie Noble, Paul Rickett, Tony Stewart and Jonathan Veal. At Featherstone: Alan Agar, Paul Coventry, Kenny Greatorex, Terry Jones, Melissa Schiele, Andy Smith and Maureen Tennant-King. At Barnsley: David Bradley, Alison Cooper, Paul Darlow, Liam Dyson, Sean Fitzpatrick, Beryl Hodgson, Kevin Hodgson, Mark Hodkinson, Mick McCarthy, Norman Rimmington and Eric Winstanley. At Bradford: Jerry Ashraf, John Dewhirst, John Helm, Peter Jackson, Mark Lawn, David Markham, James Mason, David Pendleton, Riz Rehman, Zesh Rehman and Lindsay Sutton. At Sheffield: Gary Armstrong, Dave Bassett, Clive Betts, Paul Blomfield, Keith Edwards, Anthony Garratty, John Garrett, Steve Hodkinson, Tom Whitworth, Paul Widdowson and Howard Wilkinson.

Select Bibliography

BOOKS

Allen, Pete, *Roamin' the Range Together: Living in the Shadow of Giants (1950–1980)* (Pete Allen, 2011)

Armstrong, Gary and Garrett, John, *Sheffield United FC: The Biography* (Hallamshire Publications, 2006)

Baggini, Julian, *Welcome to Everytown: A Journey into the English Mind* (Granta, 2008)

Beckett, Andy, *Promised You a Miracle: Why 1980–82 made Modern Britain* (Allen Lane, 2015)

Beckett, Francis and Hencke, David, *Marching to the Fault Line: The Miners' Strike and the Battle for Industrial Britain* (Constable, 2009)

Benson, Richard, *The Valley: A Hundred Years in the Life of a Yorkshire Family* (Bloomsbury, 2014)

Boycott, Geoffrey, *The Corridor of Certainty: My Life Beyond Cricket* (Simon & Schuster, 2015)

Caplan, Phil and Doidge, Jonathan R., *Super League: The First Ten Years* (Tempus, 2006)

Charlesworth, Simon J., *A Phenomenology of Working-Class Experience* (Cambridge University Press, 2012)

Clayton, Ian, *When Push Comes to Shove: Rugby League the People's Game* (Yorkshire Art Circus, 1993)

Clayton, Ian, *Our Billie* (Penguin, 2010)

Clayton, Ian, *Merging on the Ridiculous* (Yorkshire Art Circus, 1995)

Collins, Tony, *Rugby's Great Split: Class, Culture, and the Origins of Rugby League Football* (Routledge, 2006)

Collins, Tony, *Rugby League in Twentieth Century Britain: A Social and Cultural History* (Routledge, 2006)

Collins, Tony, *Sport in Capitalist Society: A Short History* (Routledge, 2013)

Conn, David, *The Beautiful Game?: Searching for the Soul of Football* (Yellow Jersey, 2005)

Conn, David, *The Football Business* (Mainstream, 2002)

Cooper, Andy, *Eric Taylor: A Biography* (A. Cooper Publications, 2011)

Cornwell, John, *Never Walk Behind the Bowler's Arm: Tales, Yarns and Poems from a Yorkshire City* (Calvert Wagner Promotions, 2009)

Courtenay, Tom, *Dear Tom: Letters from Home* (Black Swan, 2001)

Cunninghame Graham, Robert, *The Selected Writings of Cunninghame Graham* (Cedric Watts Associated University Presses, 1982)

De la Rivière, Richard, *Rugby League: A Critical History 1980–2013* (League Publications, 2013)

Dennis, Norman and Henriques, F., *Coal Is Our Life: Analysis of a Yorkshire Mining Community* (Routledge, 1969)

Dewhirst, John, *A History of Bradford City AFC in Objects* (Bantamspast Publishing, 2014)

Edwards, Keith and Pack, Andy, *Edwards . . . One-Nil!: The Keith Edwards Story* (Vertical Editions, 2014)

Firth, Grenville, *The Who's Who of Barnsley FC* (DB Publishing, 2011)

Fleming, Cameron, *Yorkshire Football – A History* (Scratching Shed Publishing, 2010)

Fletcher, Martin, *Fifty-Six: The Story of the Bradford Fire* (Bloomsbury, 2015)

Gamble, Andrew, *The Free Economy and the Strong State: The Politics of Thatcherism* (Palgrave Macmillan, 1988)

Gill, Alec, *Good Old Hessle Road: Stories of Hull's Trawling and Community Life* (Hutton Press Ltd, 1991)

Goldblatt, David, *The Game of Our Lives: The Meaning and Making of English Football* (Penguin, 2015)

Gray, Daniel, *Hatters, Railwaymen and Knitters: Travels through England's Football Provinces* (Bloomsbury, 2013)

Greenhalf, Jim, *It's A Mean Old Scene: A History of Modern Bradford Since 1974* (Redbeck Press, 2003)

Hadfield, David, *Up and Over: A Trek through Rugby League Land* (Mainstream, 2005)

Hamilton, Duncan, *Wisden on Yorkshire: An Anthology* (Wisden, 2011)

Hannan, Tony, *Being Eddie Waring: The Life and Times of a Sporting Icon* (Mainstream, 2008)

Hatherley, Owen, *A Guide to the New Ruins of Great Britain* (Verso, 2011)

Hatherley, Owen, *A New Kind of Bleak: Journeys through Urban Britain* (Verso, 2013)

Hatherley, Owen, *The Ministry of Nostalgia: Consuming Nostalgia (Keep Calm and Carry On)* (Verso, 2015)

Hattersley, Roy, *Goodbye to Yorkshire* (Penguin, 1978)

Hines, Barry, *A Kestrel for a Knave* (Penguin, 1976)

Hodkinson, Mark, *Life at the Top: A Season in the Premiership with Barnsley FC* (Virgin, 1998)

Hoggart, Richard, *The Uses of Literacy: Aspects of Working-Class Life* (Pelican, 1958)

Inglis, Simon, *Football Grounds of Britain* (HarperCollins, 1996)

Johnson, Anton, *King of Clubs* (Grosvenor House Publishing, 2012)

Kelner, Simon, *To Jerusalem and Back* (Macmillan, 1996)

Kuper, Simon and Szymanski, Stefan, *Soccernomics* (HarperSport, 2012)

Light, Robert (ed.), *No Sand Dunes in Featherstone: Memories of West Yorkshire Rugby League* (London League Publications, 2010)

McKinstry, Leo, *Geoff Boycott: A Cricketing Hero* (Willow, 2005)

Markham, David and Sutton, Lindsay, *The Bradford City Story: The Pain & the Glory* (Breedon Books Publishing Co, 2006)

Mills, Robert, *Field of Dreams: Headingley 1890–2001* (Great Northern Books, 2001)

Moorhouse, Geoffrey, *At the George and Other Essays on Rugby League* (Sceptre, 1990)

Parkinson, Michael, *Football Daft* (Arrow, 1973)

Pendleton, David, *Paraders: The 125 Year History of Valley Parade* (Bantamspast Publishing, 2014)

Priestley, J. B., *English Journey* (Penguin, 1977)

Priestley, J. B., *The Good Companions* (Penguin, 1969)

Rayner, Stuart, *The War of the White Roses: Yorkshire Cricket's Civil War 1968–1986* (Pitch Publishing, 2016)

Reng, Ronald, *Keeper of Dreams: One Man's Controversial Story of Life in the English Premiership* (Yellow Jersey, 2004)

Rickett, Paul, *Rotherham United: A Pictorial History* (Amberley Publishing, 2013)

Russell, Dave, *Looking North: Northern England and the National Imagination* (Manchester University Press, 2004)

Russell, Dave, *Football and the English: A Social History of Association Football, 1863–1995* (Carnegie Publishing, 1998)

Sandbrook, Dominic, *The Great British Dream Factory: The Strange History of Our National Imagination* (Allen Lane, 2015)

Scraton, Phil, *Hillsborough: The Truth* (Mainstream, 1999)

Steen, Rob and McLellan, Alastair, *500-1: The Miracle of Headingley '81* (Wisden, 2010)

Stewart, Graham, *Bang!: A History of Britain in the 1980s* (Atlantic, 2014)

Storey, David, *This Sporting Life* (Vintage, 2010)

Taylor, Matthew, *Football: A Short History* (Shire Publications, 2011)

Tempany, Adrian, *And the Sun Shines Now: How Hillsborough and the Premier League Changed Britain* (Faber & Faber, 2016)

Thorn, Tracey, *Bedsit Disco Queen: How I Grew Up and Tried to Be a Pop Star* (Virago, 2014)

Tordoff, Shaun, *City Psychos: From the Monte Carlo Mob to the Silver Cod Squad* (Milo Books Ltd, 2011)

Turner, Alwyn W., *Rejoice! Rejoice!: Britain in the 1980s* (Aurum Press, 2013)

Turner, Royce, *Coal Was Our Life: An Essay on Life in a Yorkshire Pit Town* (Perpetuity Press, 2000)

Veal, Jonathan, *Impossible Dream: The Ronnie Moore Years* (Jonathan Veal, 2013)

Wagg, Stephen and Russell, Dave, *Sporting Heroes of the North* (Northumbria Press, 2010)

Ward, Andrew and Williams, John, *Football Nation: Sixty Years of the Beautiful Game* (Bloomsbury, 2010)

Ward, Andrew and Alister, Ian, *Barnsley: A Study in Football, 1953–59* (Crowberry, 1981)

Warner, David, *The Sweetest Rose: 150 Years of Yorkshire County Cricket Club* (Great Northern Books, 2012)

Waters, Chris, *Fred Trueman: The Authorised Biography* (Aurum Press, 2012)

Whitworth, Tom, *20 Legends: Sheffield Wednesday* (Vertical Editions, 2012)

Whitworth, Tom and Olewicz, Chris, *Owls: Sheffield Wednesday through the Modern Era* (Vertical Editions, 2012)

Wilkinson, Howard, *Managing to Succeed: My Life in Football Management* (Mainstream, 1992)

ARTICLES

Conn, David, 'Follow The Money', *London Review of Books*, 30 August 2012

Craig, Olga, 'The pithead baths is a supermarket now', *Daily Telegraph*, 7 March 2004

Editorial, 'In praise of . . . Featherstone Rovers', *Guardian*, 23 August 2010

Fletcher, Martin, 'The last days of the Big K', *New Statesman*, 4 November 2015

Freedland, Jonathan, 'The Premier League is no longer England's – this country is just the backdrop', *Guardian*, 13 February 2015

Hitchens, Peter, 'Privatisation! Free trade! Shares for all! The great con that ruined Britain', *Mail on Sunday*, 3 April 2016

McMillan, Ian, 'Yorkshire found its voice in *Kes*', *Guardian*, 21 March 2016

Mason, Paul, 'The problem for poor, white kids is that a part of their culture has been destroyed', *Guardian*, 4 April, 2016

Ronay, Barney, 'Let's cream off major sports' fat to save the grassroots', *Guardian*, 26 February, 2016

Winner, David, 'Leicester City Football Club may be close to the upset of the century', *Newsweek*, 30 March 2016

Index